Test Your Knowledge Revelation Quizzing Theological Work Book

"Our Ministries"
- God's One People In Christ Ministries (GOPICM)
- The House Of The Lord People Church
  - County Jail
- Jack Howell Detention Center
  - The Texas Youth Commission
  - Shepherd's Heart
  - Feed My Sheep
- International Ministries. On-line Teaching
  - Nursing Homes
- Wesley Woods Alzheimer's Care Center
  - Regent Care Center
  - Quality Care

Annual National One People Unity Day

Other works
Books, CDS, Plays, Poems
& Inspirational Writing

"Welcome to Quizzing"

Seek and you shall find.

Study and show yourself approved.

Thought provoking, evoking, revelation, enlightening, manifestation, transformation, restorative and *salvation quizzing.*

All quizzing is taking from the "King James Version"

The Lord hath made us kings and priests unto God and His Father; to Him be glory and dominion forever and ever. Amen. Revelation 1:5 & 6. Alleluia Praise our God!

The Revelator and teaching priest

Prophetess and Pastor Dr. Mary Neal.

Contact : (254) 379-3728

E-mail godsonepeople@yahoo.com

Web: www.thehouseofthelordonthemove.com

"Test Your Knowledge Revelation Quizzing Theological Work Book"

"Many Illustrations Included"

Questions are good; if a question was never ask we might not be motivated to think.

These are evoking and provoking questions that will motivate ones thinking.

Prophetess and Pastor, Dr. Mary Neal

The Revelator and Teaching Priest

authorHOUSE®

AuthorHouse™
1663 Liberty Drive
Bloomington, IN 47403
www.authorhouse.com
Phone: 1-800-839-8640

Unless indicated, all Scripture quotations are from the,
King James Version (KJV)

New King James Version (NKJV)

Amplified Bible (AMP)

King James Version (KJV)
By Public Domain

New King James Version (NKJV)
Copyright © 1982
By Thomas Nelson, Inc.

Amplified Bible (AMP)
Copyright © 1954, 1958, 1962, 1964, 1965, 1987
By The Lockman Foundation

Published by AuthorHouse   09/21/2012

ISBN: 978-1-4772-6959-6 (sc)
ISBN: 978-1-4772-6958-9 (e)

Library of Congress Control Number: 2012917777

"Quizzing"

Test Your Knowledge Revelation Quizzing Theological Work Book

Contents Part 1

Introduction

"Wisdom is the principal thing"

Wisdom is the principal thing; therefore get Wisdom: and with all thy getting, get Understanding.

Exalt her, and she shall promote thee: she shall bring thee to honour, when thou dost embrace her. Proverbs 4:7-8

Dedication

I dedicate this book to all the Ministries and two churches I pastor, those who love the truth and all those who have a hunger and a thirst after righteousness.

King James Version (KJV)
Blessed are they which do hunger and thirst after righteousness: for they **shall** be filled. Matthew 5:6

Amplified Bible (AMP)
Blessed and fortunate and happy and [a]spiritually prosperous (in that state in which the born-again child of God [b]enjoys His favor and salvation) are those **who hunger and thirst for righteousness** (uprightness and right standing with God), for they shall be [c]completely satisfied! Matthew 5:6

Test Your Knowledge Revelation Quizzing Theological Work Book

By, Prophetess and Pastor Dr. Mary Neal

P.O. Box 9022, Waco, Texas 76714
E-mail: godsonepeople@yahoo.com
Web Page: www.thehouseofthelordonthmove.com

Other works by Dr. Mary Neal

Book: "A New Revelation From God"
Book Order: authorhouse.com & bn.com ISBN 1585003875
All other Orders: Contact: 254-379-3728 or
E-mail godsonepeople@yahoo.com
CD: "If You Want To Be Blessed"
Biblical Game: "Pick Up Your Cross and Follow Me"
Inspirational: "Poems, Prayers, Plays and Skits"

Visit me:

blogtalkradio.com/maryneal

BCNN1.com Black Christian News Worldwide Network.com.

National Feed My Sheep Ambassador

Facebook www.facebook.com/maryneal

Preach The Word Worldwide Network.com

www.myspace.com/prophetessnealwiley

Feed My Sheep Ministry www.womennpower.com

Holy Ghost Teaching Tuesdays 9:00a.m. Central Time.

Live on-the-telephone Call: 1-218-339-4300 Access code 360777#

Test Your Knowlege Revelation Quizzing Theological Work Book

Comments from one-line quizzes and endorsements

God bless you woman of God the quizzes are and have been a blessing to me.
May the Lord continue to bless your endeavors be blessed.
Barbara J. McClain-Apostle

I love this quote Sis.
Louise Rudolph

I look forward to the book. I find the quizzes to be a great blessing and helps to stretch my bible knowledge
and more so my relationship with God and my fellow man.
Truly, God ordains this ministry.
In His Care,
Dr. and Pastor George Harrison

This is Awesome Dr. Neal, cannot wait to get my copy.
I pray Gods continued blessings on you!
Sent from my iPad
Dr. Inetta J. Cooper

Yes, pastor! Run with vision
Sent from my LG phone
Pastor R. Cummings

This will be a blessing to the Body of Christ!
Dr. Patty Reese
National Chaplain
The quizzes have been very enlightening and a learning tool as well. Thank you for taking the time
to challenge the Body of Christ to be readers and continual students of the Word of God. May God
bless your endeavors!
Dr. Tamara Thomas
NPower Chief Operations Officer

Comments and endorsements from

"The House of The Lord People Church"

&

"God's One People In Christ Ministries"

The Quizzes were such a joy; I grew in spirit because I was seeking the word more and more. The quizzes are a study tool, what a great way to keep your mind stayed on The Lord. Amen! Sister Griggs.

I think the quizzes are a great tool especially in-group settings. The scriptures tells us that when two are three are gathered together in His Name (Jesus) He is in the midst. It is great to get together and study, meditate, learning about The Lord and experience His presence. Brother and Minister Griggs

Quizzing has been a blessing to me as well; I have enjoyed searching the scriptures and receiving the word and seen the hunger for truth in so many believers. I did not even stop to think that the books "A New Revelation From God" have three hundred and fourteen questions and the Biblical Game "Pick Up Your Cross And Follow Me" also has many questions as well; I have not looked for questions from either one. I did not check to see if I used these questions more than one time because, if I did, it is possible that I rephrased

them and gave more information. I can only do this through The Holy Ghost.

I thank each one of you for your comments and continuing to encourage and support this mission.

Yours truly,

Pastor and Prophetess Dr. Mary Neal

Introduction

This Quizzing book is about encouraging, building up, evoking, provoking, challenging and renewing of the mind.

Let us hold fast the profession of our faith without wavering; (for He is faithful that promised ;)

And let us consider one another to provoke unto **love** and to **good works**:

Not forsaking the assembling of ourselves together, (The body of Yahushua The Messiah/Jesus The Christ) as the manner of some is; (The Church) but exhorting one another: and so much the more, as ye see the day approaching. Hebrews 10:23-25
(Exhorting: urging, pressing, pushing, encouraging, insisting and pressuring)

Therefore, bring many son and daughter nearer to Yahweh and Yahushua.
Playfully the body of Yahushua might be mad perfect in one!

Questions are good; if a question was never ask we might not be motivated to think.
These evoking and thought-provoking questions will motivate ones thinking.

First, I am, called, chosen and determined to be faithful to the heavenly vision. Called by Yahweh/God to make known many secrets and mysteries some hidden from the foundation of the word. One calling is to root up every seed that was not, planted by Yahweh and some bad seeds have been planted from the foundation of the word.

Satan came and keeps on coming to steal, to kill, and to destroy But Yahushua/Jesus came that we might have life and that we might have it more abundantly. Satan also came for a purpose to blind the people of Yahweh/God and separate the people of Yahweh. Remember, Yahweh is The God of the living <u>not</u> The God of the dead, Satan is their god; he is the god of this world sent into the world to mislead the body. ONLY the truth acknowledged, received and followed will make man free, so let Yahweh/God be true because, His Words are true, settled in Heaven and cannot be altered. I asked The Lord this question, free from what and the answer was, free from deceptions and blindness.

If anyone, is in Yahushua The Messiah/Jesus The Christ and becomes offended because of the Word they are offended in Yahushua. These Quizzes will bring forth truth; if one is not afraid of the truth, Satan will not be able to defeat them again. Answers to Quizzing are support by scriptures.

I have been in Ministry twenty-four years and I teach and preach nine through ten times weekly sometimes more. I know what it, I to be called and separated for the kingdom of God/Yahweh. I truly have searched the Holy Word from beginning to ending repeatedly. I was taught by The Holy Ghost and continue to be educated by Him because, He is the best instructor.

But the anointing which ye have received of Him abideth in you, and ye need not that any man teach you: but as the same anointing teacheth you of all things, and is truth, and is no lie, and even as it hath taught you, ye shall abide in Him. 1 John 2:27

But The Comforter, which is The Holy Ghost, whom The Father will send in My Name, He shall teach you all things, and bring all things to your remembrance, whatsoever I have said unto you. John 14:26

> There are eighty-one quizzes is the book but each one has (3) three through (9) nine questions. We have quizzes on one page and answers on the other pages.

> ALMOST ALL THE ANSWERS SHEETS HAVE THE QUESTIONS AND ANSWERS ON THE SAME SHEETS FOR YOUR CONVENIENT.

> In the back of the book, you will discover a wealth of information given by The Holy Ghost to enlighten the bookworm, those who hunger and thirst for more wisdom, knowledge, understanding and revelation. It is a good thing if you read "A Wealth of Information" after you take or handout the quizzes. The Word reinforces all the revelation in this book, Yahushua is The Word sent by Yahweh.

Here is flavor and a few examples of subjects we will cover in Quizzing to bring the body back to the plan and purpose of Yahweh/God.

Please, see the example diagram and Quizzing #83 below.

Quizzing will enlighten us on some of the issues that Satan uses to separate the people that proclaim The Name of Yahushua/Jesus The Christ/The Messiah.

"Head of Yahushua is Yahweh" "Head of every man is Yahushua, man and the woman" "Head of woman is man" His wife only "Head of family is man" His family only But I would have you know, that the head of every man is Christ; and the head of the woman is the man; and the head of Christ is God. 1 Corinthians 11:3	This is the book of the generations of Adam. In the day that God created man, in the likeness of God made he him; ²Male and female created he them; and blessed them, and called their name Adam, in the day when they were created. ———— Acts chapter 2, we need to study the entire chapter and cross-reference it with Joel chapter 2, Number 11, and Proverbs 1. If we do so, we should understand these were people from every nation and they	¹⁷ Sanctify them through thy truth: Thy word is truth. ¹⁸ As thou hast sent Me into the world, even so have I also sent them into the world. ¹⁹ And for their sakes I sanctify Myself, that they also might be sanctified through the truth. ²⁰ Neither pray I for these alone, but for them also which shall believe on me through their word; ²¹ That they all MAY be one; as Thou, Father, art in Me, and I in Thee, that they also MAY BE ONE IN	There is NEITHER Jew nor Greek, there is NEITHER bond nor free, there is NEITHER male nor female: for ye are ALL ONE IN Christ Jesus. Galatians 3:28 What is hatred is the sight of Yahweh? MURDER Whosoever hateth his brother is a murderer: and ye know that no murderer hath eternal life abiding in him. 1 John 3:15 ————

Column 1

**Tongue:
A part of speech**

Hebrew word Glossa
Pronunciation glos-sa
A part of speech: Root
word: Of uncertain
affinity
1) the tongue, a member
of the body, an organ of
speech 2)
a tongue
a) **the language or dialect**
used by a particular
people distinct from that
of other nations

And for me, that
utterance may be given
unto me, that I may open
my mouth boldly, to make
known the mystery of the
gospel,
Ephesians 6:19

Do not misunderstand
me,
I also speak in an
unknown
language but I also
understand
what this prophesies
is relating to.

Column 2

were prophesying and all
understood the prophecy.
The prophecy can be found in
Acts 2:16-47
¹⁷And it shall come to pass in
the last days, saith God, I will
pour out of My Spirit upon
all flesh: and your sons and
your daughters shall prophesy,
and your young men shall
see visions, and your old men
shall dream dreams: ¹⁸And
on My servants and on my
handmaidens I will pour out
in those days of My Spirit;
and they shall prophesy.

For whosoever shall call upon
the name of the Lord shall be
saved. Romans 10:13

He that believeth and is baptized
shall be saved; but he that
believeth not shall be damned.
Mark 16:16

For whosoever shall call upon
The Name of The Lord shall
be saved. Romans 10:13

But for us also, to whom it shall
be imputed, if we believe on him
that raised up Jesus our Lord
from the dead; Romans 4:24

Column 3

US: that the **world may
believe that thou hast** sent **Me.**
²²And the **glory** which
Thou gavest Me I have
given them; that they **may be
one**, even as **We are One:**
²³I **in** them, and Thou in
Me, that they **may be
made perfect** in
ONE; and that the world
may know that Thou hast
sent Me, and hast **loved
them, AS
THOU HAST LOVED**
John 17:17-26

For God so loved the
world, that He gave His
only begotten Son, that
whosoever believeth {in
him} **should** not perish, but
have everlasting life.
For God sent not His Son
into the world to condemn
the world; but that the
world through Him **might**
be saved. John 3:16 &17

That **if** thou shalt confess with thy
mouth the Lord Jesus, **and** shalt
believe in thine heart that God hath
raised him from the dead, thou shalt
be saved. Romans 10:9

Column 4

He that hateth Me hateth My
Father also. John 15:23

These words spake Jesus, and
lifted up His eyes to heaven,
and said, Father, the hour is
come; glorify Thy Son, that
Thy Son also may glorify
Thee:
As Thou hast given Him
power over all flesh, that He
should give eternal life to as
many as Thou hast given Him.
And this is life eternal, that
they might know **Thee The
only True God, and
Jesus Christ, whom Thou hast
sent.**
John 17:1-3

"How the **ungodly** is justified"
But to him that worketh not,
but believeth on Him that
justifieth the ungodly, his faith
is counted for righteousness
Romans 4:5

But for us also, to whom it
shall be imputed, **If** we believe
on Him/God that raised up
Jesus our Lord from the dead;
Romans 4:24

Summary:

Yahushua The Messiah placed in my spirit to write this quizzing book and I had great joy trying to put it together! (Sometimes it was a challenge) I am blessed with three helpers, Yahweh/God The Father, Yahushua The Messiah/Jesus The Christ The Son of Yahweh and The Holy Ghost; I am using their Hebrew Names praise The Lord!

Illustrations and graphics added in order to clarify the teachings and examples of the word one, one name, one mind, one body and how two and many are made one, also the family in heaven and in earth are to be one.

I have and continue to do weekly on-line quizzing for almost two years, I continue to receive replies from on-line saying how quizzing have helped and blessed them, these quizzes were used in our church for our Wednesday nights bible studies and disciples classes and sometimes in other ministries as well. The members would get so enthusiastic, if I did not hand them out they would call me and some would show up early and work as a team to get the answers. They do encourage teamwork and loving friendships, the quizzes will be a great tool to use in Sunday school and messages. I have also used them to stimulate bible study for those who are incarcerated, in other words quizzing can be used anywhere the word is being taught. Without a doubt, they will inspire and stimulate one's mind and transform his life if he receives the truth.

The scriptures admonish us to be not . . . *conformed to this world: but be ye transformed by the renewing of your mind, that ye may prove what is that good, and acceptable, and* **perfect, will of God.** *Romans 12:2*

If you said to one, if you confess with your mouth The Lord Yahushua/Jesus and believe in your heart that Yahweh/God has raised Him/Yahushua from the dead you shalt be saved. **If he does not understand the words if, confess, shalt and do not ask for the sense of these words his understanding is futile.**

Please, remember, and is in addition. In my Book "A New Revelation From God" and in this book as well, I encourage the messengers, teachers, preaches and readers of the Word from God who do not want to be false witnesses to take a close look at words and how they can change the way one thinks and receive. Anytime one hear, believe, receive and obey Yahweh's Words they are honouring and praising Him.

For **The Father** *judgeth no man,* **but** *hath committed all judgment unto* **The Son:** *That all men* **should** *honour The Son, even as they honour The Father. He that honoureth not The Son honoureth not The Father which hath sent Him. John 5:22-23*

Keywords Search and Phrase:

Bible, Yahweh, God, Yahushua, Jesus, Messiah, Christ, son of God, Son of Man, saved, endure, word, joy, kingdom of God, love, love of God, faith, hope, charity, peace, prosperity, riches, knowledge, wisdom, understanding, one, people, overcome, justify, just, eternal life, life eternal, damnation, condemned, condemnation, abideth, one mind, spirit, our, dwell, us, *righteous*, unrighteous, holy, world, truth, word sanctify, manifest, blood, unholy, wicked, ungodly, sinners, blessed, blessing, curse, blasphemies, law, laws, lawless, commandments, Ten Commandments, finger of God, LORD, Lord, lords, God, Gods, god, gods, angels, seven spirits, living water, commandments of man, covenants, sacrifices, cross, hateth, murder, if, but, prophets, prophetess, sent, went, false teaches, false prophets, antichrist, many, first Adam, second Adam, resurrection, risen, teachers, pastors, Holy and, Holy scriptures.

Dwell, unholy, the ungodly sinners, blessed, blessing and curse, blasphemies, lawless, finger of God, Angel, angels, one in me, Sprit, spirits, living water, Sodom, Gomorrah, hateth, covenants, sacrifices, blood covenant and word covenant, You are My friend if, murder, the Spirit of God, the spirit of antichrist and how to know them, within, call them Adam, the first one sent after the resurrection, the first one Jesus appeared to after He risen, what is love according to the scripture, first thing Paul delivered according to the scriptures, and greater than I.

SOME WORDS, I CALL THE BIG <u>BUT</u> WORD AND THE BIG <u>IF</u> WORD.
"HERE ARE A FEW EXAMPLES, OF POWERFUL WORDS AND PHRASES IN THE BOOK"

Words and phrases like, if, but, and, do, in, shalt, should, shall, might, will, live, liveth, continue, endure until the end, unto, into, may, overcome, overcometh, justify, just, unjust, eternal life, life eternal, eternal damnation, abide, abideth not, one mind, one spirit, one body, same mind, our and us.

<u>**Example: Word Abideth:**</u> **The ear that heareth the reproof of life abideth among the wise**
Proverbs 15:31

He that believeth on The Son hath everlasting life: and he that believeth not The Son shall not see life; but the wrath of God **abideth** on him. John 3:36
And the servant **abideth <u>NOT</u>** in the house <u>forever</u>: but The Son **abideth** ever. John 8:35

I am the vine, ye are the branches: He that **abideth <u>IN</u> Me, and I in him**, the same bringeth forth much fruit: **without Me ye <u>can do nothing</u>**. John 15:5 (In Me) (I in Him)
He that hateth Me hateth My Father also. John 15:23

He that saith he is in the light, and *hateth his brother*, is in darkness even until now. 1 John 2:9
But he that hateth his brother is in darkness, and walketh in darkness, and knoweth not whither he goeth, because that darkness hath blinded his eyes. 1 John 2:11
Whosoever hateth his brother is a murderer: and ye <u>know</u> that <u>no</u> murderer hath *<u>eternal life abiding in</u>* him. 1 John 3:15

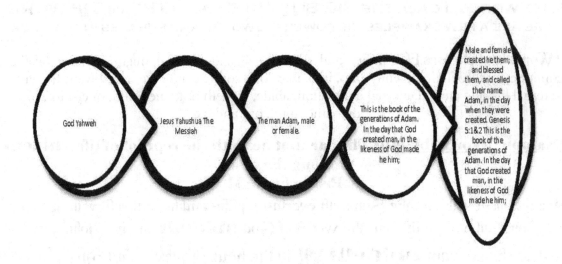

God Yahweh

Jesus Yahushua The Messiah

The man Adam, male or female.

This is the book of the generations of Adam. In the day that God created man, in the likeness of God made he him;

Male and female created he them; and blessed them, and called their name Adam, in the day when they were created. Genesis 5:1&2 This is the book of the generations of Adam. In the day that God created man, in the likeness of God made he him;

Three Thrones

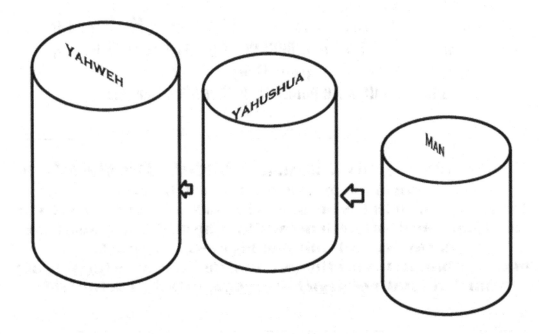

YAHWEH

YAHUSHUA

MAN

For Illustrations Only:

To **Him** THAT **Overcometh** WILL **I grant** TO **sit** WITH **Me** IN **My Throne**, **even as I** ALSO **Overcame**, AND AM **set down with My Father in His Throne**

REVELATION 3:21

JESUS SAITH UNTO HIM, I AM THE WAY, THE TRUTH, AND THE LIFE: no MAN
COMETH unto The Father, BUT BY Me.
JOHN 14:6

Ye have heard how I said unto you, I go away, **and** come **again** unto you. IF ye loved **ME**, ye
would rejoice, because I said, I go unto The Father: for My Father is greater than I. John 14:28

GODHEAD
The Head of all things is
THE FATHER. YAHWEH John 15:1

THE TRUE VINE. HEAD OF EVERY MAN
JESUS/YAHUSHUA THE MESSIAH.

THE HEAD OF YAHUSHUA THE MESSIAH IS
YAHWEH THE FATHER. JOHN 15:1

THE HEAD OF THE WOMAN IS THE MAN.

BUT ALL THE FAMILY HAVE THE FIRST NAME, I KNOW
WE SAY THE LAST NAME BUT IT IS ACTUALLY THE
FIRST NAME.

THIS IS TO SHOW IF WE ARE IN JESUS, WE ARE ALL ONE FAMILY. GAL 3:28

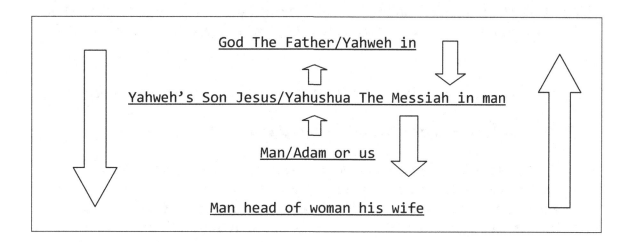

"Adam was over his wife Adam/Eve "Both Named Adam"

Male and female created he them; and blessed them, and called their name Adam, in the day when they were created. Gen. 5:1-3 But I would have you know, that the head of every man is CHRIST; **and the head of the woman is the** MAN; **and the head of Christ is God.** 1 Corinthians 11:3

"We are using this parable in John 15 to illustrate man"

"Please, keep in mind and is in addition to"

1. I AM the TRUE VINE, and MY FATHER IS THE HUSBANDMAN.
[2] Every branch {IN ME} that beareth not fruit HE taketh away: and *every branch that beareth fruit,* He **purgeth it, that it may bring forth more fruit.**
[4] {**Abide in Me,**} and I IN YOU. As the branch **cannot bear fruit of itself, except** it ABIDE IN THE VINE; **no more can ye,** EXCEPT YE ABIDE {IN ME.}
[5] I AM THE VINE, ye are the branches: He that ABIDETH IN ME, **and** I IN HIM, the same bringeth forth much fruit: for **without Me ye can do nothing.**
[3] Now ye are *clean through the word which I have spoken unto you.*

[6] IF **a man abide not in Me, he is cast forth as a branch, and is withered; and men gather them, and cast them** *into the fire, and they are burned.*

[7] If ye {abide in Me, and My words abide in you,} ye SHALL **ask what ye will, and it shall be done unto you.**

[8] HEREIN IS MY FATHER GLORIFIED, THAT YE BEAR MUCH FRUIT; SO SHALL YE BE MY DISCIPLES.

[9] **As The Father hath loved Me, so have I loved you: continue ye in My love.**

[10] If ye KEEP **My commandments, ye shall abide in My love; even as I have kept My Father's commandments, and {abide in His love.}**

[11] These things have I spoken unto you, that **My joy might remain in you, and that your joy might be full.**

[12] **This is My commandment, That ye love one another, as I have loved you.**

[13] **Greater love hath no man than this, that a man lay down his life for his friends.**

[14] **Ye are My friends,** IF **ye do whatsoever I command you.**
[15] **Henceforth I call you not servants; for the servant knoweth not what his lord doeth: but I have called you friends; for all things that I have heard of My Father I have made known unto you.**

¹⁶ Ye have not chosen Me, but I have chosen you, and ordained you, that ye should go and bring forth fruit, and that your fruit should remain: that <u>whatsoever ye shall ask of The Father in My Name</u>, He <u>may</u> give it you.

¹⁷ **These things I command you, that ye love one another.**

¹⁸ If the world hate you, ye know that it *hated Me before it hated you.*

¹⁹ IF ye were of the world, the world would love his own: BUT because ye are <u>not</u> of the world, but I have **chosen you out of the world, therefore <u>the world hateth you.</u>**

²⁰ Remember the word that I said unto you, **The servant is not greater than his lord**. IF they have persecuted ME, they will also PERSECUTE YOU; IF they have <u>kept My saying</u>, they will <u>keep yours also.</u>

²¹ But all these things will they do unto you for My Mame's sake, because they <u>KNOW NOT</u> Him that sent ME.

²² **If I had not come and spoken unto them, they** *had not had sin*: **but now they have <u>no</u> cloak for their sin.**

²³ **He that hateth Me hateth My Father also.**

²⁴ **If I had not done among them <u>the works which none other man did, they had not had sin:</u> but now have they <u>both</u> seen and hated <u>both</u> Me and My Father.**

²⁵ But this cometh to pass, that the <u>word might be fulfilled</u> that is written in their law, *They hated Me without a cause.*

²⁶ **But when <u>the Comforter is come</u>, whom I will <u>send unto you</u> from The Father**, EVEN **the Spirit of truth, which proceedeth <u>from The Father</u>, He shall <u>testify of Me:</u>**

²⁷ **And ye also <u>shall bear witness,</u> because ye have been with Me from the beginning.**

What will the Spirit of truth do? He shall <u>testify of Me:</u>

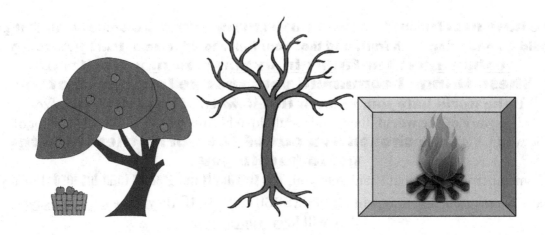

(1) What is good on this tree?
Abundant of fruits

(2) What is wrong with Mr. Tree?
No fruits, all dried up and good for nothing

(3) What will happen to Mr. Tree?
Mr. Tree shall be, cast into a furnace of fire.

One is dead and therefore fallen and one is alive and producing fruits.

I am the vine, ye are *the branches*: He that {**abideth in Me,**} <u>AND</u> **I in him,** the same

bringeth forth much fruit: for without Me ye can do nothing. John 15:5 &6

IF a man abide <u>*not in Me*</u>, he is cast forth as a branch, and is *withered*; and men gather them, and cast them into the fire, and they are burned.

As therefore **the tares are gathered and burned in the fire; so shall it be in the end of this world**. The Son of man shall send forth His angels, and they **shall** gather out of His kingdom all things that offend, and them, which do iniquity; AND shall cast them into a furnace of fire: there shall be wailing and gnashing of teeth. Matthew 13:40-42

How can one gather up the trash in his house if there was none?
"Gather OUT Of <u>His kingdom</u>"

YAHWEH/THE FATHER   YAHUSHUA/THE SON   MAN

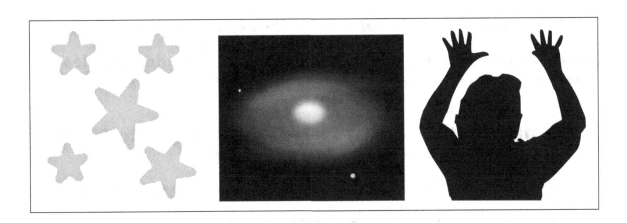

And He shall set the sheep on His right hand, but the goats on the left. Then shall The King say unto them on <u>His right hand,</u> Come, ye blessed of My Father, inherit the kingdom prepared for you from the foundation of the world: For I was an hungred, and ye gave Me meat: I was thirsty, and ye gave me drink: I was a stranger, and ye took Me in: Naked, and ye clothed Me: I was sick, and ye visited Me: I was in prison, and ye came unto Me. Then shall the righteous answer Him, saying, Lord, when saw we thee an hungred, and fed Thee? or thirsty, and gave Thee drink? When saw we Thee a stranger, and took Thee in? or naked, and clothed Thee? Or when saw we thee sick, or in prison, and came unto thee? And The King shall answer and say unto them, Verily I say unto you, Inasmuch as ye have done it unto one of the least of these My brethren, ye have done it unto Me. Then shall He say also unto them on the left hand, Depart from Me, ye cursed, <u>into everlasting fire</u>, prepared for the devil and his angels: For I was an hungred, and ye gave Me no meat: I was thirsty, and ye gave Me no drink . . . . And these shall go away into everlasting punishment: but the righteous into life eternal. Matthew 25

We should not make the choice to be on the left, if we are on the left, we are on the wrong side of God.

<u>NOW</u> THE WORKS OF THE FLESH ARE MANIFEST, *which are these; Adultery, fornication, uncleanness, lasciviousness, Idolatry, witchcraft, hatred, variance, emulations, wrath, strife, seditions, heresies, Envyings, murders, drunkenness, revellings, and <u>such like</u>: of the which I tell you <u>before,</u> as I have also told you in <u>time past</u>, that they which <u>do such things shall not inherit the kingdom of God</u>. Galatians 5:19-21*

For ye were SOMETIMES DARKNESS, but now are YE LIGHT IN THE LORD: walk as children of light:

FOR THE FRUIT OF THE SPIRIT IS IN ALL GOODNESS AND RIGHTEOUSNESS AND TRUTH

Proving what is *acceptable unto The Lord*. Ephesians 5:8-10

But the fruit of the Spirit is love, joy, peace, longsuffering, gentleness, goodness, faith, Meekness, temperance: against such there is no law.

And they that are *Christ's* have *crucified the flesh* with the *affections and lusts*.

If we live in the Spirit, let us also walk in the Spirit.

Let us not be desirous of *vain glory*, provoking one another, envying one another. Galatians 5:22-28

"This is why questions is so important"

If I abide but if, I do not abide.

"Was In the Kingdom BUT Now Out Of the Kingdom"

"There are gods many and there are lords many"

For though there be that are **called gods,** whether in heaven or in earth, (as there be gods many, and lords many,) But to us there is but one God, **The Father, of whom are all things,** and we in Him; <u>and</u> one Lord Jesus Christ, by whom are all things, and we by Him. 1 Corinthians 8:5 &6

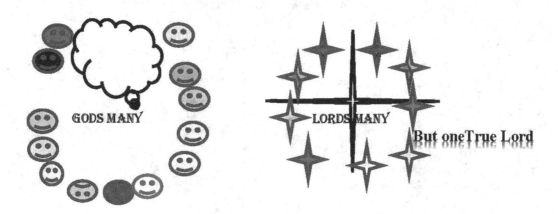

Information found in Strong's Concordance with Hebrew and Greek Lexicon

However, I research and compose this information.

ENGLISH AND HEBREW WORDS AND PRONUNCIATIONS:

The word family in Hebrew is, **Patria pa-tre-a**.
..Of whom the whole family in heaven and earth is named,
Genesis 5:1-2 both named Adam in the day that God created man *Male and female*.

Jacob had twelve sons, his son Joseph first two sons became Israel's sons.
They all had the same name or title "Israel" all the Hebrews took on the title or name Israel called the Israelites.

Esau is Edom; he is Esau the father of the Edomites, these all had the name or title Genesis 36:8 Thus dwelt Esau in mount Seir: Esau is Edom. These are the sons of Esau, who is Edom, and these are their Dukes. Genesis 36:19 Duke Magdiel, Duke Iram: these be the Dukes of Edom, according to their habitations in the land of their possession: he is Esau the father of the Edomites. Genesis 36:43

My father's first name is Wiley and every male throughout his family tree continue to carry the title of his first name Wiley, his sons and sons-sons and so on. When we are married to The Messiah/Christ males or females, we carry on His Title as we say in English Christians but I say Christ-ians meaning, the beginning sounds the same.
Research By, Prophetess and Pastor Dr. Mary Neal

Name or title for God The Father: Yahweh
Name or title for Jesus the Son of Yahweh: Root word: Yahushua and Yĕhowshuwa`
Yeh·hō·shü`·ah
Jesus: Transliteration Iēsous   Pronunciation ē-ā-sü`s
" Yasha` Yä·shah   God and gods: Theos and Theo's on both God and gods, see
examples Ps.82:6-8 & John 10:34-36

Lord and lords: Kyrios   Kü`-rē-os     on both Lord and lords    kü`-rē-os
LORD: Yĕhovah Yeh·hō·vä`
Christ: Christos Khrē-sto's
Christians: Christianos Khrē-stē-ä-no's Khrē-sto's
Joshua or Jehoshua: = "Jehovah is salvation"
1) Christ was The Messiah, The Son of God Christ = "anointed" 2) Anointed
One: Heis   Hā`s   Numeral, many or numerous.
Many: Polys   Po-lü`s
Spirit: Pneuma   Pnyü`-mä    Root Word: Pneō Pne`-ō {every spirits good and
evil} Pneuma

Some examples, on the word "ONE"

..That they all may be one . . . John 17

..Ye are all one in Christ Jesus Gal. 3:28

..That they were all of one mind . . . 2 Samuel 19:14

..Were also of one mind to make David king . . . 1 Chronicles 12:38

. . . With one mind they plot together . . . Psalm 83:5

.With one mind and one voice . . . Romans 15:6

. . . Be of one mind . . . 2 Corinthians 13:11

. . . Being like-minded . . . being one in spirit and of one mind . . .
Philippians 2:2

. . . They shall be one flesh Gen.2:24

. . . Behold, the man is become as one of us Gen . . . 3:22

There are gods many:

God, Gods, god, gods all the sounds are the same, one or more than one
and the pronunciations are the same in Hebrew.

THERE ARE LORDS MANY:

LORD, Lord, Lords, lord, lords, all the sounds are the same, one or more than one and the pronunciations are the same in Hebrew.

Spirit, spirit or spirits the pronunciation are the same in Hebrew.

We know that there are many spirits and Spirits. Ensamples, The Spirit of God, the (7) Spirits, Satan is a spirit and evil spirits but the sounds are the same, one or more than one.

However, Scripture teaches us that there **is *One True God* and** *One True Lord and God hath made that same **Jesus, whom they crucified, both** Lord and Christ.*

But to us there is but One God, The Father, of whom are all things, and we in Him; <u>AND</u> one Lord Jesus Christ, by whom <u>are all things,</u> and we *<u>by</u>* Him. 1 Corinthians 8:6

AND THIS IS LIFE ETERNAL, that they **might know** Thee **The only True God**, and Jesus Christ, whom Thou hast sent. John 17:3

For they themselves shew of us what manner of entering in we had unto you, and how ye turned to <u>God from idols</u> to serve THE LIVING AND TRUE GOD; **And to** <u>WAIT</u> for *His Son from heaven, whom He raised from the dead, even Jesus, <u>which delivered us from the wrath to come</u>.*

1 Thessalonians 1:9 &10

Therefore let <u>all</u> the house OF ISRAEL KNOW <u>assuredly</u>, that GOD HATH MADE the SAME JESUS, WHOM YE HAVE CRUCIFIED, BOTH LORD AND CHRIST. Acts 2:36

Now for <u>a long season</u> Israel <u>hath been without</u> THE TRUE GOD, **and** <u>*without*</u> *a teaching priest, and without law. 2 Chronicles 15:3*

But THE LORD IS THE TRUE GOD, He is THE LIVING GOD, and an EVERLASTING KING: at His **wrath the earth shall tremble,** and <u>the nations shall not be able to abide</u> His indignation. Jeremiah 10:10

And we <u>KNOW</u> THAT The Son of God is come, and HATH GIVEN US AN UNDERSTANDING, that we <u>*may*</u> *know Him that is True*, and we are <u>in Him that is True</u>, <u>even</u> in His Son Jesus Christ. This is The True God, <u>and eternal life</u>. 1 John 5:20

**..Of whom the whole family in heaven and earth is named,
Ephesians 3:15**

The word family in Hebrew is, Patria pa-tre-a

JACOB had twelve sons, his son Joseph first two sons became Israel's sons.

They all had the same name or title "Israel" all the Hebrews took on the title or name Israel called the Israelites.

ESAU IS EDOM; he is Esau the father of the Edomites.
THESE ALL HAD THE NAME OR TITLE "DUKES"
Genesis 36:8 Thus dwelt Esau in mount Seir: Esau is Edom.
These are the sons of Esau, who is Edom, and these are their Dukes. Genesis 36:19
Duke Magdiel, Duke Iram: these be the Dukes of Edom, according to their habitations in the land of their possession: he is Esau the father of the Edomites. Genesis 36:43

When one take a husband or wife, they both have the same name or title, when we are married to Yahushua The Messiah/Jesus The Christ, we take on His Name or Title as said in English Christians as I say Christ-ians (Meaning, the beginning of both words sounds exactly the same as,

YAH, Yahweh. YAH, Yahushua. Christ Christ-ians. Khrē-sto's **Khrē-stē-ä-no's**

Tongue: A part of speech

Hebrew word **Glossa:** Pronunciation glos-sa

A part of speech

1) the tongue, a member of the body, an organ of speech 2) a tongue
a) **The language or dialect** used by a particular people distinct from that of other nations

In order to get the revelation and understanding in the book of Acts chapter 2, we need to study the entire chapter and cross-reference it with Joel chapter 2, Number 11, and Proverbs 1.
If we do so, we should understand these were people from every nation and they were prophesying and all understood the prophecy, the scripture said, they were all filled with the Holy Ghost, and began to speak with other tongues, as the Spirit gave them utterance. "Not in but with (KJV)
Focus on these verse Numbers 11: 25 and Proverbs 1:23

And The Lᴏʀᴅ came down in a cloud, and spake unto him, and took of the spirit that was upon him, and gave it unto the seventy elders: and it came to pass, that, when the spirit rested upon them, they prophesied, and did not cease.

Proverbs 1:23
Turn you at my reproof: behold, I will pour out my spirit unto you, I will make known My words unto you.

Acts 2:5-11

[5] And there were dwelling at Jerusalem Jews, devout men, out of every nation under heaven. [6] Now when this was noised abroad, the multitude came together, and were confounded, because that every man heard them speak in his own language. [7] And they were all amazed and marvelled, saying one to another, Behold, are not all these which speak Galilaeans? [8] And how hear we every man in our own tongue, wherein we were born? [9] Parthians, and Medes, and Elamites, and the dwellers in Mesopotamia, and in Judaea, and Cappadocia, in Pontus, and Asia, [10] Phrygia, and Pamphylia, in Egypt, and in the parts of Libya about Cyrene, and strangers of Rome, Jews and proselytes, [11] Cretes and Arabians, we do hear them speak in our tongues the wonderful works of God.

Acts 10:45-48

[45] And they of the circumcision which believed were astonished, as many as came with Peter, because that on the Gentiles also was poured out the gift of the Holy Ghost. [46] For they heard them speak with tongues, and magnify God. Then answered Peter, [47] Can any man forbid water, that these should not be baptized, which have received the Holy Ghost as well as we? [48] And he commanded them to be baptized in the name of the Lord. Then prayed they him to tarry certain days.

Acts 2:4

[4] And they were all filled with the Holy Ghost, and began to speak with other tongues, as the Spirit gave them utterance.

SCRIPTURES ON UTTERANCE:

1 Corinthians 1:5 That in every thing ye are enriched by Him, in all utterance, and in all knowledge;

2 Corinthians 8:7 Therefore, as ye abound in every thing, in faith, and utterance, and knowledge, and in all diligence, and in your love to us, see that ye abound in this grace also.

Ephesians 6:19 AND FOR ME, THAT UTTERANCE MAY BE GIVEN UNTO ME, THAT I MAY OPEN MY MOUTH BOLDLY, TO MAKE KNOWN THE MYSTERY OF THE GOSPEL,

Colossians 4:3 Withal praying also for us, that God would open unto us a door of utterance, to SPEAK the MYSTERY OF CHRIST, FOR WHICH I AM ALSO IN BONDS:

Example of quizzing #83

1. What are the different readings in these two passages of scriptures?

a. And I have filled him with The Spirit of God, in wisdom, and in understanding, and in knowledge, and in all manner of workmanship, to devise cunning works, to work in gold, and in silver, and in brass. Exodus 31:2-4

b. And he hath filled him with The Spirit of God, in wisdom, in understanding, and in knowledge, and in all manner of workmanship; And to devise curious works, to work in gold, and in silver, and in brass, Exodus 35:31-32

A. **a.** EXODUS 31:2-4 AND I HAVE FILLED HIM WITH THE SPIRIT OF GOD.

TO DEVISE CUNNING WORKS, TO WORK IN GOLD, AND IN SILVER, AND IN BRASS.

EXODUS 35:31-32 **AND HE** HATH FILLED HIM WITH THE SPIRIT OF GOD.

AND TO DEVISE CURIOUS WORKS, TO WORK IN GOLD, AND IN SILVER, AND IN BRASS.

Exodus 35:30-32 **Amplified Bible** (AMP)

And Moses said to the Israelites, See, The Lord *called by name Bezalel son of Uri, the son of Hur, of the tribe of Judah; And* He has *filled him with The Spirit of God, with ability and wisdom, with intelligence and understanding, and with knowledge and all craftsmanship,*

2. When shall we understand righteousness, judgment, and discretion shall preserve us and understanding shall keep us?

A. WHEN WISDOM ENTERETH INTO OUR HEART, AND KNOWLEDGE IS PLEASANT UNTO OUR SOUL. Proverbs 2:10 Please read 2:1-11

---

2 My son, if thou wilt receive my words, and hide my commandments with thee; [2] So that thou incline thine ear unto wisdom, and apply thine heart to understanding; [3] Yea, if thou criest after knowledge, and liftest up thy voice for understanding; [4] If thou seekest her as silver, and searchest for her as for hid treasures; [5] Then shalt thou understand the fear of the LORD, and find the knowledge of God. [6] For the LORD giveth wisdom: out of his mouth cometh knowledge and understanding. [7] He layeth up sound wisdom for the righteous: he is a buckler to them that walk uprightly. [8] He keepeth the paths of judgment, and preserveth the way of his saints. [9] Then shalt thou understand righteousness, and judgment, and equity; yea, every good path. [10] When wisdom entereth into thine heart, and knowledge is pleasant unto thy soul; [11] Discretion shall preserve thee, understanding shall keep thee

---

3. Should we; the saints of The Most High God (Yahweh) have wisdom in us to do Judgment?

Q. Who was it, in the book of 1 Kings that they saw, that the wisdom of God was in him, to do judgment?

A. King Solomon. 1 Kings 3:28

And all Israel heard of the judgment which the king had judged; and they feared the king: for they saw that the **wisdom** of God was in him, to do judgment.

The Objective

"TEST YOUR KNOWLEDGE REVELATION QUIZZING THEOLOGICAL WORK BOOK"

Questions are good, if a question was never ask you might not be motivated to think, these are evoking, mind provoking questions that will motivate ones thinking.

The goal is to seek and save as many souls as possible and deliver souls out of darkness and from the attacks of Satan.

This book is for those who desire more clarification, wisdom, knowledge and understanding in the Holy Word.

Saints, do not be afraid to change your minds if your minds do not agree with the Holy Word.

And be not conformed to this world: but be ye transformed by the renewing of your mind, that ye may prove what is that good, and acceptable, and perfect, will of God. Romans 12:2

"I did not send My Word to kill you but, I did send it to destroy Satan works in you"

Have you ever tried to kill a horse when he is almost dead, or do you try to lift him up instead?

Have you ever tried to knock a lame duck down or do you pick him up before he drown?

I never tried to kick a man when he was already down but I will try to kick the one that is holding him down! **That OLD DEVIL that is, called Satan**. Because,

The thief cometh not, but for to steal, and to kill, and to destroy John 10:10

1 Paul, a servant of God, and an apostle of Jesus Christ, according to the faith of God's elect, and the **ACKNOWLEDGING OF THE TRUTH** which is after **godliness; In hope of eternal life,** which God, that **CANNOT LIE, promised before the world began**; But hath in **due times manifested His Word through preaching**, which is committed unto me according to **the commandment of God our Saviour**.
Titus 1:1-3

But whoso **KEEPETH HIS WORD**, in him **VERILY IS THE LOVE OF GOD PERFECTED**: hereby KNOW WE THAT WE ARE {IN HIM.} 1 John 2:5

And they were astonished at **HIS DOCTRINE**: for **His word was with power. Luke 4:32**

Let Yahushua be madeknown in you today, (For He saith, I have heard thee in a time accepted, and in the day of salvation have I succoured thee: behold, **now is the accepted time**; behold, **now is the day of salvation**

2 Corinthians 6:2

To reveal His Son in me, that I might preach him among the heathen; immediately I conferred not with flesh and blood: Galatians 1:16

Contents Part 2

TABLE OF CONTENTS:

QUZZING ONE THROUGH EIGHTY

Quizzing Starts Here:

1. What books and chapters can you find the word college?

2. How many times does the word collage appear in The Bible?

3. Who dwelled in the college a Prophet or Prophetess?

4. Who sent the word to King Josiah from The Lord?

5. Did King Josiah humble himself after he heard the Word from The LORD?

6. Did gender matter to him?

7. How does one purify his soul?

COLLEGE

1. What books and chapters can you find the word college?

2 Kings 22:14 & 2 Chronicles 34:22

2. How many times does the word collage appear in The Bible?

A. Twice/two times

So Hilkiah the priest, and Ahikam, and Achbor, and Shaphan, and Asahiah, went unto Huldah the prophetess, the wife of Shallum the son of Tikvah, the son of Harhas, keeper of the wardrobe; (now she dwelt in Jerusalem in the college;) and they communed with her. 2 Kings 22:14

And Hilkiah, and they that the king had appointed, went to Huldah the prophetess, the wife of Shallum the son of Tikvath, the son of Hasrah, keeper of the wardrobe; (now she dwelt in Jerusalem in the college:) and they spake to her to that effect. 2 Chronicles 34:22

3. Who dwelled in the college a Prophet or Prophetess?

A. Prophetess

Huldah the prophetess dwelt in Jerusalem in the college:

4. Who sent the word to King Josiah from The Lord?

A. HULDAH THE PROPHETESS.

5. Did King Josiah humble himself after he heard the Word from The LORD?

A. Yes. 2 Kings 22:18-20 .Because thine heart was tender, and thou hast humbled thyself before The LORD, when thou HEARDEST WHAT I SPAKE AGAINST THIS PLACE.

6. Did gender matter to him?

A. No Truth will always prevail!

7. How does one purify his soul?

A. By obeying the truth through the Spirit unto unfeigned love of the brethren.
Seeing ye have purified your souls in obeying the truth through the Spirit unto unfeigned love of the brethren, see that ye love one another with a pure heart fervently: 1 Peter 1:22

ADAM'S WOMAN

1. Did Adam go searching for a wife or did The Lord bring him a wife?

2. What was the first name Adam called the woman?

3. What was the second name Adam called the woman?

4. Why did he change the woman's name?

5. The word man is it twofold/two parts he is male or female?

6. God created the woman, blessed her and gave her a name.
Q. What name did God call the woman in the day he created her?

7. There were seven Spirits upon Christ Jesus; these seven Spirits sent down to earth why?

8. What are these seven Spirits in the book of Revelation?

So that we may boldly say, The Lord is my helper, and I will not fear what man shall do unto me. Heb. 13:6

ADAM'S WOMAN

1. Did Adam go searching for a wife or did The Lord bring him a wife?

A. And the rib, which the LORD God had taken from man, made he a
woman, and brought her unto the man. Gen. 2:22

..The woman whom thou gavest to be with me . . . 3:12

2. What was the first name Adam called the woman?

A. Woman. And Adam said, This is now bone of my bones, and flesh of my flesh:
she shall be called Woman, because she was taken out of Man. Gen. 2:23

3. What was the second name Adam called the woman?

A. Adam called his wife's name <u>EVE</u>. Gen. 3:20

4. Why did he change the woman's name?

A. HE CHANGED HER NAME BECAUSE; SHE WAS THE <u>MOTHER OF ALL LIVING</u>.
Gen 3:20

5. The word man is it twofold/two parts he is male or female?

A. And God said, Let <u>us</u> make <u>man</u> in <u>our</u> image, after <u>our</u> likeness: and let **THEM**
have dominion . . . Gen 1:26 So God created **MAN** in His own image, in the **IMAGE
OF GOD CREATED <u>HE HIM</u>; <u>MALE AND FEMALE</u>** created **HE <u>THEM</u>**. Gen.1:27. <u>IF</u> we
are in Christ, we are "**ONE**" <u>Neither</u> MALE <u>NOR</u> FEMALE: for ye **<u>ARE ALL</u>
<u>ONE</u> IN CHRIST JESUS.**

---

6. God created the woman, blessed her and gave her a name.

Q. What name did God call the woman in the day he created her?

A. **ADAM.** .. In the day that <u>God created</u> **man,** in the likeness of God <u>made he him;</u>

<u>Male and female</u> created He **THEM;** and **BLESSED THEM,** and **CALLED THEIR
NAME** <u>ADAM</u>, in the <u>day when</u> **THEY** <u>were created</u> Genesis 5:1-3

4

ADAM'S WOMAN

7. There were seven Spirits upon Christ Jesus; these seven Spirits sent down to earth why?

A. That we might have the same Spirits that was upon The Son of God! Rev. 5:6 (And I beheld, and, lo, in the midst of the throne and of the four beasts, and in the midst of the elders, stood a Lamb as it had been slain, having **seven horns and seven eyes, which are the seven Spirits of God sent forth into all the earth.** Rev. 5.6 **also Is. 11:1-3**

The spirit of The LORD shall <u>rest upon him</u>, (John 1:30-33) .I saw the Spirit descending from heaven like a dove, and it <u>abode upon Him</u>. ..Upon whom thou shalt see The <u>Spirit descending, and remaining</u> on Him.

(And I beheld, and, lo, in the midst of the throne and of the four beasts, and in the midst of the elders, **stood a Lamb** as it had been slain, having <u>**seven horns**</u> and <u>**seven eyes,**</u> which the seven Spirits of God are SENT FORTH INTO ALL THE EARTH. Rev. 5.6, Is. 11:1-3

The spirit of The LORD shall <u>rest upon Him</u>, AND John 1:30-33) .I saw the Spirit descending from heaven like a dove, and it <u>**abode upon Him**</u>. ..UPON WHOM THOU SHALT <u>SEE</u> THE <u>SPIRIT DESCENDING, AND REMAINING</u> ON HIM.

(1) Spirit of <u>The LORD,</u> (YAHWEH GOD THE FATHER) shall **rest upon Him** (THE SON OF GOD YAHUSHUA THE MESSIAH) (2) The spirit of Wisdom. (3) The spirit of Understanding. (4) The spirit of Counsel. (5) The spirit of Might. (6) The spirit of Knowledge. (7) The spirit of The Fear of The LORD.

(GOD THE FATHER) . . . Shall makes Him of quick understanding in the fear of The LORD: and He shall not judge after the sight of His eyes, neither reprove after the hearing of His ears: Is. 11:1-3

READ IS. CHAPTER 11 FOR A BETTER UNDERSTANDING AND PROVERBS CHAPTERS 1 & 4)

8. What are the seven Spirits in the book of Revelation 5?

1. POWER, 2 RICHES, 3 WISDOM, 4 STRENGTH, 5 HONOUR, 6 GLORY AND

7 BLESSING REVELATION 5:12

Praise God for The Lamb that is worthy to receive power, riches, wisdom, strength, honour, glory and blessing.

ADAM'S WOMAN

IF WE ARE FOLLOWERS OF CHRIST; CHRIST-IANS WE ARE ALSO SONS AND DAUGHTERS OF GOD AND HAVE THESE SAME SPIRITS <u>IF</u> WE LOVE GOD AND HIS SON JESUS <u>AND</u> ONE ANOTHER.

HE THAT HATH MY COMMANDMENTS, AND <u>KEEPETH THEM,</u> HE IT IS THAT LOVETH ME: AND HE THAT LOVETH ME SHALL <u>BE LOVED OF MY FATHER</u>, AND I WILL LOVE HIM, AND WILL <u>MANIFEST MYSELF</u> TO HIM. JOHN 14:21

MANIFEST MYSELF: MAKE MYSELF KNOWN, SHOW SOMETHING CLEARLY, TO MAKE SOMETHING EVIDENT.

THE MOUTH OF GOD

1. What passage in the Bible can we find this statement, Light Bread?

2. After the children of Israel departed out of the land of Egypt, where did they go?

3. Why Did The LORD lead the children of Israel through the wilderness forty years?

4. What was The LORD purpose and plan when He led them through the wilderness forty years?

5. How many times is this statement quoted in scripture, "By every word that proceedeth out of The

   Mouth of The LORD doth man live?

6. How many times is this quotation in scripture, "By every word that proceedeth out of The Mouth of God?

7. How many times is this quoted in Scripture By every Word of God?

> *Then they cried unto the LORD in their trouble, and he saved them out of their distresses. Ps. 107:13*

THE MOUTH OF GOD

ANSWERS ONLY

1. A. Number 21:5

And the people spake against God, and against Moses, Wherefore have ye brought us up out of

Egypt to die in the wilderness? for there is <u>no bread</u>, neither is there any water; and our soul loatheth this

light bread.

A. Into the **WILDERNESS OF SIN**. Exodus 16:1

3. A. TO HUMBLE THEM, TO PROVE THEM, TO KNOW WHAT WAS IN THEIR HEART, <u>WHETHER THEY WOULD KEEP HIS COMMANDMENTS OR NOT.</u> DEUT. 8:2

4. A. That He might <u>make them know</u> that man <u>doth not</u> live by bread only, but by <u>every word</u> that proceedeth out of The Mouth of The LORD <u>doth man live</u>. Duet.8:3

5. A. One time
By every Word that proceedeth out of The Mouth of The LORD doth man live. Deut. 8:3

6. A. One time
By every Word that proceedeth out of The Mouth of God. Matthew.4:4

7. A One Time
By every Word of God. Luke 4:4

THEN THEY CRIED UNTO THE LORD IN THEIR TROUBLE, AND HE SAVED THEM OUT OF THEIR DISTRESSES. PS. 107:13

THE GREAT TEMPTATIONS

1. A voice came from Heaven saying, this is My Beloved Son, in whom I am well pleased.

Matthew 3:17

Q. What happened to Jesus after His Father confessed that He was His beloved Son and He was well pleased with Him?

2. Once you are justified by faith where will you be led?

3. Once the ungodly man is justified by faith and the blood of Christ, he is reconciled to God by the death of His Son Jesus (Yahushua The Messiah) Please, read Romans chapter 4 & 5.
Q. Does God tempt him with evil?

4. What book and chapters can we find the great temptations?

5. Now that you know you will be tempted, what should you do?

6. The LORD brought the children of Israel out of the land of Egypt, and redeemed them out of the house of servants.

Q. Whom did The LORD send before the children of Israel to deliver them?

AND WHEN WE CRIED UNTO THE LORD GOD OF OUR FATHERS, THE LORD HEARD OUR VOICE, AND LOOKED ON OUR AFFLICTION, AND OUR LABOUR, AND OUR OPPRESSION DEUT.26:7

THE GREAT TEMPTATIONS

> 1. A voice came from Heaven saying, This is My Beloved Son, in whom I am well pleased Matthew 3:17.

> **Q. What happened to Jesus after His Father confessed that He was His beloved Son and He was <u>well pleased</u> with Him?**

> A. **Jesus was, led up of The Spirit into the wilderness to be tempted of the devil.**

2. Once you are justified by faith, where will you be led?

A. Into the wilderness (The world) tried of the Devil.

But, For we have not an high priest which cannot be touched with the feeling of our infirmities; but was in all points <u>tempted like as we are</u>, yet <u>without sin</u>. Heb. 4:15

3. After <u>the ungodly man is justified</u> by faith and the blood of Jesus Christ, he is reconciled to God (Yahweh) by the death of His Son. (Please, read Romans chapter 4 & 5)

Q. Does God tempt him with evil?

A. No. Let no man say when <u>he is tempted</u>, I am tempted of God: <u>for God cannot be tempted with evil</u>, <u>neither tempts he</u> <u>any man</u>: But every man is tempted, when he is <u>drawn away of his own lust</u>, and <u>enticed</u>. James 1:13 & 14

4. What book and chapters can we find the great temptations?

A. *The great temptations Deut. Chapter 7 & 29. Thou shalt not be afraid of them: but shalt well remember what the LORD thy God did unto Pharaoh, and unto all Egypt; The great temptations which thine eyes saw, and the signs, and the wonders, and the mighty hand, and the stretched out arm, whereby the LORD thy God brought thee out: so shall the LORD thy God do unto all the people of whom thou art afraid. Moreover the LORD thy God will send the hornet among them, until they that are left, and hide themselves from thee, be destroyed.*

Deuteronomy 7:18-20 And Moses called unto all Israel, and said unto them, Ye have seen all that the LORD did before your eyes in the land of Egypt unto Pharaoh, and unto all his servants, and unto all his land; The great temptations which thine eyes have seen, the signs, and those great miracles: Yet the LORD hath not given you an heart to perceive, and eyes to see, and ears to hear, unto this day. Deuteronomy 29:2-4

THE GREAT TEMPTATIONS

SAVED FROM WHAT?

5. Now that we know that we will be tempted, what should we do?

A. **SUBMIT** yourselves therefore to **GOD.** (**Obey His Word**) RESIST THE DEVIL,

(**WE NEED TO RESIST**) and **he will flee from you.** James 4:7

Pray the **p**rayer that **JESUS TAUGHT HIS DISCIPLES TO PRAY DAILY,**
ESPECIALLY LEAD US NOT INTO TEMPTATION, **BUT** deliver us from evil. Matt. 6:13
& Luke 11:4

MY FAVORITE VERSES ARE CALL AND CRIED UNTO THE LORD.

"LOOK UP CALL IN ADDITION, CRIED UNTO THE LORD:

Whosoever shall call upon The Name of The Lord shall be saved. ROMANS 10:13

BUT WHEN THE CHILDREN OF ISRAEL **CRIED UNTO THE LORD**, THE
LORD **RAISED THEM UP A DELIVERER** . . . JUDGES 3:15

Falling into temptations, suffering, diseases and whatever, if we believe and
CONTINUE TO OBEY and follow The Lord Jesus Christ. (Yahushua The Messiah)

But **do _not be deceived_ _we need to repent and obey His voice_** and sometimes it means
longsuffering. Remember, **Job received <u>double for his troubles</u> and** The LORD gave
Job <u>twice as much</u> as he had before. Job 42:10 Praise The Lord!

6. The LORD brought the children of Israel out of the land of Egypt, and <u>redeemed</u>
them out of the house of <u>servants</u>.

Q. Whom did The LORD send before the children of Israel?

A. The LORD sent <u>MOSES</u>, <u>AARON</u>, and <u>MIRIAM.</u>

DISAPPOINTED, MANY HAVE NEVER HEARD OR DID NOT RECEIVE THE REVELATION THAT <u>WOMEN WERE ALSO SENT BY THE LORD</u>!

JESUS I KNOW, AND PAUL I KNOW; BUT WHO ARE YE/YOU?

1. What does The Lord Require of His People?

2. What is required in stewards?

3. Israel cried unto The LORD many times and He rose up deliverers to deliver them.

Q. Did The LORD deliver them without confession and repentance every time?
4. Where did The LORD send Israel or to whom did He send them?
Answer found in the book of Judges Chapter 10.

5. How did they respond, after they heard the warning and judgment from The LORD?

6. What shall The LORD do for those who turn at His reproof?

7. How many times is this quoted in scriptures, I will pour out My spirit and pour out of My spirit?

8. Jesus I know, and Paul I know; but who are ye/you?

Q. Where in scripture is this quoted?

JESUS I KNOW, AND PAUL I KNOW; BUT WHO ARE YE/YOU?

ANSWERS ONLY

1. A. He hath shewed thee, **O MAN, WHAT IS GOOD;** and WHAT DOTH THE LORD require of thee, but **TO DO JUSTLY, AND TO LOVE MERCY, AND TO WALK HUMBLY WITH THY GOD?** Micah 6:8

2. A. Moreover it is **REQUIRED IN STEWARDS, THAT A MAN BE FOUND FAITHFUL.**

3. 1 Corinthians 4:2

4. A. No

Yet ye have FORSAKEN ME, AND SERVED OTHER GODS: wherefore I WILL DELIVER YOU <u>NO MORE</u>. Judges 10:13

5. A. GO AND CRY UNTO THE GODS which <u>YE HAVE CHOSEN</u>; LET THEM DELIVER YOU IN THE TIME OF YOUR TRIBULATION. Judges 10: 14

6. A. <u>**CONFESSIONS AND REPENTANT**</u>, **THEY** *ACKNOWLEDGE THEIR TRANSGRESSION AND SERVED THE LORD.*

And the children of Israel said unto The LORD, WE HAVE SINNED: *do thou unto us whatsoever seemeth good unto Thee;* **DELIVER US ONLY**, we pray Thee, this day. And they <u>PUT AWAY THE STRANGE GODS</u> FROM AMONG THEM, <u>AND</u> <u>SERVED THE LORD</u>: and <u>HIS SOUL WAS GRIEVED FOR THE MISERY OF ISRAEL</u>. Judges 10:15-16

JESUS I KNOW, AND PAUL I KNOW; BUT WHO ARE YE/YOU?

IF WE <u>CONFESS OUR SINS</u>, HE IS FAITHFUL AND JUST TO FORGIVE US OUR SINS, **AND TO CLEANSE US FROM ALL UNRIGHTEOUSNESS**. 1 John 1:9

The big but and if words: BUT IF <u>I DO NOT CONFESS AND REPENT IS HE FAITHFUL AND JUST TO FORGIVE ME?</u>

YOU ANSWER. YES OR NO ____

I SAY NO.

6. **A. I will pour out My Spirit unto you, I will make known My words unto you.** Proverbs 1:23

7. **A. Quoted three times in scriptures.** Proverbs 1:23, Joel 2:28 & Acts 2:17

8. **A.** And THE EVIL SPIRIT ANSWERED AND SAID, **JESUS I KNOW**, and **PAUL I KNOW**; **_BUT_** WHO ARE YE/YOU? *Acts 19:15*

CALL UPON THE NAME OF THE LORD/YAWEA

1. When did man begin to call upon The Name of The LORD?

2. Where in scriptures did man begin to call upon The Name of The LORD?

3. How does this scripture read in Romans 10:13 in the King James Version?

For whosoever shall call upon The Name of The Lord should, shalt, will or shall be saved.

4. Where is the first time we can see where man walked with God and had sons and daughters?

5. What is the principal thing/primary thing we need?

6. The LORD appeared to Solomon in a dream by night: and God said, Ask what I shall give thee.

Q. What did King Solomon ask for?

7. Did God give King Solomon what he asked for?

8. Did God give King Solomon more than what he asked for? (Added more than)

CALL UPON THE NAME OF THE LORD

1. When did man begin to call upon The Name of The LORD?

A. AFTER SETH HAD A SON NAMED ENOS. Genesis 4:26

2. Where in scriptures did man begin to call upon The Name of The LORD?

A. AFTER SETH HAD ENOS, .THEN BEGAN MEN TO CALL UPON THE NAME OF THE LORD.
Genesis 4:26

3. How does this scripture read in Romans 10:13 in the King James Version?

A. For whosoever **shall** call upon The Name of The Lord **SHALL BE SAVED**.
Romans 10:13

4. Where is the first time we can see where man walked with God and had sons and daughters?

A. AND ENOCH <u>WALKED WITH GOD</u> AFTER <u>HE BEGAT METHUSELAH</u> THREE HUNDRED YEARS, AND BEGAT SONS AND DAUGHTERS: Genesis 5:22

5. What is the principal thing/primary thing we need?

A. **Wisdom** is the principal thing; therefore get wisdom: and with all thy getting get **understanding**. EXALT HER, AND SHE **shall promote thee**: SHE SHALL <u>BRING THEE TO HONOUR</u>, **when** THOU DOST <u>*EMBRACE*</u> HER. Proverbs 4:7&8

6. The LORD appeared to Solomon in a dream by night: and God said, Ask what I shall give thee.

Q. What did King Solomon ask for?

A. Give therefore thy servant an <u>UNDERSTANDING HEART</u> TO <u>JUDGE THY PEOPLE</u>, THAT I MAY <u>DISCERN</u> BETWEEN <u>GOOD</u> AND <u>BAD</u>: for who is able to judge this thy so great a people? And <u>the speech pleased The LORD</u>, that Solomon had asked this thing. 1 Kings 3:9-10

CALL UPON THE NAME OF THE LORD

> 7. Did God give King Solomon what he asked for?

A. **Yes.** Behold, I have DONE ACCORDING TO THY WORDS: lo, I have given thee a wise and an understanding heart; so that THERE WAS NONE LIKE THEE BEFORE THEE, NEITHER AFTER THEE SHALL ANY ARISE LIKE UNTO THEE.
1 Kings 3:12. Praise The Lord

> 8. Did God give King Solomon more than what he asked for? (Added more than)

A. **Yes.** And I have also given thee that which thou HAST NOT ASKED, BOTH RICHES, AND HONOUR: so that there shall not be any among the kings like unto thee all thy days. AND **If** thou WILT WALK IN MY WAYS, to KEEP MY statutes and MY commandments, as thy father DAVID DID WALK, THEN I WILL LENGTHEN THY DAYS. 1 Kings 13 &14

REMEMBER, **But** SEEK YE FIRST THE KINGDOM OF GOD, AND **His righteousness**; and all THESE THINGS **shall be added** UNTO YOU. MATTHEW 6:3

Did the Serpent lie?

1. The serpent said unto the woman, For God doth know that in the day ye eat thereof, then <u>your eyes</u> <u>shall be opened,</u> **and** ye shall be **as** <u>gods</u>, knowing **good and evil.**

Q. Did the serpent lie to the woman when he made these statements?

1. Your eyes shall be opened **2.** Ye shall be as gods **3.** Knowing good and evil.

PLEASE, GIVE ONE SCRIPTURE TO SUPPORT YOUR ANSWER.

2. The LORD said unto Cain <u>If</u> thou doest well, shalt thou <u>not</u> be accepted; He also said if thou doest <u>not</u> well, sin lieth at the door. And unto thee <u>shall be his desire,</u> thou shalt <u>rule over him</u>. Genesis chapter 4

a. The LORD warned Cain but did he receive the warning?

b. Did Cain have power and authority over evil?

3. Jesus warned one of His disciples and said Satan hath desired to have you, that he may sift you as wheat.

Q. Who was that disciple?

4. The Word of God declares; . . . sin shall <u>not</u> have dominion over you.

Q. This statement found in what chapter and verse?

5. If I believe that Jesus Christ is The Son of God but do not obey His voice whose servant am I?

6. What is the kingdom of God? (*The Word definition*)

7. When anyone heareth (*continue to hear, faith cometh by hearing and hearing by the word of God*) but do not get understand, what will happen to him?

8. What is life eternal according to the scriptures? (The teaching of Jesus <u>not</u> man)

19

DID THE SERPENT LIE?

1. The serpent said unto the woman, For God doth know that in the day ye eat thereof, then your eyes shall be opened, and ye shall be as gods, knowing good and evil. Genesis chapter 3

Q. Did the serpent lie to the woman when he made these statements?

1. Your eyes shall be opened 2. Ye shall be as gods 3. Knowing good and evil.

Please, give one scripture to support your answer.

A. **No**. ..And the eyes of them **both** were opened, and they **KNEW THAT THEY WERE NAKED**. Gen. 3:7

And The LORD God said, **BEHOLD, THE MAN IS BECOME AS ONE OF US, to know good and evil**. Gen. 3:22

2. The LORD said unto Cain If thou doest well, shalt thou not be accepted; He also said if thou doest not well, sin lieth at the door. And unto thee shall be his desire. thou shalt rule over him. Gen. Chapter 4

a. The LORD warned Cain but did he receive it?

b. Did Cain have power and authority over evil?

A. No.

..It came to pass, when they were in the field, that Cain rose up against Abel his brother, and slew him. Genesis 4:8

b. Yes. Thou shalt rule over him. Gen. 4:7

3. Jesus warned one of His disciples and said Satan hath desired to have you, that he may sift you as wheat.

Q. Who was that disciple?

A. Simon Peter. And The Lord said, Simon, Simon, behold, Satan hath desired to have you, that he may sift you as wheat: Luke 22:31

4. The Word of God declares; sin shall not have dominion over you.

Q. This statement found in what chapter and verse?

A. Romans 6:14 For sin SHALL NOT HAVE DOMINION OVER YOU: for ye are NOT UNDER THE LAW, BUT under grace.

MEANING, YOU ARE NO LONGER UNDER THE LAW THAT IMPUTED/ASSIGNED SIN

DID THE SERPENT LIE?

5. If I believe that Jesus Christ is The Son of God but do not obey His voice whose servant am I?

A. The one that I obey. ..KNOW YE NOT, that **TO WHOM <u>YE YIELD YOURSELVES SERVANTS TO OBEY</u>, <u>HIS SERVANTS YE ARE</u> TO WHOM <u>YE OBEY</u>;** whether OF SIN UNTO DEATH, or of **_OBEDIENCE UNTO RIGHTEOUSNESS?_** Romans 6:16

6. What is the kingdom of God? (*The Word definition <u>not</u> man*)

A. RIGHTEOUSNESS, PEACE AND JOY IN THE HOLY GHOST.

For the kingdom of God *IS <u>NOT</u>* meat and drink; but righteousness, and peace, and joy in the Holy Ghost. Romans 14:17

7. When anyone heareth (continue to hear, faith cometh by hearing, and hearing by the word of God) but do not get understand what will happen to him?

> A. THEN COMETH THE **wicked one**, AND CATCHETH AWAY THAT WHICH **WAS** SOWN IN HIS HEART. THIS IS HE WHICH RECEIVED SEED BY THE <u>WAY SIDE</u>. MATTHEW 13:19.

THE WICKED ONE CANNOT TAKE WHAT ONE NEVER HAD right?

8. What is life eternal according to the scriptures? (The teaching of Jesus <u>not</u> man)

A. AND THIS IS <u>LIFE ETERNAL</u>, THAT THEY <u>MIGHT KNOW</u> THEE **THE ONLY TRUE GOD, and Jesus Christ, whom Thou hast sent.** JOHN 17:3

ONE MIGHT BELIEVE; MY NAME OR TITLE IS Prophetess and Pastor, Dr. MARY NEAL **BUT** DO YOU KNOW Dr. NEAL? <u>THE ONLY WAY ONE CAN KNOW ME IS TO SPEND SOME TIME WITH ME.</u>

"WHAT DID STEPHEN SEE THAT MADE THEM SO ANGRY"

1. The Lord elected Stephen because, he was a man full of faith, power and The Holy Ghost. Stephen did great wonders and miracles among the people but there arose a group disputing with him, Stephen called them stiffnecked and <u>uncircumcised in heart</u> and <u>ears</u> and said, ye do always <u>resist The Holy Ghost</u> as <u>your fathers</u> did, so do ye and he asked them a question?
Q. What was the question He asked them?

2. When you' are filed with The Holy Ghost, you can see and hear what others cannot, Stephen was filled with The Holy Ghost and saw something that others could not see.
Q. What did Stephen see?

3. Stephen had spoken many things unto them when they heard them, they were <u>cut to the heart</u> and <u>they gnashed on him with their teeth.</u>
Q What made them so angry that they stoned Stephen to death?

Philip preached unto the eunuch concerning Jesus and as they went on their way, they came unto certain water: and the eunuch said, See, here is water; <u>what doth hinder me to be</u> baptized?
Q. According to this word what <u>should</u> <u>hinder</u> one from being baptize in water?

5. What did the eunuch <u>believe</u> and what did he <u>confess/acknowledge</u>?

6. How does one know if he is born of God?

7. Jesus asked His disciples this question, Whom do men say that I The Son of Man am? They said, some say that thou art John the Baptist: some, Elias; and others, Jeremias, or one of the prophets. He saith unto them, But whom say ye that I am?
Q. Who had the revelation and knowledge of the truth and confessed/acknowledged the true?

8. Did Jesus confess and call those blessed who did not confess Him?

9. Saul was there when Stephen was stoned to death, he persecuted Jesus and His disciples; he had authority from the chief priests to bind all that call on The Name of Jesus. After Jesus appeared to Saul and he received his sight, he was baptized and filled with The Holy Ghost.

After Saul had received meat, he was strengthened and spent some days with the disciples afterward he went straightway and preached?
Q. Saul was blind but when he received his sight, he confessed/acknowledged Jesus to be?

"WHAT DID STEPHEN SEE THAT MADE THEM SO ANGRY"

1. The Lord elected Stephen because, he was a man full of faith, power and the Holy Ghost. Stephen did great wonders and miracles among the people but there arose a group disputing with him. Stephen called them stiffnecked and <u>uncircumcised in heart</u> and <u>ears</u> and said, ye do always <u>resist The Holy Ghost</u> as <u>your fathers</u> did, so do ye and he asked them a question?

Q. What was the question He asked them?
A. Which of the prophets have not **YOUR FATHERS PERSECUTED?** Acts 7:52

2. When you' are filed with The Holy Ghost, you can see and hear what others cannot, Stephen was filled with The Holy Ghost and saw something that others could not see.

Q. What did Stephen see?

A. Stephen saw **The <u>glory of God</u>, and Jesus standing <u>ON THE RIGHT HAND OF GOD</u>**. Acts 7:55

3. Stephen had spoken many things unto them, when they heard them they were <u>cut to the heart</u> and <u>they gnashed on him with their teeth.</u>
Q What made them so angry that they stoned Stephen to death?
A. Stephen confessed/acknowledged what he saw Acts 7:55-58

. . . And <u>said</u>, Behold, I <u>SEE THE HEAVENS OPENED</u>, and The Son of Man <u>standing</u> on THE <u>RIGHT HAND</u> of God. Then <u>they cried out with a loud voice</u>, and stopped their ears, and <u>ran upon him with one accord</u>, (in agreement) and <u>cast him out of the city</u>, and stoned him:

This reminds me of Job, there was a time when Job had <u>only heard</u> with <u>his ears</u> but the time came when he said in Job 42:5, I have heard of Thee <u>by the hearing of the ear</u>: but now <u>mine eye seeth Thee.</u>

4. Philip preached unto the eunuch concerning Jesus and as they went on their way, they came unto certain water: and the eunuch said, See, here is water; <u>what doth hinder me to be</u> baptized?

Q. According to this word what <u>should hinder</u>/delay or stop one from being baptize in water?

A. If they *do not* believe with *all their hearts* that *Jesus is The Son of God.*

AND PHILIP SAID, *If thou believest with all thine heart, thou mayest.* ACTS 8:37

"WHAT DID STEPHEN SEE THAT MADE THEM SO ANGRY"

That **if** thou **SHALT CONFESS WITH THY MOUTH THE LORD JESUS, AND shalt believe in thine heart** that **GOD HATH RAISED HIM FROM THE DEAD**, thou **shalt be saved**. For with the **heart man believeth** unto RIGHTEOUSNESS; and *with the mouth confession is made unto salvation.*
Romans 10:9 & 10

5. What did the eunuch believe and what did he confess/acknowledge?
A. And he answered and said **I BELIEVE THAT JESUS CHRIST IS THE SON OF GOD.** Acts 8:37

6. How does one know if he is born of God?

A. *IF one continue to believe that* JESUS IS THE CHRIST AND CONTINUE TO LOVE GOD AND CONTINUE TO LOVE ALL THOSE WHO IS BEGOTTEN OF HIM *is born of God*.

Whosoever believeth that **Jesus is The Christ** *is born of God: and every one that loveth Him that begat loveth him also that is begotten of Him.* **By this we know that we love the children of God, when** WE LOVE GOD, AND KEEP HIS COMMANDMENTS.

For this is the love of God, that **we keep His commandments**: *and* HIS COMMANDMENTS ARE NOT GRIEVOUS. 1 John 5

7. Jesus asked His disciples this question, WHOM DO MEN SAY THAT I THE SON OF MAN AM?

..They said, *some say that thou art John the Baptist:* some, *Elias*; and others, Jeremias, **or one of the prophets. He saith unto them, But whom say ye that I am?**

Q. Who had the revelation and knowledge of the truth and confessed/acknowledged the true?

A. **SIMON PETER.** ..Answered and said, **Thou art. The Christ, The Son of The living God**

Matt. 16:16

NOTICE, ONLY ONE ANSWERED

8. Did Jesus confess or call those blessed who did not confess Him?

A. **NO.** And Jesus answered and said unto **him, Blessed art thou, Simon Barjona**: for flesh and blood hath not revealed it unto thee, but My Father which is in heaven. Matthew 16:17

24

"WHAT DID STEPHEN SEE THAT MADE THEM SO ANGRY?"

9. Saul was there when Stephen was stoned to death, he persecuted Jesus and His disciples; he had authority from the chief priests to bind all that call on The Name of Jesus. After Jesus appeared to Saul and he received his sight, he was baptized and filled with The Holy Ghost.

After Saul had received meat he was strengthened and spent some days with the disciples, afterward he went straightway and preached.

Q. Saul was blind but when he received his sight, whom did he confessed/ acknowledged Jesus to be?

A. **Christ He is The Son of God.**

And straightway he preached Christ in the synagogues, that He is The Son of God.
Acts 9:20

PAUL PERSECUTED THE CHURCH FOR TEACHING AND PREACHING THAT JESUS WAS THE CHRIST THE SON OF GOD AND HE WAS PERSECUTED FOR TEACHING THE SAME.

WHEN AND IF YOU STAND ON THE TRUTH, YOU CAN ALSO LOOK FOR PERSECUTION.
BUT I CALL YOU BLESSED!

WHO IS THAT PROPHET? "SEEK YE MY FACE"

1. The LORD thy God will <u>raise up unto thee a prophet</u> from the midst of thee, of thy <u>brethren</u>,
like unto me; unto Him ye shall <u>hearken</u>.
Q. What chapter and verse can we find this statement?

2. For Moses truly said unto the fathers, A Prophet shall The Lord your God raise up unto you of your brethren, like unto me; Him shall ye <u>hear</u> in **all things** whatsoever He shall say unto you.
Q. Who is that Prophet? Please, use scripture to support your answer.

3. What will happen to every soul who does not hear The Voice of that prophet?
Please, use a scripture to support your answer.

4. What Tribe did The Lord Jesus come from?
Please, use scripture to support you answer.

5. Thou shalt <u>not</u> raise a <u>false report</u>: put <u>not</u> thine hand with the wicked to be an_____

6. Moses said unto The LORD, Behold, I am of uncircumcised lips, and how shall Pharaoh hearken unto me?
The LORD said unto Moses, See, I have made thee _____ to Pharaoh.

7. Reuben was the firstborn of Israel but because he defiled his father's bed, he lost his birthright.
Q. Who receive the birthright?

8. Joseph had two sons that were born unto him in the land of Egypt but they became whose sons?

9. How many souls came out of the loins of Jacob?

WHO IS THAT PROPHET? "SEEK YE MY FACE"

1. The LORD thy God will raise up unto thee a prophet from the midst of thee, of thy brethren,
like unto me; unto Him ye shall hearken.
Q. What chapter and verse can we find this statement?
A. Deuteronomy 18:15

2. For Moses truly said unto the fathers, A prophet shall the Lord your God raise up unto you of your brethren, like unto me; him shall ye <u>hear</u> in <u>all things</u> whatsoever he shall say unto you.
Q. Who is that Prophet?
Please, use scripture to support your answer.
A. JESUS. Unto YOU FIRST God, **having raised up His Son Jesus**, **sent Him to bless you**, in TURNING AWAY <u>EVERY ONE OF YOU FROM HIS INIQUITIES</u>. Acts 3:26

3. **What will happen to <u>every soul who</u> does not hear The Voice of that Prophet?**
Please, use a scripture to support your answer.
A. .It shall come to pass, **THAT <u>EVERY SOUL</u>, WHICH <u>WILL NOT HEAR THAT</u> <u>PROPHET</u>, SHALL BE DESTROYED FROM AMONG THE PEOPLE.** Acts 3:23

4. What Tribe did The Lord Jesus come from? Please, use scripture to support you answer.
A. JUDA. For it is <u>evident</u> that our **LORD SPRANG OUT OF JUDA**; of which **TRIBE MOSES SPAKE** nothing concerning priesthood. Hebrews 7:14 also read Gen. 49:8-12

5. Thou shalt <u>not</u> raise a <u>false report</u>: put <u>not</u> thine hand with the wicked to be an_____
A. **UNRIGHTEOUS WITNESS.** Exodus 23:1
Those who speak, teach and preach the word are witnesses.

6. Moses said unto The LORD, Behold, I am of uncircumcised lips, and how shall Pharaoh hearken unto me?
The LORD said unto Moses, See, I have made thee _____ to Pharaoh.
A. **A god.** And The LORD said unto Moses, See, I have made **thee a god to Pharaoh**: and Aaron thy brother shall be **thy prophet.** Ex. 7:1

WHO IS THAT PROPHET? "SEEK YE MY FACE"

7. Reuben was the firstborn of Israel but because he defiled his father's bed he lost his birthright.

Q. Who receive the birthright?

A. His birthright given to Ephraim and Manasseh the sons of Joseph. 1 Chronicles 5:1

Now the sons of Reuben the firstborn of Israel, (for he was the firstborn; but forasmuch as he defiled his <u>father's bed, his birthright was given unto the sons of Joseph</u> the son of Israel: and the genealogy is not to be <u>reckoned after the birthright</u>. For <u>Judah prevailed above his brethren</u>, and of him came the <u>chief ruler</u>; but the <u>birthright was Joseph's :)</u> 1 Chronicles 5:1

8. Joseph had two sons that were born unto him in the land of Egypt but they became whose sons?

A. JACOB/Israel sons.

And now **THY TWO SONS, EPHRAIM AND MANASSEH**, which were born unto thee in the land of Egypt before I came unto thee into Egypt, **ARE MINE; AS REUBEN AND SIMEON**, they shall <u>be mine</u>. Genesis 48:5

9. How many souls came out of the loins of Jacob?

A. (70) Seventy souls came out of Jacob.

. And all the souls that came out of the loins of Jacob were <u>seventy souls</u>:

for *Joseph was in Egypt already*. Exodus 1:5

ESAU AND JACOB

1. Isaac loved Esau and Rebekah loved Jacob <u>both</u> boys were under the command of their parents. Isaac sent Esau out to get the meat that he loved, "venison meat" Esau went out to the field to hunt for venison before Jacob did. Rebekah says, now therefore, my son, obey my voice according to that which I command thee.

Q. How did Jacob get the meat, the bread prepared, served his father, and his father blessed him before Esau returned?

2. Did the scripture say that The Lord cursed Jacob for this action?

If the answer is yes please, use scriptures to support your answer.

3. Is there anywhere, according to the scripture where The LORD punished Jacob for his action?

4. Did The LORD say that He loved Esau?

5. How many times have we heard this quoted, not knowing if the person is righteous or wicked, **"God is not angry with you?"**

Q. According to the scriptures, if the person is wicked is God angry?

6. How many times have we heard this quoted by man we have "no righteousness because, there is none righteous, no, not one"

Q. Why was this statement made and why are we born under sin?

Please, use scriptures to support your answers.

ESAU AND JACOB

1. Isaac loved Esau and Rebekah loved Jacob both boys were under the command of their parents. Isaac sent Esau out to get the meat that he loved, "venison meat" Esau went out to the field to hunt for venison before Jacob did. Rebekah says, now therefore, my son, obey my voice according to that which I command thee.

Q. How did Jacob get the meat, the bread prepared, served his father, and his father blessed him before Esau returned?

A. **THE LORD BROUGHT IT TO HIM.**

And Isaac said unto his son, **How is it that thou hast found it so quickly**, my son? And he said, Because **The LORD Thy God BROUGHT it to me.** Gen. 27:20

2. Did the scripture say that The Lord cursed Jacob for this action?
IF the answer is yes please, use scriptures to support your answers.

A. NO

3. Is there anywhere, according to the scripture where The LORD punished Jacob for his action?

A. No

He shall choose our inheritance for us, **THE EXCELLENCY OF JACOB WHOM HE LOVED** Psalm 47:4

4. Did The LORD say that He loved Esau?
A. No

As it is written, **Jacob have I loved,** but **Esau have I hated**. Romans 9:13
..Was **not** Esau Jacob's brother? saith The LORD: yet **I loved Jacob, And I hated Esau.**
Malachi 1:2-3

5. How many times have we heard this quoted, not knowing if the person is righteous or wicked, "God is not angry with you?"

Q. According to the scriptures, if the person is wicked is God angry?
A. Yes. If we are wicked, GOD IS ANGRY.
God judgeth the righteous, and God is angry with the wicked every day.
If he turn not, he will whet **His sword**; He hath BENT HIS BOW, and **made it ready.**
Psalm 7:11-12

6. How many times have we heard this quoted by man, we have "no righteousness because, there is none righteous, no, not one?"

Q. Why was this statement made and why are we born under sin?
Please, use scriptures to support your answers.

Esau and Jacob

What then? are we <u>better than they</u>? No, in <u>no</u> wise: for we have before <u>proved both</u> <u>Jews</u> and <u>Gentiles</u>, that they are **all under sin;** As it *is written*, THERE IS <u>NONE</u> RIGHTEOUS, NO, NOT ONE:

2. Did the scripture say that The Lord cursed Jacob for this action?

A. No

'WHY THESE STATEMENTS WERE MADE"

There is <u>none that</u> **understandeth,** <u>there is none that</u> **seeketh after God**. <u>They are</u> **all gone out of the way,** they are together **become unprofitable**; <u>there is</u> **none that doeth good, no, not one**. <u>Their</u> **throat is an open sepulchre**; <u>with their</u> **tongues they have used deceit**; the **poison of asps is under their lips**: <u>Whose</u> **mouth is full of cursing and bitterness**: Romans 3:9-14

The fool hath said in his heart, There is **NO GOD**. *They are* **corrupt, they have done abominable WORKS,** *there is* **none that doeth good**. The LORD <u>looked down from heaven</u> upon the <u>children of men,</u> **to see** if there were ANY THAT DID UNDERSTAND, and <u>SEEK GOD</u>. They are <u>all gone aside</u>, they are all together **become filthy**: <u>there is none that doeth good, no, not one</u>. Have <u>all the WORKERS OF INIQUITY NO KNOWLEDGE</u>? who *EAT UP MY PEOPLE AS THEY EAT BREAD*, and **call not upon The LORD**. Psalm 14:1-4

The **fool** hath said in his heart, *There is no God*. <u>Corrupt are they</u>, and <u>have done abominable iniquity</u>: there is <u>none that doeth good</u>. Psalm 53:1

(IF WE PRACTICE ANY OF THESE THINGS, THEY ARE UNRIGHTEOUS)

And not rather, (as we be slanderously reported, and as some affirm that we say,) Let us do evil, that good may come? whose damnation is just. What then? are we better than they? No, in no wise: for we have before proved both <u>Jews and Gentiles</u>, that they are all under sin; As it is written, There is none righteous, no, not one: Romans 3:8-10

Is the law <u>then against the promises of God</u>? God forbid: <u>for if there had been a law given</u> <u>which could have given life, verily righteousness should</u> have been by the law. But **the scripture hath concluded all under sin, that the promise by faith of Jesus Christ might be given to them that believe**. *But before faith came, we were kept under the law, shut up unto the faith which should afterwards be revealed. Galatians 3:21-23*

Esau and Jacob

As we were all born under sin because, of Adam our first father and mother Adam and Eve

(Both named Adam)

By the same method, **THE** *UNGODLY* **IS** justified by the blood **of Jesus and made righteous** when he has faith and believe the report of The Lord. Read Roman chapter 4&5

And being **fully persuaded** that, what he *had promised, He was able also to perform*. And therefore it was **IMPUTED TO HIM FOR RIGHTEOUSNESS.** Now **it** was **NOT WRITTEN FOR HIS SAKE ALONE,** that it **WAS IMPUTED TO HIM**; BUT FOR US ALSO, to whom it **SHALL BE** IMPUTED, **if we believe on Him that raised up Jesus our Lord from the dead**; Who was *DELIVERED FOR OUR OFFENCES, AND WAS RAISED AGAIN FOR OUR JUSTIFICATION.* Romans 4:21-25

AND THE SCRIPTURE WAS FULFILLED WHICH SAITH, *ABRAHAM BELIEVED* GOD, AND IT *WAS IMPUTED UNTO HIM FOR RIGHTEOUSNESS*: AND **he was called** *the Friend of God* James 2:23

"Righteous"

1. According to the scriptures, was any one righteous?

2. If my understanding is no one can be righteous, am I rightly dividing the word of truth?

3. Thou shalt not <u>wrest judgment</u>; thou shalt not <u>respect persons</u>, neither take a gift: for a gift doth _____

4. For the froward is abomination to The LORD: but His secret is with _____

5. The mouth of a righteous man is a well of life: but violence _____

6. The fruit of the righteous is a tree of life; and he that _____

7. He that receiveth a prophet in the name of a prophet shall receive a _____

8. He that receiveth a righteous man in the name of a righteous man shall receive a_____

9. For verily I say unto you, That many prophets and righteous men have desired to see those things
And to hear those things which ye hear, and have not _____

10. Then shall the righteous shine forth as the sun in the kingdom of their Father.
Who hath ears to hear, _____

11. Zacharias and Elisabeth were <u>both righteous before God</u>, walking in _____

RIGHTEOUS

1. According to the scriptures, was any one righteous?

A. **Yes.**

There were they in **GREAT FEAR**: for **God i**s in the **generation of the righteous**. Psalm 14:5

..Wilt thou also **destroy the righteous with the wicked?** Genesis 18:23

2. If my understanding is no one can be righteous, am I rightly dividing the word of truth?

A. No

3. Thou shalt not wrest judgment; thou shalt not respect,

neither take a gift: for a gift doth _____ persons

A. **Blind the eyes of the wise, and pervert the words of the righteous**. Deuteronomy 16:19

4. For **the froward is abomination to The LORD: but His secret is with** _____

A. His secret is with the righteous. Proverbs 3:32

5. The mouth of a righteous man is a well of life: but violence _____

A. **Covereth the mouth of the wicked**. Proverbs 10:11

6. The fruit of the righteous is a tree of life; and he that _____

A. **WINNETH SOULS ARE WISE**. Proverbs 11:30

7. He that receiveth a prophet in the name of a prophet shall receive a _____

A. A PROPHET'S REWARD Matthew 10:41

8. He that receiveth a righteous man in the name of a righteous man shall receive a_____

A. RIGHTEOUS MAN'S REWARD Matthew 10:41

RIGHTEOUS

9. For verily I say unto you, That many prophets and righteous men have desired to see those things which ye see, _____

   A. **AND HAVE NOT SEEN THEM.** Matthew 13:17

And to hear those things which ye hear, and have not _____

   A. **Heard them** Matthew 13:17

10. Then shall the righteous shine forth as the sun in the kingdom of their Father.

    Who hath ears to hear, _____

    A. **Let him hear**. Matthew 13:43

11. Zacharias and Elisabeth were both righteous before God, walking in _____ and ordinances of The Lord blameless.

    A. **ALL THE COMMANDMENTS** Luke 1:6

FOR THE EYES OF THE LORD ARE OVER THE RIGHTEOUS, AND HIS EARS ARE OPEN UNTO THEIR PRAYERS: BUT THE FACE OF THE LORD IS AGAINST THEM THAT DO EVIL. 1 PETER 3:12

Mercy and Grace

1. Why did Israel fear King Solomon?

2. What happen to Joshua after Moses laid his hands upon Him?

3. How many proverbs did King Solomon speak and how many songs did he compose?

4. The words mercy and grace, appears first in what book, chapter and verse?

5. The word grace, appears in what book, chapter and verse for the first time?

6. Who was the first one in scripture that <u>reads</u> "one" <u>found</u> grace?

7. Who was the servant that articulated these words?
"Thy servant hath found grace in Thy sight, and thou hast magnified Thy mercy"

8. David did that which was right in The Eyes of The LORD, and turned not aside from anything that The Lord commanded him all the days of his life, save only in the matter of?

Mercy and Grace

1. Why did Israel fear King Solomon?

A. And **all Israel heard of the judgment which the king had judged;** and they **feared the king:** for they <u>saw that</u> <u>THE WISDOM OF GOD WAS IN HIM, TO DO JUDGMENT</u>. 1 Kings 3:28

IS THE WISDOM IN US TO DO JUDGMENT? I SURE HOPE SO OTHERWISE ANYTHING GOES.

Please, read 1 Corinthians Chapter 6

..1 **Dare** any of you, having A MATTER AGAINST ANOTHER, GO TO LAW BEFORE THE UNJUST, and **not before the saints?** [2] Do ye <u>not know that the saints shall judge the world?</u> **and if** the WORLD SHALL BE JUDGED BY YOU, are **ye unworthy** to judge **THE SMALLEST MATTERS?..** 8 Nay, ye **DO WRONG**, and defraud, and that your brethren. 9 Know ye NOT THAT THE UNRIGHTEOUS SHALL NOT INHERIT THE KINGDOM OF GOD? BE NOT DECEIVED: *neither fornicators, nor idolaters, nor adulterers, nor effeminate, nor abusers of themselves with mankind,* [10] *Nor thieves, nor covetous, nor drunkards, nor revilers, nor extortioners, shall inherit the kingdom of God.*

2. What happen to Joshua after Moses laid his hands upon Him?

A. JOSHUA WAS FULL OF THE SPIRIT OF WISDOM.

And Joshua the son of Nun <u>was full of the spirit of wisdom</u>; for Moses had laid his hands upon him: and the children of Israel hearkened unto him, and <u>did as The LORD commanded Moses</u>. Deut. 34:9

3. How many proverbs did King Solomon speak and how many songs did he compose?

A. THREE THOUSAND PROVERBS: and <u>HIS SONGS WERE A THOUSAND AND FIVE</u>. 1 Kings 4:32

4. The words mercy and grace, appears first in what book, chapter and verse?

A. Genesis 19:19

Mercy and Grace

Behold now, thy servant hath found **GRACE IN THY SIGHT**, and thou **HAST MAGNIFIED THY MERCY**, *which thou hast shewed UNTO ME IN SAVING MY LIFE*; and I cannot escape to the mountain, lest some evil take me, and I die:

5. The word grace, appears in what book, chapter and verse for the first time?

A. But Noah **found grace in the Eyes of The LORD.** Genesis 6:8

6. Who was the first one in scripture that reads one found grace?

A. **NOAH.**

But Noah **found grace** in the Eyes of The LORD. Genesis 6:8

7. Who was the servant that articulated these words?

"Thy servant hath found grace in Thy sight, and thou hast magnified Thy mercy"

A. **LOT.**

And Lot said unto them, Oh, not so, My LORD: Behold now, Thy servant hath found grace in Thy sight, and thou hast **magnified Thy mercy,** *which thou hast shewed unto me in saving my life; and I cannot escape to the mountain, lest some evil take me, and I die: Behold now, this city is near to flee unto, and it* **is a little one:** *Oh, let me escape thither, (is it not a little one?) and my soul shall live* Genesis 19:18-20

I WILL TAKE THE LITTLE CITY IF THIS IS WHAT I NEED TO SAVE MY SOUL.

(I say the man and his wife was the first to receive mercy and grace, "Adam" (Remember, God call them Adam) Gen. 5:2 & 3:22, Why? Because, The LORD God did not destroy them but He did put them out of the Garden of Eden, Remember, the word "man" male or female. Read Genesis 3:22-24

8. David did that which was right in The Eyes of The LORD, and turned NOT ASIDE FROM ANYTHING that The Lord commanded him all the days of his life, save only in the matter of?

A. **URIAH THE HITTITE.**

Then Peter and the other apostles answered and said, we ought to obey God rather than men. Acts 5:29

Jesus said, Every plant, which My heavenly Father hath not planted, shall be rooted up. Matthew 15:13

THE BOOKS, UNGODLY, SINNERS AND JUDGMENT

1. Yes, I know Paul did persecute Jesus and the church but what transpired after he received his sight?

2. What did Paul preached?

3. Will the ungodly stand in the judgment, and will sinners stand in the congregation of the righteous?

4. How many books will there be when the Lord Judge His People.

5. Moses killed an Egyptian man for a purpose.

Q. Why?

Freebees

*Then they that **gladly received his word** were baptized: and the same day **there were added** unto them about three thousand souls. And they continued stedfastly in **the apostles' doctrine and fellowship**, and in breaking of bread, and in prayers. And **fear** came upon **every soul:** and **MANY WONDERS AND SIGNS WERE DONE BY THE APOSTLES**. Acts 2:41-43*

The books, Ungodly, Sinners and Judgment

1. Yes, I know Paul did persecute Jesus and the church but what transpired after he received his sight?

A. He arose and <u>was baptized</u>, when he had <u>received meat</u>, he was <u>strengthened</u>. Then was <u>Saul certain days with the disciples</u> which were at Damascus, **And straightway he preached Christ in the synagogues,**

2. What did Paul preached?

A. **That Christ is The Son of God. Acts 9:18-20**

WHY DID PAUL DO THIS EVIL THING? BECAUSE, HE DID NOT HAVE THE KNOWLEDGE HE WAS SPIRITUALLY BLIND.

3. Will the UNGODLY STAND IN THE JUDGMENT, AND WILL SINNERS STAND IN THE CONGREGATION OF THE RIGHTEOUS?

A. **According to God's Holy Word**, NO WAY.

> Therefore the <u>ungodly shall not stand in the judgment</u>, <u>nor sinners</u> in the <u>congregation of the righteous . . . Psalm 1:5-6</u>

> **Why, you cannot run a race if you are not in the race.**
> For the time is come that judgment must begin at the house of God: and *if* it first begin at us, what shall the END be of them that **obey not the gospel of God?** And **IF the righteous scarcely be saved,** where **shall the ungodly and the sinner appear?** Wherefore let them that **suffer according to the will** OF GOD COMMIT *the keeping of their souls to Him in* **well doing, as unto a faithful Creator. 1 Peter 4:17-19**

AND WHOSOEVER WAS NOT FOUND WRITTEN IN THE BOOK OF LIFE <u>WAS CAST INTO THE LAKE OF FIRE</u>. REV.20:15

4. How many books will there be when the Lord Judge His People.

A. There will be three or more books.

A. A fiery stream issued and came forth from before Him: <u>thousand thousands ministered unto Him</u>, and <u>ten thousand times ten thousand stood before Him: the judgment was set</u>, and the **books were opened.**

Daniel 7:10

The books, Ungodly, Sinners and Judgment

And I saw the dead, small and great, stand before God; and the books were opened: and another book was opened, which is the book of life: and the dead were judged out of those things which were written in the books, according to their works. Rev. 20:12

5. Moses killed an Egyptian man for a purpose.

Q. Why?

A. He saw an Egyptian beating a Hebrew, one of his brethren. Exodus 2:11

..Seeing one of them suffer wrong, he DEFENDED HIM, and avenged him that was oppressed.

He *supposed his brethren would have understood* how that God by his hand would *deliver them*: BUT THEY UNDERSTOOD NOT. Acts 7:24-26

DO YOU KNOW HIM

1. Was Moses punish for the Egyptian death?

2. Is Bethlehem also someone's name?

3. If your answer is yes, then who was Bethlehem's father?

4. According to the scripture, how is The LORD made known?

5. According to the scripture who shall be turned into hell?

I will bless The LORD at all times: His praise shall continually be in My mouth.
My soul shall make her boast in The LORD: the humble shall hear thereof, and be glad.
O magnify The LORD with me, and let us exalt His name together. Psalm 34:1-3

DO YOU KNOW HIM

1. Was Moses ever punish for the Egyptian death?

A. No

Moses was sent to be a ruler and a deliverer; to **deliver God's people out of Egypt.**

THIS MOSES WHOM THEY REFUSED, saying, <u>WHO MADE THEE A RULER AND A JUDGE</u>? the <u>same</u> did <u>God send</u> to be A <u>RULER AND A DELIVERER</u> by the hand of the angel which appeared to him in the bush Acts 7:35

2. Bethlehem is a town in the West Bank near Jerusalem.

Is Bethlehem also someone's name?

A. Yes. The sons of Salma is Bethlehem 1 Chronicles 2:54

3. If the answer is yes, then who was Bethlehem's father?

A. Salma was the father of Bethlehem. 1 Chronicles 2:51

4. According to the scripture, how is The LORD made known?

A. The LORD is known by the judgment which He executeth. Psalm 9:16

The LORD is known by the judgment which he executeth: *the wicked is* **SNARED IN THE WORK OF HIS OWN HANDS. Higgaion. Selah.**

And the Egyptians **shall know that I am The LORD, when I stretch forth mine hand upon Egypt**, and bring out the children of Israel from among them. Exodus 7:5

Thus saith The LORD, <u>In this thou shalt know</u> that I am the LORD: behold, <u>I will smite</u> with the rod that is in mine hand upon the waters which are in the river, and they shall be turned to blood.

Exodus 7:17

5. According to the scripture who shall be turned into hell?

A. The WICKED shall be turned into hell, and all the nations that forget God. For the <u>NEEDY SHALL NOT ALWAYS BE FORGOTTEN: THE EXPECTATION OF THE POOR SHALL **not** PERISH</u> FOR EVER. Psalm 9:16-17

Let God be true

1. What is the works of the flesh?

2. Who shall not inherit the kingdom of God?

3. The Holy Word says, let God be _____, but every man a _____

4. A wicked doer giveth heed to false lips; and a liar giveth ear to a naughty tongue.
Q. What is the word encouraging us <u>not</u> to do?

5. Ye shall not add unto the word which I command you, neither shall ye diminish ought from it.
Q. Ye shall not add unto the word, neither shall ye diminish ought from it. What word?

Bless The LORD, O my soul: and all that is within me, bless His Holy Name. Psalm 103:1

Bless The LORD, O my soul, and forget not all His benefits: Psalm 103:2

Bless The LORD, ye His angels, that excel in strength, that <u>do his commandments</u>, hearkening unto The <u>Voice of His Word</u>. Psalm 103:20

Bless The LORD, all <u>His works in all places</u> of His dominion: bless The LORD, O my soul. Psalm 103:22

Let God be true

1. What is the works of the flesh?

A. **Now the works of the flesh are manifest, which are these; Adultery, fornication, uncleanness, lasciviousness, Idolatry, witchcraft, hatred, variance, emulations, wrath, strife, seditions, heresies, Envyings, murders, drunkenness, revellings, and such like.** Galatians 5:19-21

2. Who shall not inherit the kingdom of God?

A. **Whoever refuse to repent/turn away from these evil deeds,** Adultery, fornication, uncleanness, lasciviousness, Idolatry, witchcraft, hatred, variance, emulations, wrath, strife, seditions, heresies,

Envyings, murders, drunkenness, revellings, and such like.

Paul says, .I tell you before, as I have also told you in time past, that they which do such things shall not inherit the kingdom of God. Galatians 5:19-21

3. The Holy Word says, let God be _____, but every man a _____

A. True & Liar

.That thou mightest be justified in thy sayings, and mightest overcome _____

A. **When thou art judged.** Romans 3:4

4. A wicked doer giveth heed to false lips; and a liar giveth ear to a naughty tongue.

Q. What is the word encouraging us not to do?

A. Add not unto His Word.

A. Add thou **not** unto *His words*, lest HE REPROVE THEE, and **thou be found a liar.**

Proverbs 17:4 & 30:6

5. Ye shall not add unto the word which I command you, neither shall ye diminish ought from it.

Q. Ye shall not add unto the word, neither shall ye diminish ought from it. What word?

A. *THE COMMANDMENTS OF THE LORD WHICH HE COMMANDED THEM TO KEEP.*

Ye *shall not add unto the word which I command you, neither shall ye diminish ought from it*, that ye *may keep the commandments of The LORD your God which I command you.*

Deuteronomy 4:2

For I testify unto every man that heareth the words of the prophecy of this book, **If any man shall add unto these things, God shall add unto him the plagues that are written in this book:** And if any man SHALL TAKE AWAY FROM THE WORDS OF THE BOOK OF THIS PROPHECY, **God shall take away his part out of the book of life, and out of the holy city, and from the things which are written in this book.** Revelation 22:18-19

Someone, anyone please, explain to me how God shall take away ONES part out of the book of life and out of the Holy City, if THEY WERE never in it? How can this thing be? GOD IS ALWAYS TRUE, SO SOMEONE IS TRYING TO DECEIVE US, THAT O SATAN IS USING HUMANKIND TO GET HIS WORK DONE. THE DEVIL IS A DECEIVER FROM THE BEGINNING.

FRUITS & LIBERTY

1. What are the fruit of the Spirit?

2. .They that are Christ's have done what?

3. If we live in the Spirit let us?

4. What book, chapter and verse can we find this statement?
"Then will I teach transgressors thy ways; and sinners shall be converted unto thee"

5. The scripture teaches us to, 'Stand fast therefore in the liberty wherewith Christ hath made us free"
But, also command us not to do what?

6. Was Paul, speaking of The Ten Commandments or something else when he wrote these words?
"And be not entangled <u>again</u> with the yoke of bondage"

FRUITS & LIBERTY

1. What are the fruit of the Spirit?
A. .THE FRUIT OF THE SPIRIT IS LOVE, JOY, PEACE, LONGSUFFERING, GENTLENESS, GOODNESS, FAITH, MEEKNESS, TEMPERANCE: AGAINST SUCH THERE IS NO LAW.

2. And they that are Christ's have done what?
A. CRUCIFIED THE FLESH WITH THE AFFECTIONS AND LUSTS.

3. If we live in the Spirit, let us?
A. *ALSO* WALK IN THE SPIRIT. Galatians 5:22-25

4. What book, chapter and verse can we find this statement?
"Then will I **TEACH TRANSGRESSORS THY WAYS***; and* **SINNERS SHALL BE CONVERTED** unto Thee"
A. Psalm 51:13

5. The scripture teaches us to, 'Stand fast therefore in the liberty wherewith Christ hath made us free"

But, also command us not to do what?
A. *And be* not *entangled* again *with the* yoke of bondage*. Galatians 5:1*
How can one be entangle again **If** he was never free in the first place? You answer.

6. Was Paul speaking of, The Ten Commandments or something else, when he wrote these words?
"And be not entangled again with the yoke of bondage"
A. **This teaching is not on the Ten Commandments, it is on circumcision.**

Behold, I Paul say unto you, that *if ye be* circumcised, *Christ shall profit you nothing.*

For I testify again to every man **that is circumcised**, that he is *a debtor to do the* *whole law*. Christ is become of no effect *unto you,* whosoever of you are justified by the law: *ye are* fallen from grace. *For we* **through the Spirit wait for the hope of righteousness by faith. For in Jesus Christ** neither circumcision availeth any thing, **nor uncircumcision; BUT** *faith which worketh by love*. Ye did run well; who **DID HINDER YOU** THAT YE **should not obey the truth?** Galatians 5:2-7

Please, read Romans chapter 4 & 5 for more information, on how the ungodly is justified by faith,
Our earthly father Abraham believed God and it was counted unto him for righteousness and he became a friend of God. Without faith it is impossible to please **God**

FRUIT & Liberty

1. In the first month, in the fourteenth day of the month, ye shall have the passover, a feast of seven days; unleavened bread shall be eaten.

Q. What is the feast of unleavened bread called?

2. Purge out therefore the old leaven, that ye may be a new <u>lump</u>, as ye are <u>unleavened</u>. For even **<u>Christ our Passover is sacrificed for us</u>:** Therefore let us <u>keep the feast</u>, not with **old leaven**, neither with the **leaven of** malice and wickedness; **but with the unleavened bread of** _____

3. Paul said, I wrote unto you in <u>an epistle</u> not to company with <u>fornicators</u>: Yet <u>not altogether</u> with the <u>fornicators of this world,</u> **or** with the covetous, or extortioners, **or** with idolaters; for then must ye needs go out of the world.

Q. Paul instructs and cautions us not to keep company with whom?

4. According to the word, if he be found that stealeth and selleth a man or if the man be in his hand he shall surely be put to _____

5. And he said, Hear now my words: If there be a prophet among you, I The LORD will make <u>Myself known unto him</u> in a vision, and <u>will speak unto him in a dream.</u>

My servant Moses is <u>not so</u>, who is faithful in all Mine house.

With him will **I speak mouth to mouth**, even <u>apparently,</u> and not in *dark speeches*; and the *similitude of The LORD* shall he behold: wherefore then were ye not afraid to speak against my servant Moses? Numbers 12:6-8

Q. Where can you find two scriptures that confirm Moses was faithful in His entire house?

6. And I thank Christ Jesus our Lord, who hath **enabled me**, for that **He counted me faithful, putting me into the ministry;**

Q. What did Paul teach before he made this statement concerning the law?

FAITHFUL PUTTING ME INTO THE MINISTRY

1. In the first month, in the fourteenth day of the month, ye shall have the Passover, a feast of seven days; unleavened bread shall be eaten. Ezekiel 45:21

Q. **What is the feast of unleavened bread called?**

A. The Passover

Now the feast of unleavened bread drew nigh, which is **CALLED THE PASSOVER**. Luke 22:1

And they went, and found as He had said unto them: and they made ready **the passover** Luke 22:13

2. Purge out therefore the old leaven, that ye may be a new <u>lump</u>, as ye are <u>unleavened</u>. For even _Christ our passover is sacrificed for us:_ Therefore let us <u>keep the feast</u>, not with <u>old leaven</u>, _neither with the leaven of malice and wickedness; but with the unleavened bread of _____

A. Sincerity <u>and</u> truth 1 Corinthians 5:8

3. Paul said, I wrote unto you in <u>an epistle</u> not to company with <u>fornicators</u>: Yet <u>not altogether</u> with the <u>fornicators of this world</u>, or with the covetous, or extortioners, or with idolaters; for then must ye needs go out of the world.

Q. **Paul instructs and cautions us not to keep company with whom?**

A. **Any man that is <u>called a brother</u> be a fornicator, or covetous, or an idolator, or a railer, or a drunkard, or an extortioner.**

But now I have written unto you **not to keep company**, if any man that is called a **brother** be a FORNICATOR, OR COVETOUS, OR AN IDOLATOR, OR A RAILER, OR A DRUNKARD, OR AN EXTORTIONER; with such an one <u>no</u> not to eat. For what have I to do to <u>judge them also that are without</u>? 1 Corinthians 5:9-11

Remember, God judge those who are not in Christ.

For what have I to do to judge them also that are _without?_ do <u>not</u> ye **<u>judge them that are within</u>**?

But them that are **<u>without God judgeth.</u>** Therefore **<u>put away from among yourselves that wicked person</u>**.

1 Corinthians 5:9-11. (_Read chapters 6 for a more perfect understand_).

FAITHFUL PUTTING ME INTO THE MINISTRY

4. According to the word, if he be found that stealeth and selleth a man or if the man be in his hand he shall surely be put to _____

A. Death

And he that stealeth a man, and selleth him, or if he be found in his hand, he shall surely be put to death Exodus 21:16

5. And He said, Hear now My words: If there be a prophet among you, I The Lord will make Myself known unto him in a vision, and will speak unto him in a dream. My servant Moses is not so, who is faithful in all Mine house. With him will **I speak mouth to mouth,** even apparently, and not in *dark speeches*; and the *similitude of The Lord* shall he behold: wherefore then were ye not *afraid to speak against my servant Moses*? Numbers 12:6-8

Q. Where can you find two scriptures that confirm Moses was faithful in all His house?

A. Hebrews 3:2 & Hebrews 3:5

Who was **FAITHFUL TO HIM THAT APPOINTED HIM,** (*God appointed Jesus 1-4)* **as also Moses** was faithful in all His house. Hebrews 3:2

And Moses verily was faithful in **all His house**, as a servant, FOR A TESTIMONY OF THOSE THINGS WHICH *WERE TO BE SPOKEN AFTER*, Hebrews 3:5

6. And I thank Christ Jesus our Lord, who hath enabled me, for that He counted me **faithful**, putting me into the ministry;

Q. What did Paul teach before he made this statement concerning the law?

Now the end of the commandment is charity out of **a pure heart, and of a good conscience,** and *of faith unfeigned:* From which some having swerved have turned aside unto vain jangling; Desiring to be teachers of the law; understanding neither what they say, nor whereof they affirm.

But we know that the law is good, if a man use it lawfully; **Knowing this,** *that the law is* **not** made **for a righteous man,** BUT **for the lawless and disobedient, for the ungodly and for sinners, for unholy and profane, for murderers of fathers and murderers of mothers, for manslayers, For whoremongers, for them that defile themselves with mankind, for menstealers, for liars, for perjured persons, and if** *there be any other thing that is contrary to sound doctrine*;

1 Timothy1:5-10 &12

BE STRONG IN THE GRACE THAT IS IN CHRIST JESUS!

1. Thou therefore, my son, be strong in the grace that is in Christ Jesus. And the things that thou hast heard of me among many witnesses, the same commit thou to _____. Wherefore, holy brethren, partakers of the heavenly calling, consider The Apostle and High Priest of **our profession, Christ Jesus;** Who was faithful to Him that appointed Him, as also Moses was faithful in all his house. *For This Man was counted worthy of more glory than Moses,* inasmuch as He who hath builded the house hath more honour than the house.

Q. Who in The Apostle and High Priest and who appointed Him?

3. A wicked doer giveth heed to false lips; and a liar giveth ear to a naughty tongue.

Add thou not unto His words, lest_____

4. According to the Holy Word who shall not inherit the kingdom of God?

5. Who are we to judge the children in the family of God or the ungodly?

1. Thou therefore, my son, be strong in the grace that is in Christ Jesus. And the things that thou hast heard of me among many witnesses, the same commit thou to _____
A. <u>**FAITHFUL**</u> **MEN, WHO SHALL BE** <u>**ABLE TO TEACH**</u> **OTHERS ALSO.** 2 Timothy 2:1 & 2

2. Wherefore, holy brethren, partakers of the heavenly calling, consider <u>The Apostle and High Priest</u> of our profession, <u>Christ Jesus;</u> Who was <u>faithful</u> to <u>Him that appointed Him</u>, as also Moses was faithful in all his house. For This Man was <u>counted worthy of more glory than Moses</u>, inasmuch as He who hath builded the house hath more honour than the house.
Q. Who in The Apostle and High Priest and who appointed Him?
A. **Jesus The Son of God is The High Priest** and God The Father appointed Him.
Hebrews 3:1-3

3. A wicked doer giveth heed to <u>false lips;</u> and a <u>liar</u> giveth ear to a <u>naughty tongue</u>. add thou <u>not</u> unto <u>His words</u>, lest _____
A. **He** <u>**reprove thee, and**</u> **thou be found a liar.** Proverbs 17:4 & 30:6

4. According to the Holy Word who shall not inherit the kingdom of God?
A. Whoever makes the wrong choices by rejecting the word and refuse to repent/turn away from these evil deeds, Paul says, of the which I tell you before, as I have also told you in time past, **that they which do** <u>**such things shall**</u> <u>**not**</u> **inherit the kingdom of God**.
Adultery, fornication, uncleanness, lasciviousness, Idolatry, witchcraft, hatred, variance, emulations, wrath, strife, seditions, heresies, Envyings, murders, drunkenness, revellings, and such like. of the which I tell you before, as I have also told you in time past, that they which do such things shall not inherit the kingdom of God.Galatians 5:19-21

5. Who are we to judge the children in the family of God or the ungodly?
Those who are not <u>adopted into the family of God</u> have not been <u>justified by faith.</u>
But to him that worketh not, but believeth on Him that justifieth the ungodly, His faith is counted for righteousness. Romans 4:5 (And being <u>fully persuaded</u> that, what he had <u>promised</u>, He was able also to perform. And therefore it was <u>imputed</u> to him for <u>righteousness.</u> Now it was not written for his sake alone, that it was <u>imputed</u> to him; <u>But for us also,</u> to whom it <u>shall be imputed,</u> <u>if</u> we <u>believe on Him that raised up Jesus our Lord from the dead;</u> Who was <u>delivered</u> for <u>our offences</u>, and was <u>raised again</u> for our <u>justification</u>). Please, read Romans 4:21-25

A. We are to judge the children of God and *He will judge those who are not in His famil*y. But them that are <u>without God judgeth.</u> Therefore <u>put away from among yourselves that wicked person.</u>
1 Corinthians 5:13

MY SPIRIT SHALL NOT ALWAYS STRIVE WITH MAN

1. And it came to pass, when men began to multiply on the face of the earth, and _____ were born unto them, That the _____ saw the _____ that they were fair; and they took them wives of all which they chose. And The LORD said, _____ for that he also is flesh: yet his days shall be an hundred and twenty years.

2. God saw that the wickedness of man was great in the earth, and that every imagination of the

thoughts of his heart was only evil continually.

Q. Did The LORD ever repent/changed His Mind that He had made man on the earth?

3. Noah found grace in The Eyes of The LORD and he was a just man.

Q. Was Noah also a perfect man?

MY SPIRIT SHALL NOT ALWAYS STRIVE WITH MAN

1. And it came to pass, when men began to multiply on the face of the earth, and _____ were born unto them, That the _____ saw the _____ that they were fair; and they took them wives of all which they chose. And The LORD said, _____, for that he also is flesh: yet his days shall be an hundred and twenty years.

A. Daughters, sons of God, daughters of men and My spirit shall not always strive with man.

Genesis 6:1-3

2. God saw that the wickedness of man was great in the earth, and that every imagination of the

thoughts of his heart was only evil continually.

Q. Did The LORD ever repent/changed His Mind; that He had made man on the earth?

A. YES.

And it repented The LORD that He had made man on the earth, and it grieved Him at His Heart. ..For it repenteth Me that I have made them. Genesis 6:5-7

3. Noah found grace in The Eyes of The LORD and he was a just man.

Q. Was Noah also a perfect man?

A. Yes.

Noah was a **just** man <u>and</u> **PERFECT IN HIS GENERATIONS**, and Noah walked with God.

But Noah found grace in the eyes of the LORD. These are the generations of Noah: Noah was a just man and perfect in his generations, and Noah walked with God. Genesis 6:8-10

Sodom and Gomorrah and the Tribe of Benjamin
Homosexuality

1. I have seen also in the prophets of Jerusalem an horrible thing:

Q. What were those horrible things He saw in the prophets of Jerusalem?

2. The prophets of Jerusalem, were unto The Lord as whom?

3. What was so wicked and sinful in Sodom and Gomorrah that The Lord destroyed the place and the people?

4. How can one know the phrase "that we may know them" the meanings is as we say to have sex with them?

5. Where can we discover more information in the New Testament that refers back to these spirits?

6. How and why did Benjamin become the smallest tribe in Israel?

SODOM AND GOMORRAH AND THE TRIBE OF BENJAMIN HOMOSEXUALITY

"Enlighten Sermon and Teaching On This Spirit"

1. I have seen also in the prophets of Jerusalem an horrible thing:

Q. What were those horrible things He saw in the prophets of Jerusalem?

A. They **commit adultery, and walk in lies**: they **strengthen also the hands of evildoers**, that *none* DOTH RETURN FROM HIS WICKEDNESS; Says, The Lord).

2. The prophets of Jerusalem, were unto The Lord as whom?

A. Sodom, and the inhabitants thereof as Gomorrah. Jeremiah 23:14

3. What was so wicked and sinful in Sodom and Gomorrah that The Lord destroyed the place and the people?

A. Men having sex *with humankind; as we say homosexuality* but I called it the same spirit that was in Sodom and Gomorrah.

And they called unto Lot, and said unto him, **Where are the men** which came in to thee this night?

Bring them out unto us, that we **may know them**. (Have sex with them) Genesis 19:5.

Please, read chapter 18 &19.

4. How can one know the phrase "that we may know them" the meanings is as we say to have sex with them?

A. And **Adam knew Eve his wife; and she conceived**, and bare Cain, and said, I have gotten a man from The LORD. Genesis 4:1

5. Where can we discover more information in the New Testament that refers back to these spirits?

A. And likewise also the men, leaving the natural use of the woman, burned in **their lust one toward another; men with men** working that **which is unseemly**, and receiving in themselves that recompence of their error which was meet. Romans 1:27

Know ye not that the unrighteous shall not inherit the kingdom of God? Be not deceived: neither fornicators, nor idolaters, nor adulterers, nor effeminate, nor abusers of themselves with mankind. 1 Corinthians 6:9.

Sodom and Gomorrah and the Tribe of Benjamin Homosexuality

"Enlighten Sermon and Teaching On This Spirit"

6. How and why did Benjamin become the smallest tribe in Israel?

A. Because, they did not only have the same spirit that was in Sodom and Gomorrah, The tribe of Benjamin **refused to put the evil from among them**; their brethren.

"Homosexuality is all about choices and judgment for the wrong choice"

The other tribes had a commandment from The Lord to destroy them. However, they did repent later on and helped the tribe of Benjamin get wives that the tribe would not be cut off forever.

This is the conclusion of the matter and why they were the smallest tribe.

Cross reference with Genesis 19, Judges 19:22-30 & Chapter 20 &21.

This information is added do to this spirit growing so rapidly.

"Pleasure in another man's sin"

Are we yet without understanding? Please, read this and I believe it will clarify this spirits we call gays, lesbians and homosexuals.

Lay **hands suddenly on no man**, neither be partaker of other men's sins: *keep thyself pure.*1Timothy 5:22

1 John 3:3 And every man that hath this hope in him purifieth himself, even as He is pure.

Some men's **sins are open beforehand**, going *before to judgment*; and some men **they follow after.** 1Timothy 5:24

What we are not to judge is in Romans 14:1-11

Him that is weak in the faith receive ye, but not to doubtful disputations. For one believeth that he may eat all things: another, who is weak, eateth herbs. Let not him that eateth despise him that eateth not; and let not him which eateth not judge him that eateth: for God hath received him. Let us not therefore judge one another any more: but judge this rather, that no man put a stumblingblock or an occasion to fall in his brother's way. But take heed lest by any means this liberty of yours become a stumblingblock to them that are weak. 1 Corinthians 8:9

Again, **When a** righteous man doth turn from his righteousness, and commit iniquity, and I lay a stumbling-block before him, **he shall die:** *because thou hast not given him warning*, **he shall die in his sin**, and his *righteousness which he hath done* shall **not be remembered**; but his blood will I require at thine hand. Ezekiel 3:20

Sodom and Gomorrah and the Tribe of Benjamin Homosexuality

"Enlighten Sermon and Teaching On This Spirit"

It was asked on yesterday, will this issue become like equal rights and black and white marrying? The answer is no way, There is nothing scriptural that supports those spirits but many that support only a man and a woman can reproduce and what happened and will happen to those who continue to live wickedly. Satan knows if 50 % of the people becomes gay that means there will be 50% less people in the world and 50% **MORE IN HELL WITH HIM.**

Every time I turn on the TV, I am hearing the statement The President made which did vex my spirit all night and continues to do so but, what about the statement made by the other one running for president that, it is ok for gays to adopt children, **how did we overlook that one**? This is even more appalling and offensive as well because, adult can make their own wicked decisions but children are to be train up in the way they should go, if these children see these wicked things going on they will think they are acceptable but no, they are not in the sight of God no matter what people believe.

This tells me, Satan has blinded both of their eyes but I also understand, these things are sent forth to judge man to see what kind of choices they will make.

No matter who you are, that support gay marriages and gays adopting children it is wrong in the sight of God, Yes, time is changing but I serve and unchangeable God who does not lie nor repent But, Jesus will repent from destroying only *if we* repent from the evil.

Know ye not that the *unrighteous shall not inherit the kingdom of God*? Be not deceived: neither fornicators, nor idolaters, ***nor adulterers, nor effeminate, nor abusers of themselves with mankind.***

What was so wicked and sinful in Sodom and Gomorrah that The Lord destroyed the place and the people?

Men having sex *with mankind, as SOME CALL* homosexuality but I called it the same spirit that was in Sodom and Gomorrah and also in the tribe of Benjamin.

Yahweh/God have mercy upon America and the nations and bring repentance.

SODOM AND GOMORRAH AND THE TRIBE OF BENJAMIN HOMOSEXUALITY

"ENLIGHTEN SERMON AND TEACHING ON THIS SPIRIT"

..THEY CALLED UNTO LOT, AND SAID UNTO HIM, **WHERE ARE THE MEN WHICH CAME IN TO THEE THIS NIGHT? BRING THEM OUT UNTO US, THAT WE MAY KNOW THEM.** (HAVE SEX WITH THEM) GENESIS 19:5.

PLEASE, READ CHAPTER 18 &19.

THIS IS HOW AND WHY BENJAMIN BECAME THE SMALLEST TRIBE IN ISRAEL BECAUSE, THEY HAD THE **SAME SPIRIT IN THEIR TRIBE AS SODOM AND GOMORRAH AND THEY REFUSED TO PUT THE EVIL FROM AMONG THEM; THEIR BRETHREN.**

WHERE CAN WE DISCOVER MORE INFORMATION IN THE NEW TESTAMENT THAT REFERS TO THESE SPIRITS AS WELL? "HOMOSEXUALITY, SODOM AND GOMORRAH"

ROMANS 1:27 AND LIKEWISE ALSO THE MEN, LEAVING THE NATURAL USE OF THE WOMAN, BURNED IN THEIR LUST ONE TOWARD ANOTHER; MEN WITH MEN WORKING THAT WHICH IS UNSEEMLY, AND RECEIVING IN THEMSELVES THAT RECOMPENCE OF THEIR ERROR WHICH WAS MEET.

1 CORINTHIANS 6:9. KNOW YE NOT THAT THE UNRIGHTEOUS SHALL NOT INHERIT THE KINGDOM OF GOD? BE NOT DECEIVED: NEITHER FORNICATORS, NOR IDOLATERS, NOR ADULTERERS, NOR EFFEMINATE, NOR ABUSERS OF THEMSELVES WITH MANKIND.

JEREMIAH 9:23&24 THUS SAITH THE LORD, LET NOT THE WISE MAN GLORY IN HIS WISDOM, NEITHER LET THE MIGHTY MAN GLORY IN HIS MIGHT, **LET NOT THE RICH MAN GLORY IN HIS RICHES:**

*BUT LET HIM THAT GLORIETH GLORY IN THIS, **THAT HE UNDERSTANDETH AND KNOWETH ME, THAT I AM THE LORD WHICH EXERCISE LOVINGKINDNESS, JUDGMENT, AND RIGHTEOUSNESS,** IN THE EARTH: FOR IN THESE THINGS I DELIGHT, SAITH THE LORD.*

HE LOVETH RIGHTEOUSNESS AND JUDGMENT: THE EARTH IS FULL OF THE GOODNESS OF THE LORD. PSALM 33:5

SODOM AND GOMORRAH AND THE TRIBE OF BENJAMIN HOMOSEXUALITY "ENLIGHTEN SERMON AND TEACHING ON THIS SPIRIT"

For I The LORD love judgment, I hate robbery for burnt offering; and I will direct their work in truth, and I will make an everlasting covenant with them. Isaiah 61:8

Hate the evil, and LOVE THE GOOD, and establish judgment in the gate: it may be that The LORD God of hosts will be gracious unto the remnant of Joseph. Amos 5:15

Behold, I set before you this day a **BLESSING AND A CURSE**; A blessing, **if** ye obey the *commandments of The Lord your God*, which I command you this day: *And **a curse, if ye will not obey The Commandments** of The Lord your God,* but turn aside out of the way which I command you this day, to go after *other gods*, which ye have not known.

And ye shall observe to do all *the statutes and judgments* which I set before you *this day*. Deut. 11:26-28 &32 Read also chapter 26-28.

*In that I command thee this day to love The LORD thy God, to walk in His ways, and TO KEEP HIS COMMANDMENTS AND HIS STATUTES AND HIS JUDGMENTS, **that thou mayest live**. Deuteronomy 30:16*

The king's strength also loveth judgment; thou dost establish equity, Thou executest judgment and righteousness in Jacob. Psalm 99:4

He doth execute the judgment of the fatherless and widow, and *loveth the stranger*, in *giving him food and raiment*. Deuteronomy 10:18

Blessed be The LORD thy God, *which delighted in thee*, to set thee on the throne of Israel: because The LORD loved Israel for ever, therefore made he thee king, *to do judgment* and justice. 1 Kings 10:9

Blessed be The LORD thy God, which delighted in thee to set thee on His throne, to be king for The LORD thy God: because Thy God loved Israel, to establish them for ever,

SODOM AND GOMORRAH AND THE TRIBE OF BENJAMIN HOMOSEXUALITY

"Enlighten Sermon and Teaching On This Spirit"

Therefore made he thee king over them, **to do *judgment and justice*.** 2 Chronicles 9:8

Philippians 1:9 And this I pray, that your love may abound yet more and more in <u>knowledge and in all judgment;</u> Philippians 1:8-10

Herein is our love made perfect, that we may have boldness in the day of judgment: because as He is, so are we in this world. 1 John 4:17

<u>**A Message from Yahweh and Yahushua,**</u> **Do you love enough to stand and correct and warn My people from Me?**

Remember, love always corrects.

O LORD, **correct me, but with judgment**; <u>not</u> in thine anger, lest thou bring me to **nothing** Jeremiah 10:24

As many as ***I love, I rebuke*** and ***chasten:*** **be zealous therefore, and repent.**
Revelation 3:19

<u>I hate</u> and <u>abhor lying</u>: but thy ***law do I love*.** Psalm 119:163

Everyone is not chosen to teach the way of The Lord, neither does Yahweh make known/manifest Yahushua to them.

He sends His pastors, teaches, prophets, prophetess, apostles and evangelists to teach and make His ways known to the people.

LET NO MAN DECEIVE YOU BY ANY MEANS: **FOR** THAT DAY SHALL NOT COME, EXCEPT THERE COME A FALLING AWAY FIRST, AND THAT MAN OF SIN BE REVEALED, THE SON OF PERDITION; 2 Thessalonians 2:3

<u>A word from The Lord Jesus:</u>

Search the scriptures; for in them YE **think ye have eternal life: and they are they which testify of Me.**

Jesus said, you have not because you ask not, *if you want to know the true ask Him:*

And ye will not come to Me, that ye **might have life. I** <u>receive</u> **not** honour **from men**. But I know you, that ye ***have not the love of God in you.***

SODOM AND GOMORRAH AND THE TRIBE OF BENJAMIN HOMOSEXUALITY

"ENLIGHTEN SERMON AND TEACHING ON THIS SPIRIT"

I am come in My Father's Name, and ye receive Me not: If another shall come in his own name, him ye will receive.

WHY, BECAUSE, MANY ARE PEOPLE PLEASERS, THEY ARE NOT SEEKING THE HONOUR FROM GOD ONLY.

How can ye believe, which receive honour ONE OF ANOTHER, and *SEEK NOT THE HONOUR THAT COMETH FROM GOD ONLY?*

Psalm 12:6 THE WORDS OF THE LORD ARE PURE WORDS: as silver tried in a furnace of earth, purified seven times.
Psalm 18:26 With the pure thou wilt shew thyself pure; AND with the forward thou wilt show thyself forward.

THE CONCLUSION OF THE WHOLE MATTER

Let up hear the *conclusion of the whole matter:* Fear God, and keep His Commandments: for this is the whole duty of man. Ecclesiastes 12:13

MY SONS AND DAUGHTERS

1. How old was Abram when The LORD appeared to him and said, I am the Almighty God; walk before Me, and be thou perfect?

2. How many years did Enoch walk with God after his son Methuselah was born?

3. How many years did Enoch live?

4. How old were Mahalalel when he died?

5. I will say to the north, Give up; and to the south, Keep not back: bring

_____

MY SONS AND DAUGHTERS

1. How old was Abram when The LORD appeared to him and said, I am the Almighty God; WALK BEFORE ME, AND BE THOU PERFECT?

A. Abram was ninety-nine years old.

And when Abram was ninety years old and nine, The LORD appeared to Abram, and said unto him, I am The **Almighty God; walk before Me, and be thou perfect**. Genesis 17:1

If He said it, you can DO it!

2. How many years did Enoch walk with God after his son Methuselah was born?

A. Enoch walked with God three hundred years.

And Enoch walked with God after he begat Methuselah three hundred years, and begat sons and daughters: Geneses 5:22

The word speaks of children, _sons and daughters_, I believe the meanings, of sons and daughters are those who are mature and follow not just believers.

Wherefore come out from among them, _and be ye separate_, saith **The Lord**, and **touch not the unclean thing**; **and I will receive you** And will be **a** Father unto you, and ye shall **be my sons and daughters,** saith The Lord Almighty. 2 Corinthians 6:17-18

And on My servants and on My handmaidens I will pour out in those days of My Spirit; and they shall prophesy: Acts 2:18

For _such an high priest became us,_ who is holy, harmless, undefiled, separate <u>from</u> sinners, and made higher than the heavens; Hebrews 7:26

Thus saith <u>The LORD, The _Holy One_ of Israel</u>, AND His Maker, Ask Me of things to come concerning _My sons,_ and concerning the work of My hands command ye Me Isaiah 45:11

3. How many years did Enoch live?

A. Enoch lived three hundred and sixty five years.

And all the days of Enoch were three hundred sixty and five years: Geneses 5:23

MY SONS AND DAUGHTERS

4. How old were Mahalalel when he died?

A. Mahalalel was 895 years old.

And all the days of Mahalaleel were eight hundred ninety and five years: and he died. Geneses 5:17

5. I will say to the north, Give up; and to the south, Keep not back: bring _____

A. My *sons* from far, and My *daughters* from the ends of the earth; Isaiah 43:6

Notice: Sons and Daughters, it does not say children.

MEANING, THOSE WHO ARE *MATURE IN YAHWEH ARE NO MORE CHILDREN, TOSSED TO AND FRO!*

{THOSE WHO ARE, ESTABLISHED, DEVELOPED, SETTLED, MATURED, COMPLETE AND ADVANCED}

> [11] And He gave some, apostles; and some, prophets; and some, evangelists; and some, pastors and teachers; [12] For the **perfecting of the saints**, for **the work of the ministry**, for the edifying of the body of Christ: [13] **Till we *all come in the unity of the faith*, and of the *knowledge of The Son of God*, unto a perfect man**, unto the measure of the stature of **the fulness of Christ:** [14] That we henceforth **be no more children, tossed to and fro**, and **carried about with every wind** of doctrine, by *the sleight of men, and cunning craftiness, whereby they lie in wait to deceive;* [15] **But *speaking the truth in love*, may grow up into Him in *all things,* which is the head, even Christ:** Ephesians 4:11-15

If I bear witness of Myself, My witness is <u>not</u> true.

1. If we come out from among sinful man (those who sin willfully after they have the knowledge of sin) and do not touch the unclean thing The Lord will receive us as_____

2. What is the testimony of Jesus?

3. He that cometh from above is above all: he that is of the earth is earthly, and <u>speaketh of the earth</u>:

He that cometh from heaven _____

4. And what He hath seen and heard, that He testifieth; and no man receiveth _____

5. He that hath received His testimony hath set to his seal that_____

6. It is also written in your law, that the testimony of _____

7. What is our righteousness according to the scriptures <u>not</u> man?

MANIFESTING QUIZZING

IF I BEAR WITNESS OF MYSELF, MY WITNESS IS <u>NOT</u> TRUE.

"TWO MEN"

1. If we come out from among sinful man (those who sin willfully after they have the knowledge of sin) and do not touch the unclean thing The Lord will receive us as_____

A. His sons and daughters

Wherefore <u>come out from among them</u>, and **be ye separate,** saith The Lord, and touch not the unclean thing; and <u>I will receive you</u>. 2 Corinthians 6:17&18

2. What is the testimony of Jesus?

A. The testimony of Jesus is the spirit of prophecy.

And I fell at his feet to worship him. And he said unto me, See thou do it not: I am thy fellowservant, and of thy brethren that have **the testimony of Jesus**: <u>worship God</u>: for the testimony of Jesus is the spirit of prophecy. Revelation 19:10

3. He that cometh from above is above all: he that is of the earth is earthly, and <u>speaketh of the earth</u>: He that cometh from heaven _____

A. Is above all John 3:31

4. And what He hath seen and heard, **that He testifieth;** and no man receiveth _____

A. His testimony John 3:32

5. He that hath <u>received</u> His testimony hath set to his seal that_____

A. God is true. John 3:33

6. It is also written in your law, that the testimony of _____

A. Two men is true John 8:17

Please, notice two men.

MANIFESTING QUIZZING

IF I BEAR WITNESS OF MYSELF, MY WITNESS IS <u>NOT</u> TRUE.

"TWO MEN"

Remember, two or three witnesses establish everything.
But if he will not hear thee, then take with thee one or two more, that <u>in the mouth of two or three witnesses every word may be established.</u> Matthew 18:16
Who are these two Men? Answer found in John Chapter 5

7. What is our righteousness according to the scriptures not man?

A. And it <u>shall</u> be our righteousness, if we observe to do all these commandments BEFORE THE LORD our God, *as He hath commanded us.* Deuteronomy 6:25

I can of Mine Own Self <u>do nothing</u>: **as I hear, I Judge**: and **My Judgment is Just**; because **I seek not Mine own will**, <u>but</u> *THE WILL OF THE FATHER which* **hath sent Me**. **If I bear** WITNESS OF MYSELF, MY *WITNESS IS not true*. THERE IS <u>**ANOTHER**</u> THAT BEARETH WITNESS OF ME; and <u>**I know that the witness which He witnesseth of Me is true.**</u> But I receive *not* testimony from man: but these things I say, that ye **might be saved.** But I have *GREATER WITNESS* THAN THAT OF JOHN: for the works which **The Father hath given Me to finish,** the same **WORKS THAT I DO, BEAR WITNESS OF ME,** that **The Father hath sent Me.** And *THE FATHER HIMSELF, which hath* **sent Me, hath borne witness of Me.** Ye **have neither heard His voice at any time**, nor **seen His shape**. And ye have **not** His word **abiding** in you: for *whom H hath sent, **Him ye believe not.*** <u>***Search the scriptures;*** for in them ye <u>think ye have eternal life:</u> and</u> they are they which testify of Me. And ye will not come to Me, that ye **might** have life. I receive **not** honour from **men.** But I know you, that ye have not the **love of God in you.** *I* <u>AM COME IN</u> *MY FATHER'S NAME,* and ye receive Me NOT: if ANOTHER shall come in his <u>own name, him ye will receive.</u> How can ye believe, which RECEIVE HONOUR ONE OF ANOTHER, and <u>**seek not the honour that cometh from God only?**</u> John 5:30-32, 34-36 and39.

Yahushua The Messiah/Jesus Christ The Son of God <u>and</u> Yahweh/ The Father The Everlasting God are these Two Witnesses! Praise Yah, Yahweh and Yahushua

"Life Eternal Manifested"

1. God's will is that all men be saved and that all men come unto the knowledge of the truth after he is justified.

What truth does God desire man to know/have knowledge?

2. Some believe the word saved and life eternal, have the same implication but according to scriptures what is life eternal?

3. God separated Paul from his mother's womb and called him by His Grace for what purpose?

4. This He ordained in Joseph for a _____ when He went out through the land of Egypt: where I heard a language that I understood not.

Psalm 96

1 O sing unto The LORD a new song: sing unto The LORD, all the earth. 2 Sing unto The LORD, bless His Name; shew forth His salvation from day to day. 3 Declare His glory among the heathen, His wonders among all people. 4For The LORD is great, and greatly to be praised: He is to be feared above all gods. 5For all the gods of the nations are idols: but The LORD made the heavens. 6Honour and majesty are before Him: strength and beauty are in His sanctuary. 7Give unto The LORD, O ye kindreds of the people, give unto The LORD glory and strength. 8GIVE UNTO THE LORD THE GLORY DUE UNTO HIS NAME: bring an offering, and come into His courts. 9 O worship The LORD in the beauty of holiness: fear before Him, all the earth. 10Say among the heathen that The LORD reigneth: the world also shall be established that it shall not be moved: HE SHALL JUDGE THE PEOPLE RIGHTEOUSLY. 11Let the heavens rejoice, and let the earth be glad; let the sea roar, and the fulness thereof. 12 Let the field be joyful, and all that is therein: then shall all the trees of the wood rejoice 13BEFORE THE LORD: FOR HE COMETH, FOR HE COMETH TO judge the earth: He shall judge the world with righteousness, and the people with His truth.

HE DIED FOR THE WORLD/THE UNGODLY BUT NOW HE IS JUDGING THE CHURCH, HIS PEOPLE. READ *Ps. 1:1 & 5. 1 Peter 4:17*
For the time is come that Judgment must begin at the house of God: and if it first begin at us, what shall the end be of them that obey not the gospel of God?

"LIFE ETERNAL MANIFESTED"

1. God's will is that all men be saved and that all men come unto the knowledge of the truth after he is justified.

Q. What truth does God desire man to know/have knowledge?

A. **FOR THERE IS ONE GOD, and One Mediator between God and men, The Man Christ Jesus**;

Who **GAVE HIMSELF A RANSOM FOR ALL**, to be <u>testified in due time.</u> 1Timothy 2:3-6

2. Some believe the word saved and life eternal, have the same implication but according to scriptures what is life eternal?

A. **And this is life eternal,** that they <u>might know Thee</u> **The only True God**, and **JESUS CHRIST,**

WHOM Thou HAST <u>SENT</u>. John 17:3 (*Remember, and is additional*)

3. God separated Paul from his mother's womb and called him by His Grace for what purpose?

A. God separated Paul and called him; **to reveal His Son Jesus in him that he might preach Him among the heathen.**

..But when it pleased God, who separated me from my mother's womb, and called me by His grace, **TO REVEAL HIS SON IN ME**, that I might preach Him among the heathen; immediately **I conferred not with flesh and blood**: Neither went I up to Jerusalem to them which were **apostles before me**; but I went into Arabia, and returned again unto Damascus. Galatians 1:15-17

And Simon Peter answered and said, **Thou art The Christ, The Son of The Living God.** And Jesus answered and said unto him, **Blessed art thou, Simon Barjona:** for <u>**flesh and blood**</u> hath not revealed it unto thee, **but MY FATHER WHICH IS IN HEAVEN.** Matthew 16:16-17

4. This He ordained in Joseph for a _____ when He went out through the land of Egypt: where I heard a <u>language</u> that I understood not.

A. **Testimony.** Psalm 81:5

HOW FAITH, IS MADE PERFECT

1. The word of The LORD said let not the wise man glory in his wisdom, neither let the mighty man glory in his might, let not the rich man glory in his riches. But He also said what one can glory in.

Q. What can we glory in?

2. Abraham believed God, and it was imputed unto him for righteousness: and he was called the Friend of God.

Q. How was his faith, made perfect?

3. Now to Abraham and his _____ were the promises made.

Q. **In this statement, were these promises made to Abraham and his seed or his seeds?**

4. To whom were these premises made?

Psalm 109

¹Hold not thy peace, O God of my praise; ²For the mouth of **the wicked** and **the mouth of the deceitful are opened against me**: they have spoken against me with a lying tongue. ³They compassed me about also **with words of hatred**; and fought against me **without a cause. ⁴For my love they are my adversaries**: but **I give myself unto prayer. ⁵And they have rewarded me evil for good, and hatred for my love.** ⁶Set thou *a wicked man over him*: and **let Satan stand at his right hand. ⁷When he shall be judged**, let him **be condemned**: and **let his prayer become sin**. ⁸Let his days be few; and let **another take his office**. ⁹Let his children be **fatherless, and his wife a widow. ¹⁰*Let his children be continually vagabonds***, and beg: let them seek their bread also out of their desolate places. **¹¹Let the extortioner catch all that he hath**; and **let the strangers spoil his labour. ¹²Let there be none to extend mercy unto him**: neither **let there be any to favour his fatherless children. ¹³let his posterity be cut off; and in the generation** following let **their name be blotted out**. ¹⁴Let the iniquity of his fathers be remembered with the LORD; and let **not** the sin of his mother be *blotted out*. ¹⁵Let them *be before the LORD continually that he may cut off the memory of them from the earth.* **¹⁶Because that he remembered not to shew mercy,** but *persecuted the poor and needy man*, that **he might even slay the broken in heart**. **¹⁷*As he loved cursing*,** so **let it come unto him**: as **he delighted not in blessing**, so let it **be far from him.** ¹⁸As he **clothed himself with cursing like as with his garment, so let it come into his bowels like water,** and like **oil into his bones**. ¹⁹Let it be unto him as the garment which covereth him, and for a girdle wherewith he is girded continually. **²⁰Let this be the reward of mine adversaries from the LORD, and of them that speak evil against my soul.** ²¹But do thou for me, O GOD the Lord, *for thy name's sake*: **because thy mercy is good, deliver thou me.** ²²For I am **poor and needy, and my heart is wounded within me.** ²³I am gone like the shadow when it declineth: I am tossed up and down as the locust. **²⁴My knees are weak through fasting**; and my flesh faileth of fatness. ²⁵I became also **a reproach unto them: when they looked upon me they shaked their heads**. ²⁶Help me, O LORD my God: O save me according to thy mercy: **²⁷That they may know that this is thy hand**; that thou, LORD, hast done it. **²⁸*Let them curse, but bless thou*: when they arise, let them be ashamed**; but **let thy servant rejoice**. ²⁹Let mine adversaries be clothed with shame, and **let them cover themselves with their own confusion, as with a mantle**. ³⁰I will greatly **praise the LORD with my mouth;** yea, I will praise him among the multitude. **³¹*For he shall stand at the right hand of the poor, to save him from those that condemn his soul.***

"HOW FAITH IS MADE PERFECT"

1. The word of The LORD said let not the wise man glory in his wisdom, neither let the mighty man glory in his might, let not the rich man glory in his riches. But He also said what one can glory in.

Q. What can we glory in?

A. Understanding Him and knowing Him that He is The LORD which exercises lovingkindness, judgment, and righteousness, in the earth and in these things He delights.

..But let him that glorieth glory in this, that he understandeth and knoweth Me, that I am The LORD which exercise lovingkindness, judgment, and righteousness, in the earth: for in these things I delight, saith the LORD. Jeremiah 9:23-24

2. Abraham believed God, and it was imputed unto him for righteousness: and he was called the Friend of God.

Q. How was his faith, made perfect?

A. FAITH IN ACTION, HIS FAITH AND HIS WORKS MADE HIM PERFECT.

Seest thou how *faith wrought with his works, and by works was faith made perfect?* James 2:22

***Even so faith*, if it hath <u>not</u> works, is dead, being alone.** James 2:17

But wilt thou know, *O vain man*, that <u>faith without works</u> is dead? James 2:20

For as the BODY *WITHOUT THE SPIRIT IS DEAD*, <u>so</u> faith without works is dead also. James 2:26

3. Now to Abraham and his _____ were the promises made.

Q. In this statement, were these promises made to Abraham and his seed or his seeds?

A. Abraham and his seed as of one. Galatians 3:16

4. To whom were these premises made?

A. CHRIST/THE MESSIAH

A. Now to Abraham and his seed were the promises made. *He saith not*, And to seeds, <u>AS OF MANY</u>; but as of one, and to thy seed, which is Christ. Galatians 3:16

Psalm 13

[1]How long wilt thou **forget me, O LORD**? for ever? how long wilt thou **hide thy face from me**? [2]How long shall **I take counsel in my soul**, *having sorrow in my heart daily*? **how long shall mine enemy be exalted over me**? [3]Consider and hear me, O LORD my God: **lighten mine eyes, lest I sleep the sleep of death**; [4]Lest mine enemy say, I have **prevailed against him**; and those that **trouble me rejoice when I am moved.** [5]But I have **trusted in thy mercy; my heart shall rejoice in thy salvation.** [6]I will sing unto the LORD, because he hath dealt bountifully with me. {*God salvation has been with man since the days of the Adams}* Adam and his wife.

"Jesus Manifested Himself"

1. Mary Magdalene was the first one Jesus appeared to after He had risen from the dead, Jesus had done something very important in her life before He appeared to her.
Q. What had Jesus accomplish in Mary Magdalene's life before He appeared to her?

2. If we have many devils in our lives, will Jesus manifest Himself to us?

3. According to the Holy Word; who is the one that continue to love Jesus and will be loved of The Father and Jesus will also love him and manifest Himself/make Himself known?

4. Who gave the disciples to Jesus and for what purpose and who did Jesus manifest His Father's Name?

Psalm 2

¹Why do the heathen rage, and the people imagine a vain thing?
²The kings of the earth set themselves, and the rulers take counsel together, against The LORD, _and_ **against His Anointed,** saying, **³Let us break** _their_ **bands asunder, and cast away** _their_ **cords from us. ⁴He that sitteth in the heavens shall laugh: The LORD** _shall have them in derision._ ⁵Then shall **He speak unto them in his wrath,** and **vex them in his sore displeasure.** **⁶Yet have** _I set My king upon My Holy hill of Zion._ ⁷I WILL DECLARE THE DECREE: THE LORD HATH _SAID UNTO ME,_ <u>THOU ART MY SON; THIS DAY HAVE I BEGOTTEN THEE.</u> _⁸ASK OF ME, AND I SHALL GIVE THEE THE_ <u>HEATHEN FOR THINE INHERITANCE,</u> _AND THE_ <u>UTTERMOST PARTS OF THE EARTH</u> _FOR THY POSSESSION._ **⁹Thou shalt break them with a rod of iron; thou shalt dash them in pieces like a potter's vessel.** ¹⁰Be <u>wise</u> now therefore, <u>O ye kings:</u> be <u>instructed,</u> <u>ye judges of the earth.</u> **¹¹Serve The LORD** <u>**with fear, and rejoice with trembling.**</u>

²Kiss The Son, LEST HE <u>BE ANGRY</u>, and <u>**ye perish from the way,**</u> **when His wrath is kindled but a little Blessed are all they that** <u>**put their trust in Him.**</u>
{I hope we can see and know this is Jesus The Messiah/Yahushua The Son of God/Yahweh}

"Jesus Manifested Himself"

1. Mary Magdalene was the first one Jesus appeared to after He had risen from the dead, Jesus had done something very important in her life before He appeared to her.

Q. What had Jesus accomplish in Mary Magdalene's life before He appeared to her?

A. JESUS HAD CAST seven devils OUT OF MARY MAGDALENE.

Now when Jesus was risen early the first day of the week, he appeared first to Mary Magdalene, out of whom he had cast seven devils. Mark 16:9

2. If we have many devils in our lives, will Jesus manifest Himself to us?

A. I believe HE WILL NOT. **The Word of God teaches us** WHO IT IS THAT CONTINUE TO LOVE JESUS <u>and who</u> will be loved of His Father **and whom Jesus will manifest Himself/make Himself known.**

3. According to the Holy Word; who is the one that continue to love Jesus and will be loved of The Father and Jesus will also love him and manifest Himself/make Himself known?

A. HE THAT HATH HIS COMMANDMENTS AND keepeth them (Continue)

He that hath My commandments, and keepeth them, he it is that loveth Me: and he that loveth Me shall be loved of My Father, and I will love him, and will manifest Myself to him. John 14:21

4. Who gave the disciples to Jesus and for what purpose and who did Jesus manifest His Father's Name?

A. God took these men out of the world and gave them to *His Son Jesus,* to teach them His Word and in the way they *should walk* and to *manifest Him.*

I have manifested Thy Name <u>unto</u> the men which Thou <u>gavest</u> Me out of the world: Thine they were, and *Thou gavest them Me*; and **they have kept Thy word.** Now THEY HAVE KNOWN THAT ALL THINGS WHATSOEVER THOU HAST GIVEN ME ARE OF THEE. For I have given unto them *the words which thou gavest Me*, and *they have received them*, and *have known surely that I came out from Thee, and* **they have believed that Thou didst send Me.** John 17:6-8

Saying, I WILL DECLARE THY NAME UNTO MY BRETHREN, <u>in the midst of the church will I sing praise unto Thee.</u> AND AGAIN, <u>I WILL PUT MY TRUST IN HIM.</u>

And again, Behold **I** <u>and</u> <u>the children which God hath</u> **given** Me. Hebrews 2:12 & 13.

And **I will wait upon The LORD, that hideth His face from the house of Jacob, and I will look for Him.**

Behold, <u>I</u> and <u>the children</u> whom The LORD hath given Me <u>are</u> for <u>signs</u> and for <u>wonders</u> in Israel from The LORD of <u>Hosts</u>, which *dwelleth in mount Zion*.

Isaiah 8:17 & 18.

"FASTING" WHAT FAST DID THE LORD CHOOSE

1. How did Jesus teach His disciples to fast?

2. The Scribes and Pharisees saw Jesus eating with publicans and sinners, they said unto His disciples, How is it that He eateth and drinketh with publicans and sinners? When Jesus heard it, He saith unto them, They that are whole have no need of the physician, but they that <u>are sick</u>: I came not to <u>call the righteous</u>, but <u>sinners to repentance</u>. The disciples of John and of the Pharisees *used to fast*: They asked Jesus this question. *Why do the disciples of John and of the Pharisees fast,* **but** <u>*Thy disciples fast not?*</u>

Q. How did Jesus respond to this question?

3. Cry aloud, spare not, lift up thy voice like a trumpet, and shew My people their transgression, and the house of Jacob their sins. Yet they seek Me daily, and delight to know My ways, as a nation that did righteousness, and forsook not the ordinance of their God: they ask of Me the ordinances of justice; they take delight in approaching to God. Wherefore have we fasted, say they, and thou seest not? wherefore have we afflicted our soul, and thou takest no knowledge? Behold, in the day of your fast ye find pleasure, and exact all your labours.

Behold, ye fast <u>for strife and debate</u>, and to <u>smite with the fist of wickedness</u>: ye shall <u>not fast</u> as ye do this day, to make your <u>voice to be heard on high</u>. Is it such a fast that <u>I have chosen</u>? a day for a man to <u>afflict his soul</u>? is it to bow <u>down his head as a bulrush</u>, and to <u>spread sackcloth and ashes under him</u>? wilt <u>thou call this a fast</u>, and an <u>acceptable day to The LORD</u>?

Q. What Fast Did The Lord Choose for them?

Psalm 62

1Truly my soul waiteth upon God: from Him cometh **my salvation. 2He only is my rock and my salvation**; <u>He is my defence</u>; I shall **not be greatly moved.** 3How long will ye **imagine mischief against a man?** ye shall be slain all of you: as a bowing wall shall ye be, and as a tottering fence. 4They only consult to cast him down from his excellency: they delight in lies: they bless with their mouth, but they curse inwardly. Selah. 5My soul, wait thou only upon God; **for my expectation is from Him.** 6He only **is my rock** and my **salvation:** He is my defence; I shall not be moved. **7In God is my salvation** and *my glory: the rock of my strength, and my refuge, is in God.* **8Trust in Him at all times;** **ye people, pour out your heart before Him:** God is a refuge for us. Selah. **9Surely men of low degree are vanity,** and *men of high degree are a lie*: to be **laid in the balance,** they are altogether lighter than vanity. **10Trust not in oppression,** and become **not vain in robbery: if riches increase,** set *not your heart upon them.* **11God hath spoken once; twice** have **I heard this; that power belongeth unto God.** 12ALSO UNTO THEE, O LORD, **belongeth mercy:** for *THOU RENDEREST TO EVERY MAN ACCORDING TO HIS WORK.*

WHAT FAST DID THE LORD CHOOSE, "THE BEST FASTT THAT WORKS"

1. How did Jesus teach His disciples to fast?
A. Jesus taught them to anoint their heads, and wash their faces. Are we following Yahushua teaching?

But thou, when <u>thou fastest, anoint thine head, and wash thy face;</u> That thou appear <u>not unto men</u> to fast, <u>but unto Thy Father which is in secret</u>: and <u>Thy Father, which seeth in secret, shall reward thee openly</u>. Matthew 6:17-19

2. The Scribes and Pharisees saw Jesus eating with <u>publicans and sinners</u>, they said unto His disciples, How is it that He eateth and drinketh with publicans and sinners? When Jesus heard it, He saith unto them, They that are whole have no need of the physician, but they that are sick: I came not to call the righteous, but sinners to repentance. The disciples of John and of the Pharisees used to fast: They asked Jesus this question. Why do the disciples of John and of the Pharisees fast, but Thy disciples fast not?

Q. How did Jesus respond to this question?
A. As long as they have <u>The Bridegroom with them, they</u> <u>cannot fast.</u>

And Jesus said unto them, **Can the children of The Bridechamber fast**, while The Bridegroom is with them? *As long as they have The Bridegroom with them, they cannot fast. and they come and say unto him,* **Why do the disciples of John and of the Pharisees fast, but thy disciples fast not?** Mark 2:16-19

3. Cry aloud, spare not, <u>lift up thy voice like a trumpet</u>, and **shew My people their transgression**, and the **house of Jacob their sins.** Yet they seek Me daily, and delight to know My ways, as a *nation that did righteousness,* and forsook not the ordinance of their God: they ask of Me the ordinances of justice; they take *delight in approaching to God. Wherefore have we fasted, say they, and thou seest not? wherefore have we afflicted our soul, and* ***thou takest no knowledge?*** *Behold, in the day of your fast ye find pleasure, and exact all your labours. Behold, ye fast for strife and debate, and to smite with the fist of wickedness: ye shall not fast as ye do this day,* to **make your voice to be heard on high**. Is it such a fast that I have chosen? **a day for a man to** *afflict his soul? is it* **to bow down his head as a bulrush, and to spread sackcloth and ashes under him?** <u>wilt</u> **thou call this a fast, and an** <u>ACCEPTABLE</u> **day to The LORD?**

<u>I love to research keywords, here are some keywords on "Acceptable"</u>

The lips of the righteous know what is acceptable: but the mouth of the wicked speaketh frowardness. Proverbs 10:32

To do justice and judgment is more acceptable to the LORD than sacrifice Proverbs 21:3

The preacher sought to find out acceptable words: and **that which was written was upright, even words of truth.** Ecclesiastes 12:10

Thus saith The LORD, In an acceptable time have I heard thee, and **in a day of salvation have I helped thee:** and **I will preserve thee, and give thee for** A COVENANT OF THE PEOPLE, to **establish the earth, to cause to inherit the desolate heritages**; Isaiah 49:8
To proclaim the acceptable year of The LORD, and the day of vengeance of our God; to comfort all that mourn; Isaiah 61:2
To preach the acceptable year of the Lord. Luke 4:19

WHAT FAST DID THE LORD CHOOSE, "THE BEST FAST THAT WORKS"

&

I love to research keywords, here are some keywords on "Acceptable"

I beseech you therefore, brethren, *by the* <u>*mercies of God,*</u> *that ye present your* **bodies a living sacrifice, holy, acceptable unto God,** *which is your reasonable service.* **Romans 12:1**

Proving what is acceptable unto the Lord. **Ephesians 5:10**

Ye also, as lively stones, ARE BUILT UP A SPIRITUAL HOUSE, AN HOLY PRIESTHOOD, TO <u>OFFER UP</u> SPIRITUAL <u>SACRIFICES,</u> ACCEPTABLE TO GOD by **Jesus Christ**. **1 Peter 2:5**

Q. WHAT FAST DID THE LORD CHOOSE FOR THEM?

A. **Is not this the fast that I have chosen**? to **loose the bands of wickedness, to undo the heavy burdens,** and **to let the oppressed go free,** and **that ye break every yoke?** Is it not to **deal** *thy bread to the hungry*, and **that thou bring the** POOR THAT ARE <u>CAST OUT</u> TO THY HOUSE? when thou **seest the naked, that thou cover him;** <u>and</u> **that thou hide** <u>not</u> **thyself from thine own flesh?**

{ Hide <u>not</u> thyself from thine own flesh? I believe this scripture is teaching us not to hide from our sins as Adam did}

I Read Is. 58:1-14 for a better understanding

Then shall thy LIGHT BREAK FORTH AS THE MORNING, and thine HEALTH SHALL SPRING FORTH SPEEDILY: and **thy** righteousness shall go before thee; *<u>The glory of The LORD shall be thy reward.</u>*

Then shalt **thou call, and The LORD shall answer;** thou shalt cry, and He shall say, Here I am.

If thou take away **from the midst of thee the yoke, the putting forth of the finger,** and speaking vanity;

And if thou draw out thy *<u>soul to the hungry</u>*, and satisfy the afflicted soul; THEN shall thy light rise in obscurity, and thy darkness be as the noon day: And THE LORD SHALL GUIDE THEE CONTINUALLY, and satisfy thy soul in drought, and <u>make fat thy bones: and thou shalt be like a watered garden, and like a spring of water, whose waters fail not.</u>

AND THEY THAT <u>SHALL BE OF THEE</u> SHALL <u>BUILD THE OLD WASTE PLACES</u>: THOU SHALT <u>RAISE UP THE FOUNDATIONS OF MANY GENERATIONS</u>; AND thou shalt be called, The repairer of the breach, <u>THE RESTORER OF PATHS TO DWELL IN.</u>

IF THOU <u>TURN AWAY THY FOOT</u> FROM THE SABBATH, FROM <u>DOING THY PLEASURE ON</u>

My Holy Day; AND *call the sabbath a delight,*

The Holy of The LORD, honourable; and shalt honour Him, NOT <u>DOING THINE OWN WAYS, NOR</u> *finding thine own pleasure,* <u>NOR</u> speaking thine <u>own</u> words:

Then shalt thou <u>delight thyself in The LORD;</u> and I will cause thee to <u>ride upon the high places of the earth,</u> and feed thee with the heritage of Jacob thy father: for

The Mouth of The LORD hath spoken it.

Isaiah 58:1-14

Praise The Lord for this fast!

"CALLED TO BE A DISCIPLE/CHRIST-IAN"

1. What book, chapter and verse does the word disciples appear for the first time?

2. They were first called, Christians/Christ-ians in _____

3. Who were, called Christians/Christ-ians? _____

4. The word of God says, .For unto you it is given in the behalf of Christ, not only to believe on Him, but_____

5. After Paul and Barnabas had taught the gospel to many in the city of Derbe, they returned again to Lystra, and to Iconium, and Antioch.

Q. Why did they return to the places where the gospel; was already preached?

1How long wilt thou forget me, O LORD? for ever? how long wilt **thou hide thy face from me?**
2How long shall I take counsel in my soul, having sorrow in my heart daily? **how long shall mine enemy be exalted over me?**
3Consider and hear me, O LORD my God: **lighten mine eyes**, lest I sleep **the sleep of death;**
4Lest mine enemy say, I have prevailed against him; and those that trouble me rejoice when I am moved.
5But I have trusted in thy mercy; my heart shall rejoice in thy salvation.
6 I WILL SING UNTO THE LORD, BECAUSE HE HATH DEALT BOUNTIFULLY WITH ME. Psalm 13:1-6

"CALLED TO BE A DISCIPLE/CHRIST-IAN"

1. What book, chapter and verse does the word <u>disciples</u> appear for the first time?
A. Isaiah 8:16. <u>**Bind up the testimony, seal the law** among **My disciples**.</u>

2. They were first called Christians/Christ-ians in _____

A. Antioch.

3. Who were, called Christians/Christ-ians? _____
A. The disciples, were called Christians **because, they were followers of Christ**.
.And the disciples were called Christians first in Antioch. Acts 11:26

THE FOLLOWERS OF CHRIST, NOT EVERYONE.

The Hebrew word for Christ is, Christos pronunciation is khrē-sto's, if we are followers of Christ we take on His Name as we say Christians but I say Christ-ians. Lets' look at the Hebrew word and pronunciation for the word Christians; Christianos the pronunciation is khrē-stē-ä-no's.

NOW LOOK AT THE WORDS SIDE BY SIDE,

Christos, Christianos. The pronunciation for the beginning sounds are the same,
khrē-sto's and khrē-stē-ä-no's but we used two different ECHOES.

4. The word of God says, .For unto you it is given in the behalf of Christ, not only to believe on Him, but _____

A. ALSO TO SUFFER FOR HIS SAKE

For unto you it is given in the behalf of Christ, not only to believe on Him, but also to suffer for His sake;
Philippians 1:29

Many times, we think we are suffering for Chris's sake but it is because of our own mistakes.

5. After Paul and Barnabas had taught the gospel to many in the city of Derbe, they returned again to Lystra, and to Iconium, and Antioch.

Q. Why did they return to these places where the gospel was already preached to these disciples?

A. To confirm the souls of the disciples and exhorting them to continue in the faith (urge them strongly and earnestly to continue in the faith, and that they must through much tribulation enter into the kingdom of God.)

*Confirming <u>the souls of the disciples</u>, and <u>exhorting them to continue in the faith,</u> and that they must **through much tribulation** ENTER INTO THE KINGDOM OF GOD. And when they had <u>ordained them elders in every church</u>, and <u>had prayed with fasting,</u> they COMMENDED THEM TO THE LORD, ON WHOM THEY <u>BELIEVED.</u> Acts 14:21-23*

SENT OR WENT & THE BIRTHRIGHT"

1. Reuben was the firstborn of Israel but he did not receive the birthright.

Q. How did Reuben forfeit his birthright?

2. Who did receive the birthright?

3. Who was the first Prophetess in scripture?

4. Was Miriam, sent by The Lord?

5. There was a Prophetess that judged Israel at one time and she said these words; then he made him that remaineth have dominion over the nobles among the people: The LORD made me have dominion over the mighty.

Q. Who was the Prophetess that spoke these words?

6. There was a man who had four daughters and they were virgins.

Q. Did theses daughter prophesy.

7. Did a woman ever Judge Israel?

"SENT OR WENT & THE BIRTHRIGHT"

1. Reuben was the firstborn of Israel but he did not receive the birthright.
Q. How did Reuben forfeit his birthright?
A. He defiled his father's bed.
Reuben, thou art my firstborn, my might, and the beginning of my strength, the excellency of dignity, and the excellency of power: Unstable as water, thou shalt not excel; because thou wentest up to thy father's bed; then defiledst thou it: he went up to my couch. Genesis 49:3 & 4

2. Who did receive the birthright?
A. THE SONS OF JOSEPH RECEIVED THE BIRTHRIGHT.
Now the sons of Reuben the firstborn of Israel, (for he was the firstborn; but forasmuch as he defiled his father's bed, his birthright was given unto the sons of Joseph the son of Israel: and the genealogy is not to be reckoned after the birthright. 1 Chronicles 5:1

3. Who was the first Prophetess in scripture?
A. MIRIAM.
.And Miriam the prophetess, the sister of Aaron, took a timbrel in her hand; and all the women went out after her with timbrels and with dances. Exodus 15:20

4. Was Miriam, sent by The Lord?
A. **Yes.**
..I SENT BEFORE THEE MOSES, AARON, AND MIRIAM. Micah 6:4

5. There was a Prophetess that judged Israel at one time and she said these words; then he made him that remaineth have dominion over the nobles among the people: The LORD made me have dominion over the mighty.
Q. Who was the Prophetess that spoke these words?
A. **Deborah.** Judges5:12 & 13.

6. There was a man who had four daughters and they were virgins.
Q. Did theses daughter prophesy?
A. Yes Acts 21:9

7. Did a woman ever Judge Israel?
A. **Yes.**
And Deborah, a prophetess, the wife of Lapidoth, she judged Israel at that time. Judges 4:4 And she dwelt under the palm tree of Deborah between Ramah and Bethel in mount Ephraim: and the children of Israel came up to her for judgment. Judges 4:5 please, read Judges Chapter 4 and 5. **Powerful!**

"HIGHLIGHTS FROM PROPHETESS DEBORAH"

BECAUSE, OF THIS PROPHETESS LEADERSHIP THE LAND HAD REST FORTY YEARS. PRAISE THE LORD!

AS DAVID WAS A PROPHET AND A FATHER IN ISRAEL SO WAS DEBORAH A PROPHETESS AND A MOTHER IN ISRAEL. Judges 5:7

Then sang Deborah and Barak the son of Abinoam on that day, saying, Praise ye The Lord for the avenging of Israel, when the people **willingly offered themselves. Hear, O ye kings; give ear, O ye princes**; I, **even I, will sing unto The Lord**; I will sing praise to The Lord God of Israel. *LORD, WHEN THOU WENTEST OUT OF SEIR*, when **thou marchedst out of the field of Edom**, **the earth trembled, and the heavens dropped,** the clouds also dropped water. The mountains melted from before The Lord, even that Sinai from before The Lord God of Israel. In the days of Shamgar the son of Anath, in the days of Jael, the highways were unoccupied, and the travellers walked through byways. The inhabitants of the villages ceased, **they ceased in Israel, until that I Deborah arose, that I arose a mother in Israel.** They chose new gods; then **was war in the gates**: was there a shield or spear seen among forty thousand in Israel? **My heart is toward the governors of Israel**, that offered **themselves willingly among the people. Bless ye The Lord.** *Speak, ye that ride on white asses, ye that sit in judgment, and walk by the way.* They that are delivered from the noise of archers in the places of drawing water, **there shall they rehearse the righteous acts of the Lord, even the righteous acts toward the inhabitants of His villages in Israel**: then shall the people of The Lord go down to the gates. **Awake, awake, Deborah: awake, awake, utter a song:** arise, Barak, and lead thy captivity captive, thou son of Abinoam. *Then He made him that remaineth have dominion* over the nobles among the people: **THE LORD MADE ME HAVE DOMINION OVER THE MIGHTY**. Judges 1-14

Curse ye Meroz, said the angel of The Lord, curse ye bitterly the inhabitants thereof; **because they came not to the help of The Lord, to the help of The Lord against the mighty.**

BLESSED ABOVE WOMEN SHALL JAEL the wife of Heber the Kenite be, **blessed shall she be above women in the tent.** He *asked water, and she gave him milk; she brought forth butter in a lordly dish.*

She put her hand to the nail, and her right hand to the workmen's hammer; and with the hammer she smote Sisera, she smote off his head, when she had pierced and stricken through his temples.

At her feet he bowed, he fell, he lay down: at her feet he bowed, he fell: where he bowed, there he fell down dead.

So let all thine enemies perish, O Lord: but let them that love Him be as **THE SUN** when **he** goeth forth in **his might.** And the land had **rest forty years**. Judges 5

"Controversial Questions" Truth Is Exposed

1. One of the most controversial questions among believers today is can one's name be blotted out of the book of the living?

2. According to the scripture who names will not be blotted out of the book of life?

3. What scriptures give us knowledge, wisdom and most of all understanding; on who will <u>not</u> be blotted out and who will be saved in the life to come?

4. Where can one find a reference to this statement, a man's foes shall be they of his own household?

5. Jesus said, repent or else I will come unto thee quickly and fight with what?

REMEMBER,

And it shall come to pass in the last days, saith God, I will pour out of My Spirit upon all flesh: and **your sons and your daughters shall prophesy**, and your young men shall see visions, and your old men shall dream dreams: **AND ON MY SERVANTS** and **on My handmaidens <u>I will pour out in those days of My Spirit; and they shall prophesy:</u>** And I will shew wonders in heaven above, and signs in the earth beneath; blood, and fire, and vapour of smoke: The sun shall be turned into darkness, and the moon into blood, before the great and notable day of The Lord come: **And it shall come to pass, that whosoever shall call on The Name of The Lord shall be saved.**
ACTS 2:17-21. (READ CHAPTER 2)

And it shall come to pass afterward, that I will pour out My spirit upon all flesh; and **your sons and your daughters shall prophesy**, your old men shall dream dreams, your young men shall see visions: And also upon the servants and upon the **handmaids in those days will I pour out My spirit.** And I will shew wonders in the heavens and in the earth, blood, and fire, and pillars of smoke.
The sun shall be turned into darkness, and the moon into blood, before the great and **terrible day of The LORD come. AND IT SHALL COME TO PASS, THAT WHOSOEVER SHALL CALL ON THE NAME OF THE LORD SHALL BE DELIVERED: for** in mount Zion and in Jerusalem shall be deliverance, *<u>as The LORD hath said, and in the remnant whom The LORD shall call</u>*. JOEL 2:28-32

CONTROVERSIAL QUESTIONS "TRUTH IS EXPOSED"

1. One of the most controversial questions among believers today is can one's name be blotted out of the book of the living?

A. **Yes**. LET THE WORD OF GOD BE TRUE AND MAN'S UNDERSTANDING BE A LIAR.

Romans 3:3-5 Says, .**For what if some did not believe**? shall their unbelief make the faith of God without effect? God forbid: yea, **let God be true, but every man a liar**; as it is written, **THAT THOU MIGHTEST BE JUSTIFIED IN THY SAYINGS, AND MIGHTEST OVERCOME WHEN THOU ART JUDGED**. But if our **unrighteousness commend the righteousness of God,** what shall we say? Is God unrighteous who taketh vengeance? (I speak as a man)

A. Yet now, **if thou wilt forgive their sin**; and **if not, blot me, I pray thee, out of thy book** which Thou hast written.

A. And The LORD said unto Moses, **WHOSOEVER HATH SINNED AGAINST ME, HIM WILL I BLOT OUT OF MY BOOK**. (*We need to be very careful and not reject the word of truth*). Exodus 32 &33

A. Let Me alone, that I may destroy them, **AND BLOT OUT THEIR NAME FROM UNDER HEAVEN**: and I will make of thee a nation mightier and greater than they. Deuteronomy 9:14

A. The LORD will not spare him, but then the anger of The LORD and His jealousy shall smoke against that man, and all the curses that are written in this book shall lie upon him, and **THE LORD SHALL BLOT OUT HIS NAME FROM UNDER HEAVEN**. Deuteronomy 29:20

A. **LET THEM BE BLOTTED OUT OF THE BOOK OF THE LIVING**, and not *BE WRITTEN WITH THE RIGHTEOUS*. Psalm 69:28

A. Let his posterity be cut off; and in the generation following **LET THEIR NAME BE BLOTTED OUT**. Psalm 109:13

2 According to scripture who names will not be blotted out of the book of life?

A. **The overcomers and continue to overcome until the end.**

A. He that **OVERCOMETH, THE SAME SHALL BE CLOTHED IN WHITE RAIMENT;** and **I will NOT blot out his name out of the book of life, BUT I will confess his name before My Father, and before His angels**. Revelation 3:5

3. What scriptures give us knowledge, wisdom and most of all understanding; on who will not be blotted out and who will be saved in the life to come?

A. But he that **SHALL ENDURE UNTO THE END**, the **SAME** shall **BE SAVED**. Matthew 24:13

A. And ye shall be hated of all men for My Name's sake: but *he that shall endure unto the end,* the same shall be saved. Mark 13:13

STAY IN THE RACE AND RUN ALL THE WAY UNTIL THE END, YOU CAN MAKE IT IF YOU TRY!

"Controversial Questions" Truth Is Exposed

4. Where can one find a reference to this statement, a man's foes shall be they of his own household?

A. For I am come to set a man at variance against his father, and the daughter against her mother, and the daughter in law against her mother in law. AND A MAN'S <u>FOES SHALL BE THEY OF HIS OWN HOUSEHOLD</u>. HE THAT LOVETH FATHER OR MOTHER MORE THAN *ME IS <u>NOT WORTHY OF ME</u>:* and HE THAT *LOVETH SON OR DAUGHTER MORE THAN ME IS NOT WORTHY OF ME.* Matthew 10:34-37

A. For the *<u>son dishonoureth the father</u>, the <u>daughter riseth up against her mother</u>,* the *<u>daughter in law against her mother in law</u>;* a man's enemies are the men of his own house. Micah 7:6

5. Jesus said, repent or else I will come unto thee quickly and fight with what?

A. THE SWORD OF MY MOUTH.

Repent; or else I will come unto <u>thee quickly</u>, and will **fight against them with the sword of My mouth.** Revelation 2:16

PRAISE GOD, HE IS USING HIS WORD TO DESTROY THAT O DEVIL CALLED SATAN.

REMEMBER, .FOR **THE WORD OF GOD IS QUICK, AND POWERFUL, AND SHARPER THAN ANY TWOEDGED SWORD,** PIERCING EVEN TO THE DIVIDING ASUNDER OF SOUL AND SPIRIT, AND OF THE JOINTS AND MARROW, AND IS A DISCERNER OF THE THOUGHTS AND INTENTS OF THE HEART. HEBREWS 4:12

AND HE HAD IN HIS RIGHT HAND SEVEN STARS: AND *OUT OF HIS MOUTH WENT A SHARP TWOEDGED SWORD*: AND HIS COUNTENANCE WAS AS THE SUN SHINETH IN HIS STRENGTH. REVELATION 1:16

"CONTROVERSIAL QUESTIONS" TRUTH IS EXPOSED

In Jesus
CIRCLE

OUT of
Jesus

Satan wants you out of the circle because, he cannot get in Jesus so, he wants you to <u>walk out the door.</u>

The circle will not move but you can walk out of the circle because, you have **free choices**. The door is open. The lost son had a father but he made a choice to **leave home**.

We also have a Father who loves us; IT IS TIME FOR THE WASTERS TO COME BACK HOME; *YOUR FATHER IS LOOKING AND WAITING FOR YOUR RETURN*.

And when he cometh home, he calleth together his friends and neighbours, saying unto them, Rejoice with me; for I have found my sheep which was lost. I say unto you, that likewise joy shall be in heaven over one sinner that repenteth, more than over ninety and nine just persons, which need no repentance. Luke 15:6, 7 &10

"WISDOM"

1. What had Jesus done to cause His fame to go throughout all Syria?

2. Jesus came into His own country and He taught them in their synagogue, insomuch that they were astonished, and said, Whence hath this man this wisdom, and these mighty works?

Q. Why Jesus did not do many mighty works there?

3. There came of all people to hear the wisdom of Solomon, from all kings of the earth, which had heard of <u>his wisdom</u>. The queen of Sheba also heard of the fame of Solomon concerning <u>The Name of The LORD and she came to prove him with hard questions.</u>

Q. How did Jesus respond to this statement?

4. The LORD said unto Jonah Arise, go to Nineveh, that great city, and cry against it; for their wickedness is come up before Me. Nineveh <u>received the word from The LORD</u> and they <u>repented</u> at the preaching of Jonas.

Q. How did Jesus respond to this statement?

"Wisdom"

1. What had Jesus done to cause His fame to go throughout all Syria?
A. Jesus taught in their synagogues, and preached the ***gospel of the kingdom, and***

healed all manner

of sickness and all manner of disease among the people. Matthew 4:23. (In additional, read 9:35).

2. Jesus came into His own country and He taught them in their synagogue, insomuch that they were astonished, and said, **Whence hath this man this wisdom, and these mighty works?**
Q. Why Jesus did not do many mighty works there?
A. BECAUSE THEY WERE *OFFENDED IN HIM* AND *BECAUSE OF THEIR UNBELIEF.*
Matthew 13:57 & 58

3. There came of all people to hear the wisdom of Solomon, from all kings of the earth, which had heard of <u>his wisdom</u>. THE QUEEN OF SHEBA ALSO HEARD OF THE FAME OF SOLOMON CONCERNING <u>THE NAME OF THE LORD AND SHE</u>

<u>CAME TO PROVE HIM WITH HARD QUESTIONS.</u>
Q. How did Jesus respond to this statement?

A. A GREATER THAN SOLOMON IS HERE.
The queen of the south shall rise up in the judgment with this generation, and shall <u>condemn it</u>: for she came from the uttermost parts of the earth to <u>hear the wisdom of</u>

<u>Solomon</u>; and, behold, a greater than Solomon is here. Matthew 12:42

4. The LORD said unto Jonah Arise, go to Nineveh, that *great city*, and *cry against it; for their wickedness is come up before Me*. Nineveh *received the word from The*

***LORD* and they <u>repented</u> at the preaching of Jonas.**
Q. How did Jesus respond to this statement?

A. *A greater than Jonas is here.*
The men of Nineveh *shall rise in judgment* with this generation, and shall condemn it: ***because they repented at the preaching of Jonas***; and, behold, a greater than Jonas is here. Matthew 12:41

"Be Wise and Don't Even Think It"

1. Who created darkness and evil?

2. What hath The LORD set before all His People?

3. How can one in The Lord be, eternally blessed?

4. How can one in The Lord be, eternally curse?

"Be Wise and Don't Even Think It"

1. Who created darkness and evil?

A. The Lord

The Lord said, I form the light, and create darkness: I make peace, and <u>create evil</u>:

The LORD do <u>all these things</u>. Isaiah 45:7
Cross-reference with Matthew 10:34

THINK NOT that *I am come to <u>send peace on earth</u>*: I came ***not to send peace***, but <u>a sword</u>. For I am come to set a man at variance <u>against his father,</u> and <u>the daughter against her mother</u>, and the daughter in law <u>against her mother in law</u>. And a man's <u>foes shall be they of his own household</u>.

He that loveth father or mother more than Me is <u>not worthy of Me</u>: and he that loveth son or daughter more than Me is not worthy of Me. Matthew 10:34-37

Matthew 3:9 And think <u>not</u> to say within yourselves, We have Abraham to our father: for I say unto you, that <u>**God is able of these stones to raise up children unto Abraham**</u>.

Matthew 5:17 **Think <u>not</u> that I am come to <u>destroy the law,</u> or <u>the prophets</u>: I am <u>not</u> come to destroy, but to fulfil.**

Matthew 10:34 **Think not that I am come to <u>send peace on earth</u>: I came <u>not to</u> send peace, but a <u>sword</u>.**

Matthew 24:44 THEREFORE BE YE ALSO READY: for in SUCH AN HOUR AS YE THINK NOT The Son of man COMETH.

Luke 12:40 **Be ye therefore ready also: for The Son of man cometh at an hour when ye think not.**

2. What hath The LORD set before all His People?
A. A blessing and a curse
BEHOLD, I SET BEFORE YOU THIS DAY A BLESSING AND A CURSE . . .
Deuteronomy 11:26

3. How can one in The Lord be, eternally blessed?

A.If he obey *The Commandments of The Lord our God*. Deuteronomy 11:27 *blessing, if ye obey The Commandments of The LORD your God*, which I command you this day:

Cross-reference with Revelation 22:14-15 & Matthew 5:3-12.

BLESSED ARE THEY THAT DO HIS COMMANDMENTS, THAT *THEY may* HAVE <u>RIGHT TO THE</u> *tree of life*, AND <u>MAY</u> enter in through the gates into the city.
WHO WILL NOT ENTER?

"BE WISE AND DON'T EVEN THINK IT"

FOR **_WITHOUT_** ARE DOGS, AND SORCERERS, AND WHOREMONGERS, AND MURDERERS, AND IDOLATERS, AND WHOSOEVER <u>LOVETH AND MAKETH A LIE.</u>

4. How can one in The Lord be, eternally curse?

A. IF ONE DOES NOT *OBEY* The Commandments of The Lord our God. And A CURSE, <u>IF</u> YE WILL <u>NOT OBEY</u> *The Commandments of The LORD your God*, but turn aside out of the way *which I command you this day*, to *go after other gods*, which *ye have not known*. Deuteronomy 11:28

Cross-reference with Matthew 5:19-21

<u>Whosoever</u> **therefore** SHALL BREAK ONE OF THESE LEAST COMMANDMENTS, and SHALL TEACH MEN SO, he shall be called the LEAST *IN THE KINGDOM OF HEAVEN*. BUT whosoever SHALL <u>DO</u> AND <u>TEACH</u> THEM, THE SAME SHALL BE CALLED GREAT IN THE KINGDOM OF HEAVEN. For I say unto you, *That except your righteousness shall exceed the righteousness of the scribes and Pharisees, ye shall* <u>IN NO CASE</u> ENTER <u>*INTO*</u> THE KINGDOM OF HEAVEN.

Ye have heard that it was said of them of old time, Thou shalt not kill; and whosoever shall *kill shall be in danger of the judgment:*

But I say unto you, **That** *whosoever is* <u>ANGRY WITH HIS BROTHER</u> <u>WITHOUT A CAUSE</u> *shall be* in danger *of the judgment:* **and whosoever shall say to** *his brother***, Raca, shall be in** *danger of the council:* **but whosoever shall say,** *Thou fool***, be** <u>in danger</u> **of hell fire**
Matthew 5:21 & 22

In addition, said <u>ALSO MANY TIMES</u> *in the New,* THOU SHALT NOT KILL.

<u>*NOTICE IN DANGER,*</u> **When one does not repent he is in danger because, life eternal is not** <u>abiding</u> **at that time.**

Let the word be true!

Please, read Matthew 5 and Deuteronomy chapters 26-28 for a better revelation.

1. How did the elders obtain a good report?

2. Jesus said unto His disciples ye believe in God but He also said to them believe_____

3. There are many trying to get to The Father without going through the right door.

Q. How can one be sure they have entered through the right door?

Many believe when they receive Jesus into their hearts this is all required to receive eternal life.

4. Does the Bible give more than one example of faith, if so where can you discover them?

"NOW FAITH IS THE SUBSTANCE AND THE RIGHT DOOR"

1. How did the elders obtain a good report?

A. By faith Hebrews 11:1

2. Jesus said unto HIS DISCIPLES YE BELIEVE IN GOD but HE ALSO SAID TO THEM BELIEVE_____

A. ALSO IN ME. JOHN 14:1

3. There are many trying to get to The Father without going through the right door.

Q. How can one be sure they have entered through the right door?

A. ONLY IF THEY BELIEVE ON GOD THAT RAISED JESUS FROM THE DEAD.

JESUS SAITH UNTO HIM, I am the way, the truth, and the life: *no man* cometh unto The Father, but by Me.

John 14:6. Also, cross-reference with John Chapter 10 for more clarifications.

Many believe when they receive Jesus into their hearts this is all required to receive eternal life.

4. Does the Bible give more than one example of faith, if so where can you discover them?

A. Yes. Many Hebrews Chapter 11

---

¹**Now faith is the substance of things hoped for,** the evidence of <u>THINGS</u> not seen. ²For by it <u>the elders obtained a **good report**</u>. ³Through <u>faith we understand that the worlds were framed by the word of God</u>, so that <u>things</u> which <u>are seen</u> were not made of things which do appear. ⁴By faith <u>Abel offered unto God a more excellent sacrifice than Cain</u>, by which <u>he obtained witness that he was righteous</u>, God <u>testifying of his gifts</u>: and by it he being dead yet speaketh. ⁵By <u>faith Enoch was translated that he should not see death</u>; and was **not found**, because God <u>had translated him</u>: for before his translation he had <u>this testimony</u>, **that he pleased God**. ⁶**But without faith it is impossible to please Him**: for he that <u>cometh to God</u> must **believe that He is, and** that **He is a rewarder of them that diligently seek Him.**⁷By <u>faith Noah,</u> **being warned of God of things not seen as yet, moved with fear, prepared an ark to the saving of his house;** by the which <u>he condemned the world,</u> and **became heir of the righteousness which is by faith.** 8By faith Abraham,

when he was called to go out into a place which **he <u>should</u> AFTER RECEIVE FOR AN INHERITANCE, OBEYED**; and he went out, not knowing whither he went. ²<u>By faith</u> he sojourned in the LAND OF PROMISE, as in a strange country, dwelling in tabernacles with <u>Isaac and Jacob,</u> **THE HEIRS WITH HIM OF THE SAME PROMISE:** ¹⁰For he looked for a city which **hath foundations, whose builder and maker is God.** ¹¹Through *faith also Sara herself received strength to conceive seed, and was delivered of a child when she was past age, because she judged him faithful who had promised.* ¹² Therefore sprang there even of ONE, and him as good as dead, so many as the stars of the sky in multitude, and as the sand which is by the sea shore innumerable.

13THESE ALL DIED IN FAITH, not having received the promises, but having seen them afar off, and were persuaded of them, and embraced them, and confessed that they were strangers and pilgrims on the earth. *14FOR THEY THAT SAY SUCH THINGS DECLARE PLAINLY THAT THEY SEEK A COUNTRY.15AND TRULY, IF THEY HAD BEEN*

"NOW FAITH IS THE SUBSTANCE AND THE RIGHT DOOR"

mindful of that country from whence they came out, they might have had opportunity to have returned. [16]But now they **desire a better country**, that is, **an heavenly**: wherefore **God is not ashamed to be called their God**: for He hath prepared for them a city. **[17]By faith Abraham, when he was tried, offered up Isaac: and he that had received the promises offered up his only begotten son. [18]Of whom it was said, That in Isaac shall thy seed be called: [19]Accounting that God was able to raise him up, even from the dead; from whence also he received him in a figure.**

[20]By faith Isaac blessed Jacob and Esau concerning things to come. [21]By faith Jacob, when he was a dying, blessed both the sons of Joseph; and worshipped, leaning upon the top of his staff. [22]By faith Joseph, when he died, made mention of the departing of the children of Israel; and gave commandment concerning his bones. [23]By faith Moses, when he was born, was hid three months of his parents, because they saw he was a proper child; and they were not afraid of the king's commandment.

[24]By faith Moses, when he <u>was come to years</u>, refused to <u>be called the son of Pharaoh's daughter</u>; [25]Choosing rather to suffer affliction with the people of God, than to enjoy the pleasures of <u>sin for a season</u>; [26]Esteeming <u>the reproach of Christ</u> greater riches than the <u>treasures in Egypt</u>: for he had respect unto the recompence of the reward. [27]By faith he forsook Egypt, not fearing the wrath of the king: for he endured, as seeing him who is invisible. [28]Through faith he kept the Passover, and the sprinkling of blood, lest he that destroyed the firstborn <u>should</u> touch them.**[29] By faith they passed through the Red sea as by dry land:** which the Egyptians assaying to do were drowned. [30]By faith the walls of Jericho fell down, after they were compassed about seven days.

[31]By faith the harlot Rahab perished not with them that <u>believed not,</u> when she had received the spies with peace.

[32]And what shall I more say? for the time would fail me to tell of Gedeon, and of Barak, and of Samson, and of Jephthae; of David also, and Samuel, and of the prophets: [33]Who through faith subdued kingdoms, wrought righteousness, obtained promises, stopped the mouths of lions.

[34]Quenched the violence of fire, escaped the edge of the sword, out of weakness were made strong, waxed valiant in fight, turned to flight the armies of the aliens.

[35]Women received their dead raised to life again: and others were tortured, not accepting deliverance; that they might obtain a better resurrection: [36]And others had trial of cruel mockings and scourgings, yea, moreover of bonds and imprisonment:

[37]They were stoned, they were sawn asunder, were tempted, were slain with the sword: they wandered about in sheepskins and goatskins; being destitute, afflicted, tormented;

[38](Of whom the world was not worthy:) they wandered in deserts, and in mountains, and in dens and caves of the earth. [39]And these all, *having obtained a good report* through faith, received <u>not</u> the promise: [40]God having provided some better thing for us, *that they without us should not be made perfect*.

"HOW THREE BECOMES ONE"

1. Jesus said the one that loveth Him (continue to love Him), shall be loved of His Father and He would manifest Himself to him.

Q. How did Judas respond to this statement?

2. How did Jesus reply to Judas's question?

3. At that day ye shall know that **I am in My Father**, and YE IN ME, and I IN YOU.

Q. Can you position The Father, Jesus and you in the right circle? John 14:10-20

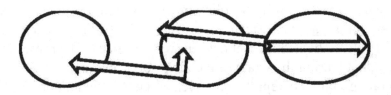

4. Did Jesus give something to Judas to cause Satan to enter into him?

5. Did Jesus called; Judas His friend?

6. We are friends of Jesus, **if** we **do** whatsoever He commands us.

Q. What book, chapter and verse support this statement?

"HOW THREE BECOMES ONE"

1. Jesus said the <u>one that</u> loveth Him (CONTINUE TO LOVE HIM), shall <u>be loved</u> <u>of His Father</u> and He would manifest Himself to him.

Q. How did Judas respond to this statement?

A. Judas saith unto Him, NOT ISCARIOT, LORD, **how is it that thou wilt manifest Thyself unto us, and not unto the world?** John 14:22

2. How did Jesus reply to Judas's question?

A. Jesus answered and said unto him, IF A MAN LOVE ME, HE WILL KEEP MY WORDS: ***AND MY FATHER WILL LOVE HIM,*** and WE WILL <u>come unto him,</u> **and** make **Our abode** with him.
John 14:23

3. At that day ye shall know that I AM IN MY FATHER, and YE IN ME, **and I in you.** John 14:10-20

Q. Can you position The Father, Jesus and you in the right circle?
(Remember, the implication of the word "and" is in addition).

Jesus in Man #3.   Man in Jesus #2.   Jesus in God #1.

THIS IS HOW THREE BECOMES ONE IN THE SPIRIT!

4. Did Jesus give something to Judas to cause Satan to enter into him?

A. Yes.

HE IT IS, TO **whom** <u>I</u> **shall** <u>GIVE</u> **a sop,** **when I have dipped it.** AND WHEN HE HAD DIPPED THE SOP, **He gave it to Judas Iscariot,** THE <u>SON OF SIMON.</u> AND AFTER THE SOP SATAN ENTERED INTO HIM. THEN <u>SAID JESUS</u> UNTO HIM, *THAT THOU DOEST,* <u>*DO*</u> *QUICKLY.* JOHN 13:26-27

WE SHOULD KNOW WHY THIS TRANSPIRED.

I speak not of you all: I know whom I have chosen: but that **the scripture may be fulfilled,** He that eateth bread with Me hath lifted up his heel against Me. John 13:18

5. Did Jesus called; Judas His friend?

A. YES. Yea, MINE OWN FAMILIAR FRIEND, IN WHOM I TRUSTED, which DID EAT OF MY BREAD, HATH LIFTED UP HIS HEEL AGAINST ME. Psalm 41:9
I speak not of you all: <u>I KNOW WHOM I HAVE CHOSEN</u>: **BUT *that the scripture may be fulfilled*,** HE THAT EATETH BREAD WITH ME HATH LIFTED UP HIS HEEL AGAINST ME. John 13:18

"HOW THREE BECOMES ONE"

6. We are friends of Jesus, **IF** we **DO whatsoever** He commands us.

Q. What book, chapter and verse support this statement?

A. **Ye are My friends, IF ye DO whatsoever *I command you.*** John 15:14

Many say we do not need to do any works, because Jesus finished it for us. The Devil is a lie.

> JOHN 15:15 **HENCEFORTH** I call you *not* servants; for **the servant knoweth** *not* what his lord doeth: BUT *I HAVE CALLED YOU FRIENDS; for all things* THAT I HAVE HEARD OF MY FATHER I HAVE MADE KNOWN UNTO YOU.
>
> 16 **Ye have not chosen Me**, BUT *I have chosen you*, AND ORDAINED YOU, THAT YE SHOULD GO AND BRING FORTH FRUIT, AND THAT YOUR FRUIT **should remain**: that *whatsoever ye shall ask of The Father in My Name, He may give it you.*
>
> 17 These things I command you, *that ye love one another.*
>
> 18 *If the world hate you, ye know that it hated me before it hated you.*
>
> 19 If ye were of the world, the world would love his own: but *because ye are not of the world*, but I have chosen you out of the world, therefore the world hateth you.
>
> 20 Remember the word that I said unto you, The servant is *not greater* than his lord. **IF THEY HAVE PERSECUTED ME, THEY WILL ALSO PERSECUTE YOU;** *if* they have ***KEPT MY SAYING***, THEY ***WILL KEEP YOURS ALSO.***
>
> 21 But all these things will **they do unto you for My name's Sake**, *because* THEY KNOW NOT *HIM* THAT *SENT ME.*
>
> 22 If I had not come and spoken unto them, they had not had sin: but now they have no cloak for their sin.
>
> 23 **He that hateth Me** hateth MY FATHER ALSO.
>
> 24 **If I had not done among them the works which none other man did, they had not had sin:** BUT NOW HAVE THEY BOTH SEEN AND HATED BOTH ME AND MY FATHER.
>
> 25 But this cometh to pass, that *the word might be fulfilled that is written in their law, They hated me without a cause.*
>
> 26 But when the **Comforter is come, whom I will send unto you from The Father,** *even **THE SPIRIT OF TRUTH***, which **proceedeth from** The Father, ***HE SHALL TESTIFY OF ME:*** 27 *And ye also shall bear witness, because ye have been with me from the beginning.*

'Seeking those things which are above"

1. .And he went out to meet Asa, and said unto him, Hear ye me, Asa, and all Judah and Benjamin; The LORD is with you, while ye be with Him; and if ye seek Him, He will be found of you;

He used the big but and if word. Q. But?

2. For a long season, Israel had been without three things.

Q. Can you name these three things?

3. When Israel was in trouble, they turned unto The LORD God of Israel and they sought Him.

Q. In this verse, did they find him?

4. Asa had a disease in his feet, until his disease was exceeding great; yet in his disease he sought not to The LORD.

Q. Whom did Asa seek after?

5. If ye then be risen with Christ, seek those things which are above.

Q. What are those things Paul encourages us to seek, after?

'SEEKING THOSE THINGS WHICH ARE ABOVE"

1. ..And he went out to meet Asa, and said unto him, **Hear ye me, Asa,** and **all Judah and Benjamin;** *The LORD is with you, while ye be with Him*; and IF <u>YE SEEK HIM</u>, HE WILL BE FOUND OF YOU;

He used the big but and if word. Q. But?

A. .**But** <u>IF</u> **ye forsake him,** <u>HE WILL</u> **forsake you.** 2 CHRONICLES 15:2

2. For a long season, Israel had been without three things.
Q. **Can you name these three things?**
1. TRUE GOD
2. TEACHING PRIEST
3. WITHOUT LAW 2 CHRONICLES 15:2-3.

3. When Israel was in trouble, they turned unto The LORD God of Israel and they sought Him.

Q. **In this verse, did they find him?**

A. YES.

But when they in their trouble **did turn** unto The LORD God of Israel, AND SOUGHT HIM, HE WAS FOUND OF THEM. 2 Chronicles 15:4.

4. Asa had a disease in his feet, until his disease was exceeding great; yet in his disease he sought NOT TO THE LORD.

Q. **Whom did Asa seek after?**

A. *THE PHYSICIAN* 2 Chronicles 16:13

5. If ye then be risen with Christ, seek those things which are above.

Q. **What are those things Paul encourages us to seek, after?**

A. THE FATHER ***AND*** CHRIST JESUS THE SON OF GOD.

IF ye then be risen with Christ, ***SEEK THOSE THINGS*** which are above, ***where Christ sitteth*** on ***the right hand of God.*** Set your AFFECTION ON **THINGS ABOVE,** not on things on the earth. For ye are dead, and your LIFE IS HID <u>WITH CHRIST</u> <u>*IN GOD*</u>. WHEN **CHRIST**, <u>*WHO IS OUR LIFE, SHALL APPEAR, THEN SHALL YE ALSO APPEAR WITH*</u> **Him in glory**. Colossians 3:1-3

"Righteousness like a mighty stream"

1. "We will not be satisfied until justice rolls down like waters and <u>righteousness</u> like <u>a mighty stream.</u>"

Q. Righteousness like a mighty stream or righteousness as a mighty stream, is this quotation scriptural?

If the answer is yes please, use scripture to support your answer.

2. Ye who turn judgment to wormwood, and_____

3. Hate the evil, and love the good, and_____

4. Why does the scripture teach us to seek good and not evil?

"We sing, we pray, we shout, we even fallout"

5. Will there be a time, <u>if</u> we continue to live in sin and do not repent after we have the knowledge of the truth/sin willfully, that The Lord will say take away from Me the noise of thy songs?

"RIGHTEOUSNESS LIKE A MIGHTY STREAM"

1. "We will not be satisfied until justice rolls down like waters and <u>righteousness</u> like <u>a</u>

<u>mighty stream</u>."

Q. Righteousness like a mighty stream or righteousness as a mighty stream, is this quotation scriptural?

If the answer is yes please, use scripture to support your answer.
A. YES.

But let <u>judgment</u> run down as waters, <u>and righteousness as a mighty</u>
<u>stream</u> Amos 5:24
To understand this statement let judgment run down as waters, and

righteousness as a mighty stream Please, read Amos Chapter 5

2. Ye who turn judgment to wormwood, and_____
A. Leave off righteousness in the earth. Amos 5:7 please, read 6-9
SEEK THE LORD, AND YE SHALL LIVE; LEST HE BREAK OUT LIKE FIRE IN THE HOUSE OF
JOSEPH, *and devour it, and there be none to quench it in Bethel.*
YE WHO TURN JUDGMENT TO WORMWOOD, AND LEAVE OFF
RIGHTEOUSNESS IN THE EARTH,
<u>Seek Him</u> that maketh the seven stars and Orion, and turneth the shadow of death into
the morning, and maketh the day dark with night: that calleth for the waters of the sea,
and poureth them out upon the face of the earth: **The LORD is His Name:**
That strengtheneth the spoiled against the strong, so that the spoiled shall come against
the fortress.

3. Hate the evil, and love the good, and_____
A. <u>Establish judgment in the gate</u>: it may be that The LORD God of hosts will be
gracious unto the remnant of Joseph. Amos 5:15

4. Why does the scripture teach us to seek good and not evil?
A. THAT WE MAY LIVE AND SO THE LORD, THE GOD OF HOSTS WILL BE
WITH US.
That ye may live: and so The LORD, The God of hosts, shall be with you, as ye have
spoken. Amos 5:14

<u>"We sing, we pray, we shout, we even fallout"</u>

**5. Will there be a time, <u>if</u> we continue to live in sin and do not repent after we have the
knowledge of the truth/sin willfully, that The Lord will say take away from Me the
noise of thy songs?**

A. YES.

TAKE *THOU AWAY FROM ME THE NOISE OF THY SONGS,* <u>***for I will not hear the***</u>
<u>***melody of thy viols.***</u> AMOS 5:23

"THE KNOWLEDGE OF THE TRUTH"

1. What is good and acceptable in the sight of God our Saviour?
Who <u>will</u> have all men to <u>be saved</u>, and to come unto the knowledge of the truth?
For there is _____ and _____ between_____
_____

2. **Wherefore, I desire that ye faint not at my tribulations for you, which is your glory. For this cause I bow my knees unto The Father of our Lord Jesus Christ, of whom the_____**

3. **So they read in the book in the law of God distinctly, and gave the sense, and caused them to _____**

4. **Does the scripture teaches the sinners or the ungodly is justified by faith?**

5. **But to him that worketh not, but believeth on him that justifieth the ungodly, his faith is?**

"THE KNOWLEDGE OF THE TRUTH"

1. What is good and acceptable in the sight of God our Saviour?
who <u>will</u> have all men to <u>be saved</u>, AND To come unto the knowledge of the truth?
For there is _____ and _____ between_____
God and men _____the Man Christ Jesus;

A. ONE GOD, One Mediator, GOD AND MEN, THE MAN CHRIST JESUS.
WHO GAVE <u>HIMSELF A RANSOM FOR ALL</u>, TO BE <u>TESTIFIED IN DUE TIME</u>.
1 TIMOTHY 2:3-6.
It is due time!

And they overcame him by <u>the blood of the Lamb</u>, AND <u>by the word of their</u> <u>testimony</u>; AND <u>THEY LOVED</u> not <u>THEIR LIVES</u> unto the death. Revelation 12:11

2. .Wherefore I desire that ye faint not at my tribulations for you, which is your glory.
For this cause I bow my knees unto The Father of our Lord Jesus Christ, of whom the_____
A. WHOLE FAMILY *in heaven and earth is named*. Ephesians 3:13-14

3. SO THEY READ IN THE BOOK IN THE LAW OF GOD DISTINCTLY, AND GAVE THE SENSE, AND CAUSED THEM TO _____
A. UNDERSTAND THE READING. NEHEMIAH 8:8

4. Does the scripture teaches the sinners or the ungodly is justified by faith?
A. .**The ungodly**
For when we were yet **without strength**, in due time CHRIST DIED FOR THE UNGODLY. Romans 5:6

5. .But to him that <u>worketh not</u>, BUT BELIEVETH ON HIM THAT JUSTIFIETH <u>THE</u> <u>UNGODLY</u>, his faith is?
A. *Counted for righteousness.* Romans 4:5

PLEASE, READ CHAPTER 4 & 5 TO GET A BETTER UNDERSTANDING OF THIS VERSE.
ROMANS 4-5
NOTICE THE PHRASE "JUSTIFIETH THE UNGODLY"

LET'S TAKE A LOOK AT HOW THIS PHRASE IS USED IN SCRIPTURES"

"THE KNOWLEDGE OF THE TRUTH"
"UNGODLY"

But God commendeth His love toward us, in that, while we **were yet** <u>sinners, Christ died for us.</u> *MUCH MORE THEN, BEING NOW JUSTIFIED BY HIS BLOOD*, WE <u>SHALL BE SAVED</u> FROM <u>WRATH *THROUGH*</u> HIM. For if, when we **were** <u>enemies,</u> we were <u>reconciled to God by the</u> DEATH OF HIS SON, MUCH MORE, **BEING RECONCILED, WE SHALL BE** <u>SAVED BY</u> HIS life. Romans 5:8-10

2 Samuel 22:5 When the waves of death compassed me, **the floods of ungodly men** made me afraid;

2 Chronicles 19:2 And Jehu the son of Hanani the seer went out to meet him, and **said to king Jehoshaphat, Shouldest thou help the ungodly,** and <u>LOVE THEM THAT HATE THE LORD</u>? therefore is wrath upon thee from before The LORD

Job 16:11 God hath delivered me **to the ungodly**, and turned me over into the hands of the wicked.

Psalm 1:1 **BLESSED IS THE MAN THAT** WALKETH NOT IN THE COUNSEL OF THE UNGODLY, **NOR STANDETH IN THE WAY OF SINNERS,** nor sitteth in the seat of the scornful.

Psalm 1:4 **THE UNGODLY ARE NOT SO**: but are like the chaff which the wind driveth away.

Psalm 1:5 *Therefore the ungodly shall not stand in the judgment,* <u>NOR</u> *sinners in the congregation of the righteous.*

Why, *BECAUSE THE UNGODLY NEVER INTER INTO THE RACE, HE IS ALREADY CONDEMNED.*

For God sent **not** His Son into the world to condemn the world; **but** that the world through Him **MIGHT** *be saved.* He **that believeth on Him is not condemned: but** He that **believeth not** IS CONDEMNED ALREADY, *BECAUSE HE HATH NOT BELIEVED IN THE NAME OF THE ONLY BEGOTTEN SON OF GOD*. And this is the **condemnation,** that *light is come into the world,* and <u>men</u> *loved darkness rather than light,* BECAUSE THEIR <u>DEEDS WERE EVIL</u>. **²⁰For** *every one that doeth evil hateth the light,* neither cometh to the light, *LEST HIS DEEDS SHOULD BE REPROVED.* John 3:17-20

Psalm 1:6 **FOR THE LORD** <u>KNOWETH THE WAY OF THE RIGHTEOUS</u>: **but t**he way of **THE UNGODLY SHALL PERISH.** Psalm 3:7 Arise, O LORD; **save me**, O My God: for thou hast **smitten all mine enemies upon the cheek bon**e; thou hast **broken the teeth of the ungodly.**

Psalm 18:4 The sorrows of death compassed me, and the floods of **UNGODLY MEN** made me afraid.

"The knowledge of the truth"
"Ungodly"

Notice the two groups, UNGODLY in addition SINNERS:

Psalm 43:1 Judge me, O God, and plead my cause against an **ungodly nation:** O deliver me from the deceitful and unjust man.

Psalm 73:12 Behold, **these are the ungodly,** who prosper in the world; they increase in riches.

Proverbs 16:27An **ungodly man diggeth** up evil: and in his lips there is as a burning fire.

Proverbs 19:28 An **ungodly witness** SCORNETH JUDGMENT: and THE MOUTH OF THE WICKED DEVOURETH INIQUITY.

Romans 4:5 But to him **that worketh not, but believeth on Him** that JUSTIFIETH THE UNGODLY, his **faith is counted for righteousness.**

1 Timothy 1:9 Knowing this, that **the law is not made for a RIGHTEOUS man, BUT for the lawless and disobedient, for the ungodly and for sinners, for unholy and profane, for murderers of fathers and murderers of mothers, for manslayers,**

And if the RIGHTEOUS SCARCELY BE SAVED, where shall THE UNGODLY AND THE SINNER APPEAR?

2 Peter 2:5 And **spared not the old world,** but SAVED NOAH THE EIGHTH PERSON, a PREACHER OF RIGHTEOUSNESS, bringing in the **flood upon the world of the ungodly;**

2 Peter 2:6 And *turning the cities of Sodom and Gomorrha into ashes* condemned them with an overthrow, making them an **ensample** unto those that **after should live ungodly;**

2 Peter 3:7 But the heavens and the earth, which are now, by the same word are kept in store, *RESERVED UNTO FIRE AGAINST THE DAY OF JUDGMENT AND PERDITION OF UNGODLY MEN.*

Jude 1:4 For there are certain men crept in unawares, who were before of old *ordained to this condemnation*, UNGODLY MEN, TURNING THE GRACE OF OUR GOD INTO LASCIVIOUSNESS, AND DENYING THE ONLY LORD GOD, AND OUR LORD JESUS CHRIST.

Jude 1:18 How that they told you there should be MOCKERS IN THE LAST TIME, who **should walk after their own ungodly lusts.**

106

"Heavy Revelation and Manifestation"

"If I am a Deceiver let God be true and every man a liar, including me"

1. What is the patience of the saints?

2. According to the scriptures, can one lose his reward or receive a partial reward?

3. Why does one choose to believe a lie?

4. Do these words have the same meaning should, shall and shalt?

HEAVY REVELATION AND MANIFESTATION"
"IF I AM A DECEIVER LET GOD BE TRUE AND EVERY MAN A LIAR, INCLUDING ME"

1. What is the patience of the saints?
A. THEY THAT KEEP THE COMMANDMENTS OF GOD, AND THE FAITH OF JESUS.

Here is the patience of the saints: HERE ARE THEY THAT KEEP THE COMMANDMENTS OF GOD, AND THE FAITH OF JESUS. Revelation 14:12

2. According to the scriptures, can one lose his reward or receive a partial reward?
A. YES

LOOK TO YOURSELVES, THAT WE LOSE NOT THOSE THINGS WHICH WE HAVE WROUGHT, *BUT THAT WE RECEIVE A FULL REWARD.* 2 John 1:8

3. Why does one choose to believe a lie?
A. I TRULY BELIEVE, NO I KNOW IT IS BECAUSE, WE DO NOT WANT TO BE TRANSFORMED. THEREFORE, WE ALLOW SATAN TO BLIND OUR EYES.

He hath blinded their eyes, and hardened their heart; that they should not see with their eyes, nor understand with their heart, and be converted, and I SHOULD HEAL THEM. John 12:40

IN WHOM THE GOD OF THIS WORLD HATH BLINDED THE MINDS of them which BELIEVE NOT, LEST THE LIGHT OF THE GLORIOUS GOSPEL OF CHRIST, who is the image of God, should shine unto them. 2 Corinthians 4:4

But he that hateth his brother is in darkness, and *WALKETH IN DARKNESS, AND KNOWETH NOT WHITHER HE GOETH,* because *THAT DARKNESS HATH BLINDED HIS EYES.* 1 John 2:11

One scripture for sure being misquoted and incorrectly translated has caused many to stumble and continue to do so, JOHN 3:16 HAS BEEN MISQUOTED AND *INACCURATELY* TRANSLATED IN MANY BIBLES FOR YEARS.

John 3:16 For God so loved the **WORLD**, that *He gave His only begotten Son*, THAT WHOSOEVER BELIEVETH IN HIM SHOULD NOT PERISH, BUT HAVE EVERLASTING LIFE.

(SHOULD NOT} IT DOES NOT SAY (*SHALL NOT*) BUT SOME TRANSLATIONS HAVE *SHALL NOT.*

FURTHERMORE, THE MEANING OF THE WORD BELIEVETH IS TO CONTINUE AND THE WORD SAID *IN ME.*

THE WORD SAID BELIEVETH (IN ME} THERE IS NOTHING IN THIS ONE { }
ONE CANNOT ABIDE IN A PLACE, EXCEPT HE WAS THERE BEFORE.

HEAVY REVELATION AND MANIFESTATION"
"IF I AM A DECEIVER LET GOD BE TRUE AND EVERY MAN A LIAR, INCLUDING ME"

WE ARE TO ABIDE IN HIM.
"PEOPLE OF GOD YOU DID NOT PLANT THIS SEED, SO DO NOT BE AFRAID TO ENDED"

Satan gave Eve partial truth in Geneses 3:4, WHEN HE SAID UNTO THE WOMAN, YE SHALL <u>NOT SURELY DIE</u>. EVE AND ADAM DID NOT DIE A *PHYSICAL DEATH AT THAT TIME BUT THEY DIE A <u>SPIRITUAL DEATH.</u>* ARE WE TEACHING THE SAME ERR TODAY? I BELIEVE WE ARE, NO I <u>KNOW WE ARE</u>

Matthew 24:13 Says, BUt he that <u>SHALL ENDURE unto THE END</u>, the same <u>shall</u> be saved.

Mark 13:13, AND YE SHALL BE HATED OF ALL MEN FOR MY NAME'S SAKE: BUt HE THAT <u>SHALL ENDURE</u> UNTO <u>THE END</u>, the same <u>shall be saved</u>.

4. Do these words have the same meaning should, shall and shalt?

A. **NO**

FOR YEARS, I BELIEVED THE TEN COMMANDMENTS SAID, THOU SHALL NOT BUT IN (KJV) IT IS SHALT NOT

REMEMBER, EVERYTHING WAS WRITING FOR OUR EXAMPLE.

Remember, Judas called and chosen and anointed but he was also lost, to fulfill the scripture.
This is a perfect example, to teach us that we can also be cut off.

BEHOLD THEREFORE THE GOODNESS AND SEVERITY OF GOD: ON THEM WHICH FELL, SEVERITY; BUT TOWARD THEE, GOODNESS, **if** THOU continue IN **his** goodness: *OTHERWISE* **thou also shalt be cut off**. ROMANS 11:22

BUT THE <u>WICKED</u> *SHALL BE CUT OFF FROM THE EARTH,* AND <u>THE TRANSGRESSORS</u> SHALL BE ROOTED OUT OF IT. PROVERBS 2:22
Who are TRANSGRESSORS? lawbreakers, those who break the laws of God, continuing to cast His word behind their backs.

"PAST, PRESENT AND FUTURE"
Again, deceivers let God be true and every man a liar including me"

1. For though there be that are called _____ whether in heaven or in earth, as there be _____ and _____But to us there is but _____, of whom are all things, and we in Him; and _____ by whom are all things, and we by Him.

2. Are these statements true and can they be supported by scripture "all our past, present and future sins are forgiving?

3. If we **ARE IN CHRIST JESUS,** we are brethren and sometimes the brethren go away from the truth.

Q. If we convert the brethren, are we saving his soul from hell?

4. Is this statement true of false "The blood of Jesus Christ cleanseth us from all our sin even <u>if</u> we do not confess and repent?

"PAST, PRESENT AND FUTURE"
AGAIN, DECEIVERS LET GOD BE TRUE AND EVERY MAN A LIAR INCLUDING ME"

1. For though there be that are called _____ whether in heaven or in earth, as there be _____ and _____ But to us there is but_____, of whom are all things, and we in Him; and _____ by whom are all things, and we by Him.

A. **gods, gods many, and lords many, One God The Father,** ONE LORD JESUS CHRIST.

2. Are these statements true and can they be supported by scripture "ALL OUR PAST, PRESENT AND FUTURE SINS ARE FORGIVING?

A. NO, N*ot true according to these scriptures.*

Romans 3:25 Says, Whom God hath set forth to be a propitiation through faith in His blood, to declare *His righteousness* FOR *the remission of sins that are past.*

2 Peter 1:9 Says, But he that LACKETH THESE THINGS IS BLIND, AND CANNOT SEE AFAR OFF, and hath *forgotten* that he was purged from his old sins.

THE BIG BUT WORD

But when the **righteous turneth** away from **his righteousness,** and committeth iniquity, and **doeth** according to all the **abominations that the wicked man doeth,** shall he live? *All his righteousness that he hath done shall not be mentioned: in his trespass that he hath trespassed,* and **in his sin that he hath sinned,** in them SHALL HE DIE. Ezekiel 18:24

PLEASE, READ EZEKIEL CHAPTER 2, 3, 18, 33 & 34 FOR CLARIFICATION ON THIS SUBJECT.

[17] For the time is **come that judgment must begin at the house of God**: and IF IT FIRST BEGIN AT US, what shall the end be of them that obey not the gospel of God? [18] And *if the righteous scarcely be saved,* where shall the ungodly and the sinner appear? [19] WHEREFORE LET THEM THAT SUFFER ACCORDING TO THE WILL OF GOD COMMIT THE KEEPING OF THEIR SOULS to him in WELL DOING, AS UNTO A FAITHFUL CREATOR. 1 Peter 4:17-19

Depart from me, ye evildoers: for I will keep the commandments of My God.
Psalm 119:115

AND THEN WILL I PROFESS UNTO THEM, I NEVER KNEW YOU: *DEPART FROM ME,* ye THAT WORK INIQUITY. Matthew 7:23

Then shall He say also unto them ON THE LEFT HAND, Depart from Me, ye CURSED, INTO EVERLASTING FIRE, PREPARED FOR THE DEVIL AND HIS ANGELS: Matthew 25:41

"PAST, PRESENT AND FUTURE"

3. **If we are, in Christ Jesus, we are brethren (brothers and sisters) and sometimes *the brethren go away from the truth*.**
Q. If we convert the brethren, are we saving his soul from hell?
A. Absolutely.

TAKE NOTICE. THIS IS A BROTHER BUT HE IS A sinner.

BRETHREN, **if any of you do err from the truth,** and ONE CONVERT HIM;
Let him **know,** that **he which converteth the sinner from the error of his way shall save a soul from death, and shall hide a multitude of sins.** James 5:19-20

James 5:19-20 (NKJV)
Says, BRETHREN, if anyone among you **wanders from the truth,** and SOMEONE TURNS HIM BACK, LET HIM KNOW that he WHO TURNS A SINNER FROM THE ERROR OF HIS WAY WILL SAVE A SOUL FROM DEATH AND COVER A MULTITUDE OF SINS.

4. Is this statement true of false "The blood of Jesus Christ cleanseth us from all our sin even if we do not confess and repent?

A. FALSE

But **if** we walk in the light, as HE IS IN THE LIGHT, WE HAVE FELLOWSHIP ONE WITH ANOTHER, *AND THE BLOOD OF JESUS CHRIST* HIS SON CLEANSETH US FROM ALL SIN. 1 JOHN 1:7

IF WE CONFESS OUR SINS, HE IS FAITHFUL AND JUST TO FORGIVE US OUR SINS, AND TO CLEANSE US FROM ALL UNRIGHTEOUSNESS.

THE KEYWORD IS IF WE DO THIS. 1 JOHN 1:9

ALL *UNRIGHTEOUSNESS IS SIN*: AND THERE IS A SIN NOT UNTO DEATH 1 JOHN 5:17

LET'S' LIVE OUR LIVE WITH CONFESSION AND REPENTANCE AND WE WILL see the mercy and the grace of Yahweh and Yahushua.
FOR GODLY SORROW WORKETH REPENTANCE to salvation not to be repented of: but **the sorrow of the world worketh death.** 2 Corinthians 7:10

"REVELATION AND TEACHING QUIZ"

1. A wonderful and horrible thing is committed in the land.
Q. What was that wonderful and horrible thing that was committed?

2. After The Lord brought Israel out of the land of Egypt, He did not command them to offer burnt offerings or sacrifices but, He did commanded something from them.

Q. What did The Lord command from Israel after He made them free from bondage?

3. Who voiced these words and why did he come down?

I have surely seen the affliction of My people which are in Egypt, and have heard their cry by reason of their taskmasters; for I know their sorrows;

.

4. Who was the first Prophet in the scriptures?

PLEASE, USE SCRIPTURES TO SUPPORT YOUR ANSWER.

"REVELATION AND TEACHING QUIZ"

1. A wonderful and horrible thing is committed in the land.
Q. What was that wonderful and horrible thing that was committed?
A. **THE PROPHETS PROPHESY FALSELY,** and the priests bear rule by their means; and My people love to have it so: and what will ye do in the end thereof? Jeremiah 5:30-31

2. After The Lord brought Israel out of the land of Egypt, He did not command them to offer burnt offerings or sacrifices but, He did commanded something from them.
Q. What did The Lord command from Israel after He made them free from bondage?
A. **Obey My Voice, and I will be your God, and ye shall be My people:** AND WALK YE IN ALL THE WAYS THAT I HAVE COMMANDED YOU, THAT IT MAY BE WELL UNTO YOU. **But they hearkened not,** nor *inclined their ear, but walked in the counsels and in the imagination of their evil heart, and went backward, and not forward.* Jeremiah 7:22-24

3. Who voiced these words and why did he come down?
I have surely seen <u>the affliction of My people</u> which are in Egypt, and have <u>heard their cry</u> by reason of their taskmasters; for <u>I know their sorrows;</u>

A. **The LORD spoke these words.** HE CAME DOWN TO DELIVER THEM OUT OF THE HAND OF THE EGYPTIANS, and to bring them up out of that land unto a good land and a large, unto a land flowing with milk and honey; unto the place of the Canaanites, and the Hittites, and the Amorites, and the Perizzites, and the Hivites, and the Jebusites. Exodus 3:7-8

4. Who was the first Prophet in the scriptures?
PLEASE, USE SCRIPTURES TO SUPPORT YOUR ANSWER.
A. THE LORD, "YAHUSHUA" THE SON OF GOD, WHOM GOD MADE BOTH **Lord** AND **Christ!**
God Spoke to Adam by His Son and to the Prophets and *NOW SPEAKING TO US BY HIS SON.*

The Angel is The Son of God The Lord Jesus, **God spoke to The Lord Jesus** and *The Lord Jesus spoke to Moses* and *Moses spoke to Aaron his brother.*
(And THE LORD SAID unto **Moses,** SEE, I HAVE MADE THEE **a god** to Pharaoh: and AARON THY **brother shall be thy prophet.** Exodus 7:1
THE WORD PROPHET APPEARS THE FIRST TIME IN GENESIS 20:7 **Abraham was a prophet,** .Now therefore restore the <u>man his wife;</u> **for he is a prophet.** And The **Angel** of The LORD appeared unto <u>him</u> in a flame of fire out of the midst of a bush: Exodus 3:2
*(Some believe **Adam was the first prophet** because he <u>talked</u> and <u>walked with God</u> in the garden of Eden).*

114

"REVELATION AND TEACHING QUIZ"

But, Remember let **us** make man <u>and</u> man has become **as One of Us** and the **WORD gods in scriptures. Genesis 3.**

THIS IS "YAHUSHUA" THE SON OF GOD AND THE LORD JESUS IS THE **first**

Prophet!

NO MAN HATH SEEN GOD AT ANY TIME, <u>THE ONLY BEGOTTEN SON,</u> WHICH IS IN <u>THE BOSOM OF THE FATHER,</u> HE HATH DECLARED HIM. John 1

No man HATH <u>SEEN GOD AT ANY TIME.</u> 1 John 4:12

AND **The Father Himself,** WHICH **hath <u>sent Me</u>,** HATH **borne witness of Me.** YE <u>HAVE NEITHER HEARD</u> **His voice at any time,** *NOR SEEN HIS SHAPE.* John 5:37

<u>WOULD YOU AGREE,</u> *IF I AM SPEAKING AND YOU ARE LOOKING AT ME, HOW CAN I SAY, YOU HAVE NEITHER HEARD MY VOICE AT ANY TIME, NOR SEEN MY SHAPE?*

WE MUST BE IN THE SPIRIT IN ORDER TO UNDERSTAND. YAHUSHUA/JESUS IS NOT A DECEIVER NOR HIS FATHER YAHWEH.

It is also written in your law, that THE TESTIMONY of **two *men* is true. I Am ONE** THAT BEAR <u>WITNESS OF MYSELF</u>, **and** THE <u>FATHER THAT SENT ME</u> BEARETH <u>WITNESS OF ME</u>.

John 8:17 & 18

Two Men

Jesus answered them, **IS IT <u>NOT WRITTEN IN YOUR LAW,</u> I said, Ye are gods?** John 10:34

And THE ANGEL OF THE LORD appeared unto him in a flame of fire out of the midst of a bush:

Exodus 3:2

(And **The LORD said** unto Moses, **SEE, I have <u>made thee a god</u>** to Pharaoh: **and** <u>Aaron</u> thy brother shall be **thy prophet.** Exodus 7:1

And Moses said, I will now turn aside, and see this great sight, why the bush is not burnt.

And **WHEN <u>THE LORD SAW</u>** that he turned ASIDE TO SEE, <u>GOD CALLED</u> UNTO HIM OUT OF THE MIDST OF <u>THE BUSH</u> (Remember, THE <u>ANGEL</u> OF THE LORD)

And The LORD said, I have surely seen the affliction of My people which are in Egypt, and have heard their cry by reason of their taskmasters; for I know their sorrows

Exodus 3:2-8

AND I <u>AM COME DOWN TO DELIVER</u> THEM out of the hand of the Egyptians.

"REVELATION AND TEACHING QUIZ"

He shall send His angel before thee.. Genesis 24:7

Behold, **I SEND AN ANGEL** before thee, to keep thee in the way, and to bring thee into the place which I have prepared. Exodus 23:20

And **I WILL SEND AN ANGEL BEFORE THEE**. Exodus 33:2

The LORD Thy God will *raise up unto thee a Prophet from the midst of thee*, OF THY BRETHREN, **like unto me;** UNTO HIM YE SHALL HEARKEN Deuteronomy 18:15

For Moses truly said unto the fathers, A prophet shall The Lord your God raise up unto you of your brethren, like unto me; **Him shall ye hear in all things** whatsoever **He shall say** unto you. Acts 3:22

AND IT SHALL COME TO PASS, THAT EVERY SOUL, WHICH WILL NOT HEAR THAT PROPHET, SHALL BE DESTROYED FROM AMONG THE PEOPLE. Acts 3:23

This is that Moses, which said unto the children of Israel, **A PROPHET SHALL THE LORD YOUR GOD RAISE UP UNTO YOU OF YOUR BRETHREN, LIKE UNTO ME; HIM SHALL YE HEAR.** Acts 7:37

"JESUS IS THIS PROPHET"

God, who at sundry times and in divers manners spake in time past unto the fathers by the prophets, HATH IN THESE LAST DAYS SPOKEN UNTO US BY HIS SON, whom **He** hath **appointed heir of all things**, by whom also *He made the worlds;* Who being the brightness of His glory, and **the express image of His person,** and upholding all things by the **word of His power**, when **He had by HIMSELF PURGED OUR SINS, sat down on the right hand of The Majesty on high:** Hebrews 1:1-3

For then must He often have suffered since the foundation of the world: BUT *NOW ONCE IN THE END OF THE WORLD* hath *He appeared to put away sin by the sacrifice of Himself.* Hebrews 9:26

> **REMEMBER, THIS WORLD HAD NOT ENDED; THIS WAS AT THE END OF THE OTHER WORLD.**

But we see Jesus, who was made a little lower than the angels for the suffering of death, crowned with glory and honour; that He by the grace of God should taste death for every man. For it became Him, for whom are all things, and by whom are all things, in **bringing many sons unto glory,** to make the *captain of their salvation perfect* through sufferings. For both He that sanctifieth and they who are sanctified are **all of one: for which cause He is not ashamed to call them brethren,** Saying, I will declare Thy Name unto My brethren, in the midst of the church will I sing praise unto thee. And again, I will put My trust in Him. And again, Behold I and the children which *God hath given Me.*

Forasmuch then as the children are partakers of flesh and blood, He also Himself likewise took part of the same; that through death *He might destroy him that had the power of death, that is, the devil;*

And deliver them who through fear of death were **all their lifetime subject to bondage.** For verily He took not on Him the nature of angels; but *He took on Him the seed of Abraham.* Wherefore in all things it **behoved Him to** be made like *unto His brethren*, that He might be **a merciful and faithful high priest in things pertaining to God,** to make reconciliation for the sins of the people.

For in that He Himself hath suffered being tempted, He is able to succour them that are tempted. Hebrews 2:9-18

"EGYPT MY PEOPLE"

1. Who spoke these words, I have sinned this time: The LORD is righteous, and I and my people are wicked?

2. Did The LORD ever call Egypt His people and called them blessed?

3. Does the word "hosts" suggest that this is more than one?

4. Gilead is Mine, and Manasseh is Mine; Ephraim also is the strength of Mine head; Judah is My_____

5. The_____shall not depart from Judah, nor a lawgiver from between his feet until_____; and unto him shall the gathering of the people be.

6. The princes digged the well, the nobles of the people digged it, by the_____,with their staves. And from the wilderness they went to Mattanah:

7. And he provided the first part for himself, because there, in_____was he seated; and he came with the heads of the people, he executed the justice of the LORD, and his judgments with Israel.

8. For The LORD is our judge,_____, The LORD is our king;_____.

9. There is_____: who art thou that judgest another?

"EGYPT MY PEOPLE"

1. Who spoke these words, I have sinned this time: The LORD is righteous, and I and my people are wicked?
A. Pharaoh. Exodus 9:27

2. Did The LORD ever call Egypt His people and called them blessed?
A. Yes.

Whom The LORD of Hosts <u>shall bless,</u> saying, **Blessed be Egypt My people,** and Assyria the *work of My hands, and Israel Mine inheritance.* Isaiah 19:25.

3. Does the word "hosts" suggest that this is more than one?
A. Yes.
Look at the words **all** the <u>hosts</u>.
And it came to pass at the end of the four hundred and thirty years, even the selfsame day it came to pass, that **all** the **hosts** of The LORD went out from the land of Egypt. Exodus 12:41

4. Gilead is Mine, and Manasseh is Mine; Ephraim also is the strength of Mine head; Judah is My_____
A. **LAWGIVER.** Psalm 60:7 & Psalm 108:8

5. The____shall not depart from Judah, nor a lawgiver from between his feet until_____;
and unto him shall the gathering of the people be.
A. **SCEPTRE. UNTIL SHILOH COME.** Genesis 49:10

6. The princes digged the well, the nobles of the people digged it, by the_____, with their staves. And from the wilderness they went to Mattanah:
A. **DIRECTION OF THE LAWGIVER.** Numbers 21:18

7. And he provided the first part for himself, because there, in _____was he seated; and he came with the heads of the people, he executed the justice of the LORD, and his judgments with Israel.
A. **A PORTION OF THE LAWGIVER.** Deuteronomy 33:21

8.For The LORD is our judge, _____, The LORD is our king;
_____.

A. **THE LORD IS OUR LAWGIVER. HE WILL SAVE US.** Isaiah 33:22

"EGYPT MY PEOPLE"

LAWGIVER

9. There is_____: who art thou that judgest another?

A. ONE LAWGIVER WHO IS ABLE, TO SAVE AND TO DESTROY. JAMES 4:12

Do not, misunderstand the phrase who art thou that judgest another.

We need to read this chapter to get a better understanding of this saying. James 4:11, Speak not <u>evil one of another</u>, brethren. He that <u>speaketh evil of his brother</u>, and judgeth his brother, speaketh evil *of the law*, <u>and judgeth the law</u>: but <u>if</u> thou judge the law, thou art not a <u>doer</u> of <u>the law</u>, but <u>a judge</u>.

THIS STATEMENT HAS TO DO WITH FOOD.

"SEEK FOR ME"

1. Will The Lord Hide His Face so one can seek after Him?

2. If someone continue to reject the word, will there comes a time he or she will not be able to find The Lord?

3. The LORD spoke these words "And ye shall seek Me, and find Me, when ye shall search for Me with_____

4. The LORD of hosts shall be exalted in _____ and God that is Holy shall be sanctified in_____

---

[7]The law of the LORD is perfect, CONVERTING THE SOUL: the testimony of the LORD is sure, making wise the simple.

[8]The statutes of the LORD are right, rejoicing the heart: THE COMMANDMENT OF THE LORD IS PURE, enlightening the eyes.

[9]THE FEAR OF THE LORD IS CLEAN, ENDURING FOR EVER: THE JUDGMENTS OF THE LORD ARE TRUE AND RIGHTEOUS ALTOGETHER.

[10]MORE TO BE DESIRED ARE THEY THAN GOLD, YEA, THAN MUCH FINE GOLD: sweeter also than honey and the honeycomb.

[11]*MOREOVER BY THEM IS THY SERVANT WARNED:* and IN KEEPING OF THEM *THERE IS GREAT REWARD.*

[12]Who can understand his errors? cleanse thou me from secret faults.
[13]Keep back thy servant also from presumptuous sins; let them not have dominion over me: then shall I be upright, and I shall be innocent from the great transgression.

[14]Let the words of my mouth, and the meditation of my heart, be acceptable in thy sight, O LORD, my strength, and my redeemer.

Psalms 19:7-19

"SEEK FOR ME"

1. Will The Lord Hide His Face so one can seek after Him?
A. **Yes.**
.. I WILL <u>WAIT UPON THE LORD</u>, THAT HIDETH HIS FACE FROM THE HOUSE OF JACOB, AND <u>I WILL LOOK</u> FOR HIM. Isaiah 8:17.

2. If someone continue to reject the word, will there comes a time he or she will not be able to find The Lord?
A. **Yes.**
YE <u>SHALL SEEK ME</u>, and SHALL <u>NOT FIND ME</u>: and where I am, thither ye <u>cannot come</u>. John 7:34
Then said Jesus again unto them, I go My way, and YE <u>SHALL SEEK ME</u>, AND SHALL DIE IN YOUR SINS: WHITHER I GO, YE <u>CANNOT COME</u>. John 8:21

THERE IS A SIN UNTO DEATH:
KNOW YE NOT, THAT TO WHOM YE YIELD YOURSELVES SERVANTS TO OBEY, HIS SERVANTS YE ARE TO WHOM YE OBEY; WHETHER OF SIN UNTO DEATH, or OF RIGHTEOUSNESS OBEDIENCE UNTO? Romans 6:16
If ANY MAN SEE *HIS BROTHER* SIN A SIN WHICH IS not unto death, he shall ask, and HE SHALL GIVE HIM LIFE for them that sin not unto death. There is a sin unto death: I *do not say that* he shall pray for it. 1 John 5:16
SEEK YE THE LORD while He may be found, call ye upon Him while He is near: Isaiah 55:6

3. The LORD spoke these words "And ye shall seek Me, and find Me, when ye shall search for Me with_____
A. **All your heart.** Jeremiah 29:13
..HE IS A REWARDER OF THEM THAT <u>DILIGENTLY SEEK</u> HIM. HEBREWS 11:6

4. The LORD OF HOSTS <u>shall be exalted in</u> _____ AND GOD THAT IS HOLY shall be sanctified in_____
A. **JUDGMENT, RIGHTEOUSNESS.** Isaiah 5:16

"Teaching and preaching Quiz"

1. Many believe and teach that The Lord is married to the backsliders and He will not divorce them nor put them away "put them out if they commit adultery"

Q. Does scriptures support this believe?

2. If we cause the righteous to go astray in an evil way, what will be our reward?

3. They say, If a man put away his wife, and she go from him, and become another man's, shall he return unto her again? shall not that land be greatly polluted?

Q. How did The LORD respond to this question?

"TEACHING AND PREACHING QUIZ"

1. Many believe and teach that The Lord is married to the backsliders and He will not divorce them nor put them away "put them out if they commit adultery"

Q. Does scriptures support this believe?

A. **NO**

And I saw, when for all the causes whereby **BACKSLIDING ISRAEL COMMITTED ADULTERY** I HAD **PUT HER AWAY, AND GIVEN HER A BILL OF DIVORCE**; YET HER TREACHEROUS SISTER JUDAH And it came to pass through *the lightness of her whoredom*, that she defiled the land, and committed *adultery with stones and with stocks*. And yet for all this **her treacherous sister Judah** hath not turned unto Me with her whole heart, but feignedly, saith The LORD. And **THE LORD SAID UNTO ME,** The backsliding Israel hath justified herself more than tracherous Judah.

Go and proclaim these words toward the north, and say, ***RETURN, THOU BACKSLIDING** ISRAEL, SAITH THE LORD; AND I WILL NOT CAUSE MINE ANGER TO FALL UPON YOU: FOR I AM MERCIFUL, SAITH THE LORD, AND I WILL **not keep** ANGER FOR EVER.*

Praise The Lord! Just confess and repent and He will. no longer be angry

Only acknowledge thine iniquity, that thou *hast transgressed against The LORD Thy God*, and hast scattered thy ways to the strangers under every green tree, and *ye have not obeyed My voice*, saith The LORD. ***Turn, O backsliding children,*** saith The LORD; for *I AM MARRIED UNTO YOU:* Jeremiah 3:9-14.

Thus saith The LORD, *Where is the bill of your mother's divorcement*, whom *I have put away?* or which of My creditors is it to *whom I have sold you*? Behold, FOR YOUR INIQUITIES HAVE YE SOLD YOURSELVES, and FOR YOUR TRANSGRESSIONS IS YOUR MOTHER PUT AWAY. Isaiah 50:1

Please, read Jeremiah chapter 3 through 7 for a better revelation and understanding.

2. If we cause the righteous to go astray in an evil way, what will be our reward?

A. WE WILL FALL INTO OUR OWN PIT.

Many teach there is non-righteous.

Whoso causeth the righteous to go astray in an evil way, he shall fall himself into his own pit: but *the upright shall have good things in possession.* Proverbs 28:10

3. They say, If a man put away his wife, and she go from him, and become another man's, shall he return unto her again? shall not that land be greatly polluted?

Q. How did The Lord answer this question?

A. But **THOU HAST PLAYED THE HARLOT WITH MANY LOVERS;** yet RETURN AGAIN TO ME, saith The LORD. Jeremiah 3:1

"Shout Alleluia"

FIRST, I am not being offensive nor malicious; I only love and rejoice in the truth.

Charity rejoiceth not in iniquity, but rejoiceth in the truth. 1 Corinthians 13:6
FOR THE TRUTH SAKE, THIS QUESTION IS TO BRING FORTH TRUTH.

1. How many times does the word Alleluia appear in scripture? (KJV) and (NKJV)

2. Why did the voice of many people in heaven say, Alleluia Salvation, and glory, and honour, and power, unto The Lord our God?

3. What is the meaning of the word Hallelujah in some translations?

(Example, Amplified Bible

"SHOUT ALLELUIA"

First, I am not being offensive nor malicious; I only love and rejoice in the truth. Charity rejoiceth not in iniquity, but rejoiceth in the truth. 1 Corinthians 13:6
For the truth sake, this question is to bring forth truth.

1. How many times does the word Alleluia appear in scripture? (KJV) and (NKJV)
A. ALLELUIA APPEARS FOUR TIMES IN SCRIPTURES. (*I can only see four times*)
And after these things I heard a great voice of much people in heaven, saying, *Alleluia; Salvation, and glory, and honour, and power, unto The Lord our God*:
Revelation 19:1
And again they said, *Alleluia And her smoke rose up for ever and ever.*
Revelation 19:3
And the four and twenty elders and the four beasts fell down and worshipped God that sat on the throne, saying, Amen; Alleluia. Revelation 19:4
And I heard as it were the voice of a <u>great multitude</u>, and <u>as</u> the voice of <u>many waters</u>, and as the <u>voice of mighty thunderings</u>, saying, Alleluia: *for The Lord* God omnipotent reigneth. Revelation 19:6
2. Why did the voice of many people in heaven say, Alleluia Salvation, and glory, and honour, and power, unto The Lord our God?
A. BECAUSE, OF <u>JUDGMENT</u> ON THE GREAT WHORE "BABYLON"
For true and righteous are His judgments: for He hath judged the great whore, which did <u>corrupt the earth with her fornication</u>, and hath <u>avenged the blood of His servants at her hand.</u>
Revelation 19:2
3. What is the meaning of the word Hallelujah in some translations?
(Example, Amplified Bible says,
A. PRAISE THE LORD, **found twenty three times in the Amplified Bible.**
HALLELUJAH IS THE TRANSLITERATION OF A HEBREW TERM THAT MEANS, **"Praise ye The Lord"**
I did not discover in my research where Hallelujah or Alleluia is the <u>Height Praise</u>.

Transliteration	' Pronunciation
Hallēlouïa	häl-lā-lü-ē-ä

Praise ye The Lord, Hallelujah and Praise Yahh and Ya.
(If I cannot find it, I will not teach it. Let The Word of God be true)
"Whatever we do, we should do for the glory of God"

And that every <u>tongue</u> <u>should</u> confess that Jesus Christ is Lord, to the <u>GLORY OF GOD THE FATHER</u>. PHILIPPIANS 2:11 (*Every tongue:/every language*)

Wherefore receive ye <u>one another, as Christ also received us</u> to THE GLORY OF GOD. Romans 15:7
Whether therefore ye eat, or drink, or whatsoever ye DO, DO ALL TO THE GLORY OF GOD. 1 Corinthians 10:31
For all things are for your sakes, that the abundant grace might through the thanksgiving of many redound to the glory of God. 2 Corinthians 4:15

"REVEALING THE FATHER AND THE SON OF GOD"

1. If God is not a man, that He should lie; neither the son of man, that He should repent, who was it that repented that He had made man? Numbers 23:19

2. Someone was setting on the throne but no man in heaven, nor in earth, neither under the earth, was able to open the book, neither to look thereon and he wept much.

Q. Who was sitting on the throne? Revelation chapters 4 & 5

3. In Revelation 4:10 who are the twenty-four elders worshiping?

And I saw in the right hand of Him that sat on the throne a book written within and on the backside, sealed with seven seals. And I saw a strong angel proclaiming with a loud voice,

Who is worthy to open the book, and to loose the seals thereof?

Someone was worthy to take the book out of the hand of the one setting on the throne.

B. Who was worthy?

4. Why are they <u>singing a new song</u> and <u>what is this New Song</u>? Revelation 5

"REVEALING THE FATHER AND THE SON OF GOD"

1. If God is <u>not a man</u>, that <u>He</u> should <u>lie</u>; neither the son of man, that He should repent, who was it that repented that He had made man? Numbers 23:19

A. **The LORD changed His Mind**. Pray and ask for revelation<u>; I believe it was The Son of The Living and everlasting God.</u> **Notice neither the son of man.**

And it repented The LORD that He had made man on the earth, and it **grieved Him at His heart.** And The LORD said, <u>I will destroy man whom I have created from the face of the earth;</u> both man, and beast, and the creeping thing, and the fowls of the air; for it repenteth Me that I have made them.

Genesis 6:6-7

And to make **all men see what is the fellowship of the mystery**, which *from the beginning of the world hath been hid in God,* **who created all things by Jesus Christ:** Ephesians 3:9

For **by Him were all things created**, that are in heaven, and that are in earth, visible and invisible, whether they be thrones, or dominions, or principalities, or powers: all *things were created* by Him, and for Him:

Colossians 1:16.

Thou art worthy, O *Lord*, to receive **glory and honour and power**: for thou hast *created all things, and for thy pleasure they are and were created.* Revelation 4:11

2. Someone was setting on the throne but no man in heaven, nor in earth, neither under the earth, was able to open the book, neither to look thereon and he wept much.

Q. Who was sitting on the throne? Revelation chapters 4 & 5

A. *God The Father*

3. In Revelation 4:10 who are the twenty-four elders worshiping?

A. *God The Father.*

And I saw in the **RIGHT HAND OF HIM THAT <u>SAT</u> ON THE THRONE A BOOK WRITTEN WITHIN AND ON THE BACKSIDE, SEALED WITH SEVEN SEALS. AND I SAW** *A STRONG ANGEL PROCLAIMING WITH A LOUD VOICE,*

Who is worthy to open the book, and to loose the seals thereof?

Someone **WAS WORTHY TO TAKE THE BOOK OUT OF THE HAND OF THE ONE SETTING ON THE THRONE.**

B. Who was worthy to take the book?

A. *The Lion of the tribe of Judah! Yahushua The Messiah/Jesus Christ The Son of The Living God.* Revelation 5:5

Here is wisdom, ***God, was seated on His throne*** *and* *Yahushua The Messiah/* **Jesus** *came and took the book out of* *Yahweh /His Father's hand.* <u>*AMAN*</u>

REVELATION AND WISDOM CONTINUE

4. Why are they singing a new song and what is this New Song? Revelation 5
A. THEY HAD A NEW REVELATION BEFORE THEY ONLY WORSHIPED GOD

But NOW, THEY ARE ALSO WORSHIPING THE LAMB OF GOD, GIVING THEM *both* HONOUR.
THEY COULD NOT HONOUR WHOM THEY COULD <u>NOT SEE</u>. HE STOOD UP AND THEY SAW HIM.

That all men should **honour** *The Son, even as they honour The Father. He that* **honoureth** <u>not</u> *The Son honoureth not The Father which* hath sent Him. John 5:23

I receive not honour from men. **John 5:41**
How can ye **believe, which receive honour one of another,** and seek not the honour **that cometh from God only?** John 5:44
Jesus answered, **I have not a devil;** *but* **I HONOUR MY FATHER, *and ye do dishonour Me.***
John 8:49
Jesus answered, **IF I HONOUR MYSELF, MY honour is <u>NOTHING</u>: IT IS <u>*MY FATHER THAT HONOURETH ME*</u>, OF WHOM YE SAY, THAT HE IS YOUR GOD:**
John 8:54

IF ANY MAN <u>SERVE</u> ME, **let him follow Me;** AND <u>*WHERE I AM, THERE SHALL ALSO MY SERVANT BE*</u>. IF ANY MAN <u>SERVE</u> ME, **HIM WILL MY FATHER HONOUR.**
JOHN 12:26

God will honour those who honour His Son.

Revelation 5 And one of the elders saith unto me, **Weep not:** behold, **The Lion of the tribe of Judah, the Root of David, hath prevailed to open the book, and to loose the seven seals thereof.**
And I beheld, and, lo, <u>in the midst of the throne</u> and of <u>the four beasts, and in the midst of the elders,</u> **stood a Lamb as it had been slain,** having seven horns and seven eyes, WHICH ARE THE SEVEN SPIRITS OF GOD **SENT** FORTH INTO ALL THE EARTH. And HE CAME and TOOK THE BOOK OUT OF THE RIGHT HAND of Him that <u>sat</u> upon the throne.

"REVELATION AND WISDOM CONTINUE"

Yahushua takes the book our of Yahweh's hands!

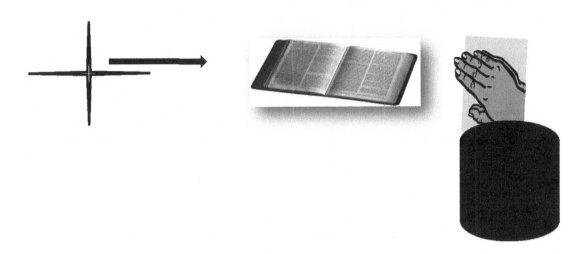

And when **He had taken the book**, the four beasts and four and **twenty elders fell down before** The Lamb, having every one of them harps, and golden vials full of odours, which are the **PRAYERS OF SAINTS**. *And* THEY SUNG A NEW SONG, *saying,* **Thou art worthy to take the book,** *and to open the seals thereof: for* **Thou wast slain**, *and* HAST REDEEMED US TO GOD BY THY BLOOD OUT OF EVERY KINDRED, AND TONGUE, AND PEOPLE, AND NATION; And HAST MADE US UNTO OUR GOD **kings and priests:** and we shall *reign* on the earth. And I beheld, and I heard the voice of many angels round about the throne and the beasts and the elders: and the number of them was ten thousand times ten thousand, and thousands of thousands; *Saying with a loud voice,* **Worthy is The Lamb that was slain to receive power, and riches, and wisdom, and strength, and honour, and glory, and blessing. And every creature which is in heaven, and on the earth, and** under the earth, and such as are in the sea, and all that are in them, heard I saying, *Blessing, and honour, and glory, and power,* be unto

HIM THAT SITTETH UPON THE THRONE, **and** unto **The Lamb** for ever and ever. And the four beasts said, Amen. A*nd the four and twenty elders fell down and worshipped him that liveth for ever and ever.*

▌Pray we can clearly see Yahweh/God The Father and/in addition Yahushua/ Jesus His Son The Lord Jesus Christ.

Praise God for making His Son known unto me! Halleluiah

"FEAR AND REVERENCE"

1. The Holy Word teaches us to fear God; some believe the meaning, of this word is to reverence God.

Q. According to scripture, does fear and reverence have the same meaning?

2. Jesus said; He receives not honour from men and If He honour Himself, His honour is nothing.

If I receive honour, someone else is honoring me. Right

Q. If Jesus did not honour Himself neither received honour from man, them whom did he receive it from?

Please, use scripture to support your answer.

3. They said that Jesus had a Devil; how did He respond to this statement?

4. If someone said that you had a Devil, how would you reply?

5. If any man serves Jesus and follow Him, what will The Father give Him?

"FEAR AND REVERENCE"

1. The Holy Word teaches us to fear God; some believe the meaning, of this word is to reverence God.

Q. According to scripture, does fear and reverence have the same meaning?

A. Definitely not

Wherefore we **receiving a kingdom which cannot be moved, *let us have grace, whereby we may serve God acceptably* with reverence AND godly fear**: Hebrews 12:28

But fear not thou, O My servant Jacob, and **be not dismayed, O Israel..**
Fear thou not, O Jacob My servant, saith The LORD: for I am with thee. Jeremiah 46:27 & 28

How does this sound, reverence not, O Jacob My servant, saith The LORD: for I am with thee?
Fear means exactly to fear. if you said to a child do not touch the hotplate and he touched it anyway. the next time he just might obey why? fear because. he was burned

Deliver me, I pray thee, from the hand of my brother, from the hand of Esau: for **I FEAR HIM.**
Genesis 32:11.

Here we can see we should not fear man but we should fear God

Jesus said. But I will forewarn you whom ye shall fear: Fear Him And I say unto you *MY FRIENDS, Be not* afraid of them that kill the body, and AFTER THAT HAVE NO MORE THAT THEY CAN do. **But I will forewarn you whom ye shall fear**: FEAR HIM, which *AFTER HE HATH KILLED* HATH POWER TO CAST INTO HELL; yea, I SAY UNTO YOU, **Fear Him.** MEANING, FEAR ONLY YAHWEH/GOD AND **NOT** MAN. Luke 12:4-5

Therefore thou shalt keep the commandments of The LORD thy God, to walk in His ways, and to *fear Him.* Deuteronomy 8:6

2. Jesus said; He receives not honour from men and If He honour Himself, His honour is nothing.
If I receive honour, someone else is honoring me. Right
Q. If Yahushua/Jesus did not honour Himself neither received honour from man, them whom did he receive it from?
Please, use scripture to support your answer.
A. **Yahweh/ God The Father.**

"FEAR AND REVERENCE"

For He <u>received from</u> God The Father honour and glory, when there came <u>such a voice</u> to Him <u>from</u> The <u>Excellent Glory</u>, THIS IS MY BELOVED SON, in whom *I AM WELL PLEASED.*
2 Peter 1:17

How can ye <u>believe,</u> which **receive honour one of another**, and ***seek not the honour that cometh from God only?*** John 5:44
Jesus answered, **If I <u>honour Myself</u>, My honour is nothing**: It Is My Father that honoureth Me; of whom ye say, that <u>He is your God</u>: John 8:54

3. They said that Jesus had a Devil; how did He respond to this statement?
A. Jesus answered, I <u>have not a devil</u>; **but** <u>I HONOUR MY FATHER</u>, and ye **DO DISHONOR ME.**
John 8:49

4. If someone said that you had a Devil, how would you reply?
My reply would be I have not a Devil; I honour The Father and His Son.

That all men <u>should</u> honour The Son, even as they honour The Father. He that honoureth not <u>The Son</u> honoureth not The Father which hath sent Him. John 5:23
I can honour my parents for fifty years but that does not imply I will continue to do so. {Honoureth is to continue}

5. If any man serves Jesus and follow Him, what will The Father give Him?
A. YAHWEH THE FATHER WILL GIVE HIM HONOUR.

If any man serve Me, let him follow Me; and where I am, there shall also My servant be: if any man serve Me, him will My Father honour. John 12:26

"BAPTISM"

1. Where did the first baptism take place according to the scripture?

2. Does baptism save anyone according to the scriptures?

3. Can disciples (followers of Yahushua Messiah/Jesus Christ) believe on God and baptized in water but, never heard or received The Holy Ghost?

"Baptism"

1. Where did the first baptism take place according to the scripture?
A. In the cloud and in the sea

And the children of Israel **went into the midst of the sea** upon the dry ground: and the waters were a wall unto them on their right hand, and on their left. Exodus 14:22

If you said, it does not say they were baptized you are correct but this is why looking for more information on the subject is essential to get a better understanding. Now read 1 Corinthians 10:1-5

Moreover, **brethren,** I would not that ye **should be ignorant,** how that **all our fathers were under the cloud,** and all passed through the sea; **And were all baptized unto Moses in the** *cloud* **and** *in the sea*;

And did all **eat the same spiritual meat;** And did **all drink the same spiritual drink**: for **they drank of that spiritual Rock that followed them**: AND that **Rock was Christ/The Messiah.** But with **many of them God was NOT well pleased**: for they were **overthrown in the wilderness.**
1 Corinthians 10:1-5
Remember, Yahweh/God was well pleased with The Messiah.

2. Does baptism save anyone according to the scriptures?
A. **YES** it does, when baptized we are buried with Christ and raised in newness of life.
The like figure whereunto even baptism doth also now save us (*not the putting away of the filth of the flesh, but the answer of a good conscience toward God,*) **by the resurrection of Jesus Christ/Yahushua Messiah** 1Peter 3:21

Buried with Him in baptism, wherein also ye are **risen with Him through the faith of the operation of God, who hath raised Him from the dead.** Colossians 2:12

Therefore **we are buried with Him** *by baptism* into death: *that like as Christ was raised up from the dead by the glory of The Father, even so we also should walk in newness of life.* Romans 6:4

3. Can disciples (followers of Yahushua Messiah/Jesus Christ) believe on God and baptized in water but, never heard or received The Holy Ghost?
A. **YES.**

And it came to pass, that, while Apollos was at Corinth, Paul having passed through the upper coasts came to Ephesus: and **finding certain disciples,** He said unto them, **Have ye received The Holy Ghost SINCE YE BELIEVED?** And they said unto him, We have **NOT** so much **as heard** whether there be **any Holy Ghost**. And *he said unto them, Unto what then were ye baptized? And they said, Unto John's baptism.*

Then said Paul, ***John verily baptized with the baptism of repentance***, saying unto the people, **{Man's baptism}**that they **should believe on Him** which *should come after Him*, that is, **on Christ**

"BAPTISM"

Jesus. When they ***heard this***, they WERE BAPTIZED IN THE NAME OF THE LORD JESUS And when Paul had **laid his hands upon them, THE HOLY GHOST CAME ON THEM**; and they **spake with tongues,** and **PROPHESIED.** And all the men were about <u>twelve.</u>

NOTICE:
THEY SPAKE <u>with</u> TONGUES ACCORDING TO KJV, IT DOES <u>NOT</u> <u>PROCLAIM</u> THEY SPAKE <u>*IN*</u> TONGUES. ACTS 19:1-7

TONGUE: A part of speech

Hebrew word: Glossa Pronunciation glos-sa

TONGUES: *a language or dialect used by people from every nations under heaven as we can see in Acts 10:46*

And there were *dwelling at Jerusalem* JEWS, DEVOUT MEN, OUT OF <u>EVERY</u> <u>NATION</u> UNDER <u>HEAVEN</u>. Now when this was noised abroad, the multitude came together, and were confounded, because that every man heard **them speak in his own language.** Acts 2:5-7

Please, notice this verse,

Then they that **gladly received his word** ***were baptized:*** and the same day there ***were added*** unto them about <u>three thousand</u> *souls*.
Acts 2:41
Please, focus on what they prophesied in Acts 2:21-43.

135

"BAPTISM CERTIFICATE" By, Prophetess and Pastor Dr. Mary Neal
Title: Dying to the first Adam and putting on the second Adam, The Lord from heaven I Cor. 15

This certifies that _____ has confessed Romans 10:9 and believes that
Jesus Christ is The Son of God,
That **if** thou shalt confess with thy mouth The Lord Jesus, and shalt believe
in thine heart that God hath raised Him from the dead, thou shalt be saved.
For with the heart man believeth unto righteousness; and with the mouth
confession is made unto salvation. *Romans 10:9-10*
And as they went on their way, **they came unto a <u>certain water</u>:** *and the eunuch said,*
See, <u>here is water</u>; what <u>doth hinder me</u> to <u>be baptized</u>?
And Philip said, **If thou believest with <u>all thine heart</u>, thou mayest.** *And* **he answered
and said,** *I believe that Jesus Christ is The Son of God.* Acts 8: 36 & 37

**.and was baptized in The Name of The Father/Yahweh, and of The Son/Yahushua,
and of The Holy Ghost**
*Go ye therefore, and teach all nations, baptizing them in The Name of The Father,
and of The Son, and of The Holy Ghost Matthew 28:19*

Baptized _____ day of _____ _____
Church: _____ of _____ _____

Pastor: —

In whom also ye are circumcised with the circumcision <u>made **without hands**</u>, **in putting
off the body of the sins of the flesh** by the **circumcision of Christ: Buried with Him
in baptism,** wherein **also ye are risen with Him through <u>the faith</u> of the operation of
God**, who **hath raised Him from the dead**. [13]And you, <u>being dead in your sins</u> and <u>the
uncircumcision of your flesh</u>, hath He quickened together <u>with</u> Him, having **forgiven you
all trespasses**; Colossians 2:11-13
If ye then be risen with Christ, **seek those things which are above**, where **Christ sitteth
on the right hand of God**. Set your <u>**affection on things above**</u>, **not** on *things on the
earth*. For ye *are dead, and your life is hid with Christ in God*. When Christ, who is
our life, shall appear, then shall **ye also appear with Him in Glory**. Colossians 3:1-3
What shall we say then? **<u>Shall we continue in sin</u>**, that **<u>grace may abound</u>**? *<u>God forbid</u>*.
How shall we, that are dead to sin, <u>**live any longer therein**</u>? Know ye not, that so many of
us as **<u>were baptized into Jesus Christ were baptized into His death</u>**? **<u>Therefore we are
buried with Him by baptism into death</u>**: that **<u>like as Christ was raised up from the dead
by the glory of The Father</u>**, <u>even so we also</u> **should walk in <u>newness of life</u>**. [5]For **if** we have
been **<u>planted together in the likeness of His death</u>**, we shall be also **<u>in the likeness of His
resurrection</u>**: **Knowing this, that our old man is <u>crucified with</u> Him**, *that **the body of sin
might be destroyed**,* that henceforth **we <u>should not</u> *serve sin***. For he **that <u>is dead</u> is freed
from sin**. Now **<u>if</u> we be dead with Christ, we believe that we shall also**: Knowing that **Christ
being raised from the dead** *dieth no more;* death hath **no more dominion over Him**.
Romans 6:1-8

Which sometime were disobedient, when once <u>the longsuffering of God waited in the days
of Noah</u>, while the <u>ark was a preparing</u>, wherein few, that is, **eight souls were saved by
water**. ***<u>The like figure</u>*** <u>whereunto even</u> **baptism doth also now save us** (<u>not the putting
away of the filth of the flesh</u>, **but** <u>the answer of **a good conscience toward God**,</u>) **by the
resurrection of Jesus Christ**: 1 Peter 3:20-21

"Two parables of an hundred sheep"

1. Jesus used these two parables of an hundred sheep, "having an hundred sheep, if he lose one of them" and "have an hundred sheep, and one of them be gone astray" leave the ninety and nine.

Q. Where can we find these parables and what is the most important different concerning them that can change the consequence?

2. And the Philistines were afraid, for they said, God is come into the camp. And they said, Woe unto us! for there hath not been such a thing heretofore. Woe unto us! who shall deliver us out of the hand of these?

Q. Who shall deliver us out of the hand of these might gods or mighty Gods?
B. These are the gods or the Gods that smote the Egyptians with all the plagues in the wilderness?

3. There is joy in heaven over one sinner that repenteth, more than over ninety and nine just persons, which need no repentance.

The son had a Father, as Yahweh/God is our Father **if** we are in Yahushua Messiah/Jesus Christ.

The lost son confessed his sins when he said, father I have <u>sinned against heaven, and in thy sight</u>, and am <u>no more worthy</u> to be <u>called thy son.</u> But the father said to his servants, Bring forth the best robe, and put it on him; and put a ring on his hand, and shoes on his feet: And bring hither the fatted calf, and kill it; and let us eat, and be merry: For this my son WAS DEAD, and **is alive again;** he **was lost,** and **is found.**
And they *began to be merry.*

As we would say today, His father gave him a big party; his elder son was in the field and as he came and drew nigh to the house, he heard musick and dancing. *<u>His elderly son was angry and would not go in:</u>* therefore came his father out, and intreated him, he answering said to his father, Lo, these **many years do I serve thee, neither transgressed I at any time thy commandment**: and **yet thou never gavest me a kid, that I might make merry with my friends:** But as soon as this THY SON WAS COME, which hath **devoured thy living with harlots,** thou hast **killed for him the fatted calf.** Luke 15:7-30
This parable teaches us how we also have a Father but sometimes leave Him and waste our lives but **when** and **if we repent** and <u>**come back to Him there is Joy in heaven.**</u>

Q. What did the father give to his elderly son that he did not give to the one that devoured his living? "The waster"

4. **For I know the thoughts that I think toward you, saith The LORD.**
Q. What are His thoughts?

"TWO PARABLES OF AN HUNDRED SHEEP"

1. Jesus used these two parables of an hundred sheep, "having an hundred sheep, if he lose one of them" and "have an hundred sheep, and one of them be gone astray" leave the ninety and nine.
Q. Where can we find these parables and what is the most important different concerning them that can change the consequence?
A. Luke 15:4 & Matthew 18:12-13.

Luke says, <u>UNTIL</u> he find it. But, Matthew says and <u>IF</u> so be that he find it.
The Parable in Matthew teaches us, the sheep went astray and one went into the mountains to seek after him **BUT IT DECLARES, IF SO BE THAT HE FIND IT.**

One might say how you know, because, of the big If word "if so be that he find it. What man of you, having an hundred sheep, **if** he lose one of them, doth not leave the ninety and nine in the wilderness, and go after that which <u>is lost</u>, until **HE FIND IT**? Luke 15:4

How think ye? if a man have an hundred sheep, and one of them <u>be gone astray</u>, doth he not leave the ninety and nine, and goeth into the mountains, and seeketh that which is gone astray?

And <u>if</u> so be that he find it, verily I say unto you, **HE REJOICETH MORE OF THAT SHEEP, THAN OF THE NINETY AND NINE WHICH WENT <u>NOT</u> ASTRAY.** Matthew 18:12-13

Remember, .All we like sheep have **gone astray;** we have turned **every one to his own way;** and *THE LORD HATH LAID ON HIM THE INIQUITY OF US ALL.* Isaiah 53:6

2. And the Philistines were afraid, for they said, God is come into the camp. And they said, Woe unto us! for there **hath not been such a thing heretofore.** Woe unto us! who shall deliver us out of the hand of these?
Q. Who shall deliver us out of the hand of these might gods or mighty Gods?
A. **Mighty Gods**
B. These are the gods or the Gods that smote the Egyptians with all the plagues in the wilderness?

B. These are The Gods

3. There is joy in heaven over one sinner that repenteth, more than over ninety and nine just persons, which need no repentance.
The son had a Father, as Yahweh/God is our Father **if** we are in Yahushua Messiah/Jesus Christ.
The lost son confessed his sins when he said, father I have <u>sinned against heaven,</u> <u>and in thy sight,</u> and am <u>no more worthy</u> to be <u>called thy son.</u> But the father said to his servants, Bring forth the best robe, and PUT IT ON HIM; AND PUT A RING ON HIS HAND, AND SHOES ON HIS FEET: AND BRING HITHER THE FATTED CALF, AND KILL IT; AND LET US EAT, AND BE MERRY: For this my son WAS DEAD, and is alive again; he was lost, and is found.
And they *began to be merry.*

"TWO PARABLES OF AN HUNDRED SHEEP

As we would say today, *His father gave him a big party*; his elder son was in the field and as he came and drew nigh to the house, _he heard musick and dancing_. _His elderly son was angry and would not go in:_ therefore came his father out, and intreated him, he answering said to his father, **Lo, these many years do I**

serve thee, **neither transgressed I at any time thy commandment**: and **yet thou never gavest me a kid,** that **I might make merry with my friends:** But as soon as this THY SON WAS COME, which hath **devoured thy living with harlots,** thou hast **killed for him the fatted calf**. Luke 15:7-30

This parable teaches us how we also have a Father but sometimes leave Him and waste our lives but **when** and **if we repent** and **come back to Him there is Joy in heaven.**

Q. What did the father give to his elderly son that he did not give to the one that devoured his living? "The waster"

A. *All his possessions*

And he said unto him, Son, thou art ever with me, and all that I have is thine. Luke 15:31.

This parable and example should teach us when we come to God; it is all ways better not to return back into Egypt/the world and bring the old man back to life again, the one that did not leave home received **All his father's possessions.**

Jesus said, *All things that The Father hath are Mine*: therefore said I, that He shall take of Mine, and shall shew it unto you. John 16:15

4. For I know the thoughts that I think toward you, saith The LORD.
Q. What are His thoughts?

A. *Thoughts of peace*, and _not_ of _evil_, to give you _an expected end_ Jeremiah 29:11

"MANIFESTATION QUIZZING"

1. There is a nondenominational group called The Churches of Christ.

   Q. Is this quotation scriptural, The Churches of Christ?

2. Where in scripture does Tertius identify himself as writing an epistle?

3. Did Jesus appear before The Father to put away sin in this world or the old world?

4. Did Christ every glorified Himself to be made a high priest or did He glorified someone beside Himself?

5. To whom did Jesus manifest His Father's Name?

   B. What things did some know?

6. Did Jesus pray for the ones that God had given him first or the world first?

   (The book of John)

"MANIFESTATION QUIZZING"

1. There is a nondenominational group called The Churches of Christ.
Q. Is this quotation scriptural "The Churches of Christ"?
A. Yes.
Salute one another **with an holy kiss. The churches of Christ** salute you. Romans 16:16

2. Where in scripture does Tertius identify himself as writing an epistle?
A. Romans 16:22. I Tertius, **WHO WROTE THIS EPISTLE**, salute you in The Lord.

3. Did Jesus appear before The Father to put away sin in this world or the old world?
A. **THE OLD WORLD** Remembers this world **HAS NOT ENDED.**

For then must He often have suffered since THE **foundation of the world**: BUT NOW ONCE IN THE *end of the world* HATH HE APPEARED TO PUT AWAY SIN BY THE SACRIFICE OF HIMSELF.
Hebrews 9:26

God, who at sundry times and in divers manners spake in time past unto the fathers by the prophets, Hath in these last days spoken unto us by His Son, whom He hath appointed heir of all things, by whom also He made the worlds; Hebrews 1:*1-2*

I have glorified Thee on the earth: I have finished the work which **Thou gavest Me to do**. And now, O *Father, glorify Thou Me* **with Thine own self** with the glory **which I had with** *Thee before the world was*. JOHN 17:4 &5

4. Did Christ every glorified Himself to be made a high priest or did He glorified someone beside Himself?
A. He never took that honor unto Himself; HE ALWAYS *GLORIFIED THE FATHER IN HEAVEN*.
And no man **taketh this honour unto himself, but he that is called of God,** as was Aaron. **So also Christ glorified not Himself to be made an high priest;** but HE THAT SAID UNTO Him, Thou art My Son, to day have I begotten Thee. Hebrews 5:4 & 5

5. To whom did Jesus manifest His Father's Name?
A. **To the men His Father gave Him.**
I have manifested Thy Name unto the men which thou gavest Me out of the world: Thine they were, and Thou *gavest* them Me; and they have kept Thy Word. John 17:6

"MANIFESTATION QUIZZING"

B. What things did some know?
A. **Now they have known that all things whatsoever Thou hast given Me are of Thee**.
FOR I HAVE GIVEN UNTO THEM *the words which thou gavest Me;* and they **have received them**, and have *known surely that I came out from thee,* and they *have believed that Thou didst send Me.*
John 17:7 & 8

6. Did Jesus pray for the ones that God had given him first or the world first?
(*The book of John*)
A. **I pray for them**: I pray **not for the world**, BUT for them which **Thou hast given Me**; for they are Thine.
And **ALL MINE** ARE THINE, and **Thine are Mine;** and **I AM GLORIFIED IN THEM**.
And now I am no more in the world, but these are in the world, and **I come to Thee**. **Holy Father, keep through Thine Own Name those whom**

Thou *hast given* Me, that they may be ONE, as WE are.
While I was WITH THEM IN THE WORLD, I KEPT THEM IN THY NAME: those that ***Thou gavest Me I have kept, and none of them is lost***, BUT the **son of perdition**; that the scripture **might be fulfilled**. And now come I to Thee; and these things I speak in the world, that they might have **My joy fulfilled in themselves**. I have given them **Thy Word**; and the world hath hated them, because they are **not of the world**, *even as I **am not of the world***. I pray not that Thou shouldest take them out of the world, but that thou *shouldest keep them from the evil.* John 17:9-15

Father, I will that they also, whom Thou hast GIVEN ME, BE WITH ME WHERE I am: that they may behold My glory, which Thou hast given Me: for Thou *lovedst Me before the foundation of the world.* John 17:2

Praise Yahweh/God The Father, for His Son Jesus Christ/Yahushua the Messiah who continue to bring many sons and daughters to glory and unto God The father!

Praise Yahh, Yah, *Yĕhovah and* yeh·hō·vä'
My research says, the meanings are the same.
I can understand **Yah**weh and **Yah**ushua. The beginning of **both** name sounds the same. **Remember, I am come in *My Father's name.* John 5:43**
Beware of Him, and obey His voice, provoke Him not; for He will not pardon your transgressions: for *My Name is in Him* Exodus 23:21 Wow! Christ and Christ-ians Wow Sensational!

"MAKING PLAIN THE MYSTERIES OF GOD"

1. Alluding to Paul writing, How that by revelation He made known unto me the mystery; (as I wrote afore in few words, Whereby, when ye read, ye may understand my knowledge in the mystery.

Q. What was Paul's knowledge in the mystery hiding from the beginning of the world?

2. That which we have seen and heard declare we unto you, that ye also may have fellowship with us:

Q. And truly, their fellowships were with whom?

3. The mystery hidden, <u>from ages</u> and from <u>generations is manifest</u> to whom?

4. It is the glory of God to conceal a thing but what is the honour of a kings?

"Making plain The Mysteries Of God"

1. Alluding to Paul writing, How that by revelation He made known unto me the mystery; (as I wrote afore in few words, Whereby, when ye read, ye may understand my knowledge in the mystery.

Q. What was Paul's knowledge in the mystery hiding from the beginning of the world?

A. *How God created all things by Jesus Christ.*

And to make **all men see what is the fellowship of the mystery, which from the beginning of the world hath been hid in God, who created all things by Jesus Christ:** Ephesians 3:9

2. That which we have <u>seen</u> and <u>heard</u> declare we unto you, that ye also <u>may</u> have <u>fellowship with us</u>:

Q. And truly, their fellowships were with whom?

A. *God The Father, in addition <u>with</u>* His Son Jesus Christ. 1 John 1:3

3. The mystery hidden, <u>from ages</u> and from <u>generations is manifest</u> to whom?

A. His saints, His holy apostles and prophets by the Spirit.

EVEN THE MYSTERY WHICH HATH BEEN HID FROM AGES AND FROM GENERATIONS, **but now is made manifest to his saints:** To whom God would make known what is the riches of the glory of this mystery among the <u>Gentiles</u>; *which is Christ in you, the hope of glory*: Whom we preach, <u>warning every man, and teaching every man in all wisdom;</u> **that we may present every man** *<u>PERFECT</u>* IN CHRIST JESUS. Colossians 1:26-28

(REMEMBER, .O SON OF MAN, I HAVE SET THEE A WATCHMAN UNTO THE HOUSE OF ISRAEL; THEREFORE THOU SHALT *HEAR THE WORD AT MY MOUTH, AND* WARN THEM FROM ME . . .)

Ezekiel 33

Which in other ages *was not* made known unto the sons of men, as it is now revealed unto **His holy apostles** and **prophets by The Spirit**. Ephesians 3:51

That your faith **should not** stand in **the wisdom of men,** *but* **in the power of God.** *Howbeit we speak wisdom among them that are* **perfect**: yet not the <u>wisdom of this world,</u> nor of the *princes of this world*, that come to nought: But we **speak the wisdom of God in a mystery,** *even the hidden wisdom, which God ordained before the world unto our glory*: Which none of the **princes of this world knew**: *for had they known it, <u>they</u> would not <u>have</u> crucified The Lord of glory.*

But as it is written, *Eye hath not seen, nor ear heard, neither have entered into the heart of man, the things which God hath prepared for them that love Him.* **But God hath revealed them unto us by His Spirit:** for THE SPIRIT SEARCHETH ALL THINGS, yea, the deep things of God.

1 Corinthians 2:5-10

4. It is the glory of God to conceal a thing but what is the honour of kings?

A. The honour of kings is to search out a matter. Proverbs 25:2

The secret things belong unto The LORD our God: but those things which **are revealed belong unto us and to our children for ever, that we** *<u>may do all the words of this law</u>*. Deuteronomy 29:29

Notice: *<u>not</u>* <u>works</u> but words of the law.

"OUR RIGHTEOUSNESS"

1. After Moses came down from Mount Sinai with the two tables of testimony in his hand, this skin of his face shone.
Q What makes a man's face shone/shine?

2. *It is not hidden from thee, neither is it far off. It is not in heaven, that thou shouldest say, Who shall go up for us to heaven, and bring it unto us, that we may hear it, and do it? Neither is it beyond the sea, that thou shouldest say, Who shall go over the sea for us, and bring it unto us, that we may hear it, and do it? But the word is very nigh unto thee, in thy mouth, and in thy heart, that thou mayest do it.*
Deuteronomy 30:12-14
Q. Where can we find a reference to this scripture?

3. This statement noted in scriptures five times or more "which if a man do, he shall live in them"
Q. Can you name these five places?

4. Moses describeth the righteousness which is of the law, that the man which doeth those things shall live by them.
Q. Where did Moses describe what would be our righteousness?

5. **Why The LORD would humble Israel and allowed them to suffer?**

6. **What are we to teach the people of God to observe and we should observe and do?**

"OUR RIGHTEOUSNESS"

1. After Moses came down from mount Sinai with the two tables of testimony in his hand, this skin of his face shone.

Q What makes a man's face shone/shine?

A. *A man's wisdom* maketh his face to shine. Ecclesiastes 8:1

2. It is not hidden from thee, neither is it far off. It is not in heaven, that thou shouldest say, Who shall go up for us to heaven, and bring it unto us, that we may hear it, and do it? Neither is it beyond the sea, that thou shouldest say, Who shall go over the sea for us, and bring it unto us, that we may hear it, and do it? But the word is very nigh unto thee, in thy mouth, and in thy heart, that thou mayest do it. Deuteronomy 30:12-14

Q. Where can we find a reference to this scripture?

A. Romans 10:6-10.

But the righteousness which is of faith speaketh on this wise, *Say not in thine heart*, Who shall ascend into heaven? (*that is, to bring Christ down from above:*)

Or, **Who shall descend into the deep? (that is, to bring up Christ again from the dead.)** But what saith it? The word is **nigh thee,** *even in thy mouth, and in thy heart*: that is, **the word of faith, which we preach;**

That if thou shalt confess with thy mouth The Lord Jesus, AND shalt believe in thine heart that God hath raised Him from the dead, thou shalt be saved. For with *the heart man believeth unto righteousness*; and with **the mouth** *confession is made **UNTO** salvation*.

Some are teaching, just say the *sinner prayer and you shall or you will be saved and some say just believe John 3:16 and you shall or will be saved.* **Are these testimonials scriptural? No.**

Read Romans 10:6-10 again and Romans 10:13, Mark 16:16.

John 3:16 Teaches, **For God so loved the WORLD,** that **He gave His only begotten Son**, that **whosoever believeth { IN HIM} SHOULD** not perish, **but HAVE EVERLASTING LIFE.**

This scripture teaches, how God so loved the **world** and gave His Son for the **world** and if one **believeth (continue to believe}** in Him **not** out of Him **SHOULD** NOT PERISH. THE **UNGODLY IS JUSTIFIED** BY FAITH, AS ABRAHAM OUR FATHER WAS, NOT THE **SINNERS.** READ ROMANS CHAPTER 4 &5

NOW READ THESE SCRIPTURES.

Therefore the ungodly shall *not stand in the judgment,* **nor** SINNERS **in the congregation of the righteous.** Psalm 1:5

For The LORD KNOWETH THE WAY OF THE RIGHTEOUS: but **the way of the ungodly** *shall perish*.

Psalm 1:6

And if the righteous scarcely be saved, *where shall the* **ungodly** AND **the sinner appear?**

1 Peter 4:18

"Our Righteousness"

3. This statement noted in scriptures five times or more "which if a man do, he shall live in them"

Q. Can you name these five places?

A. **Leviticus 18:5** Ye shall therefore keep My statutes, and My judgments: which if a man do, he shall live in them: *I am The LORD.*

Nehemiah 9:29 And testifiedst against them, that thou mightest bring them again unto thy law: yet they dealt proudly, and hearkened not unto Thy commandments, but sinned against Thy judgments, (*which if a man do, he shall live in* them;) and withdrew the shoulder, and hardened their neck, and would not hear.

Ezekiel 20:11 And I gave them My statutes, and shewed them My judgments, *which if a man do, he shall even live in them.*

Ezekiel 20:13 But the house of Israel rebelled against Me in the wilderness: they walked not in My statutes, and they despised My judgments, which if a man do, he shall even live in them; and my sabbaths they greatly polluted: then I said, I would pour out My fury upon them in the wilderness, to consume them.

Ezekiel 20:21 Notwithstanding **the children rebelled against Me: they walked not in My statutes, neither kept My judgments to do them, which if a man do, he shall even live in them; they polluted My sabbaths:** then I said, I would pour out my fury upon them, **to accomplish My anger against them in the** wilderness.

4. Moses **DESCRIBETH THE RIGHTEOUSNESS WHICH IS OF THE LAW,** that the man which doeth those things shall live by them.

Q. Where in scriptures did Moses described what would be our righteousness?

A. Deuteronomy 6:25.

AND IT shall BE OUR RIGHTEOUSNESS, IF WE <u>OBSERVE TO DO</u> ALL THESE COMMANDMENTS BEFORE THE LORD OUR GOD, AS HE HATH COMMANDED.

5. Why The LORD would humble Israel and allowed them to suffer?

A. That He might make something know to them, that man cannot continue to live by bread only, but by **every word that proceedeth out of The Mouth of The LORD doth man live.**

(And He humbled thee, and suffered thee to hunger, and fed thee **with manna, which thou knewest not,** neither did thy fathers know; that **He might make thee know that man doth not live by bread only, but by every word that proceedeth out of The Mouth of The LORD <u>DOTH</u> MAN LIVE Deuteronomy 8:3**

6. What are we to teach the people of God to observe and we should observe and do?

A. EVERYTHING HE COMMANDED.

Teaching them to observe all things whatsoever I have commanded you: and, lo, I am with you always, even unto the end of the world. Amen. Matthew 28:20

"Our Righteousness"

And thou shalt <u>remember that thou</u> **wast a bondman in Egypt:** and thou SHALT OBSERVE AND DO THESE STATUTES. Deuteronomy 16:12

They CLAVE TO <u>THEIR BRETHREN</u>, <u>THEIR NOBLES</u>, AND **ENTERED INTO A CURSE**, and into **an oath**, to walk in <u>God's law</u>, which was <u>given by Moses</u> the servant of God, **and** TO OBSERVE AND do **all the commandments** OF THE LORD **our** Lord, <u>and</u> His **judgments and** His **statutes;** Nehemiah 10:29

What was the curse?

I believe it can be found in the "statutes" *Nehemiah 10:30-39*
But, let us look at what action they took before. Nehemiah 10:28

And the rest of the people, the priests, the Levites, the porters, the singers, the Nethinims, and all they that had **separated themselves** **FROM THE PEOPLE OF THE LANDS** unto <u>the law of God</u>, their wives, their sons, and their daughters, every one having knowledge, and having understanding:

Nehemiah 10:30-39

---

[30] And that we **would not give our daughters unto the people of the land**, not take **their daughters for our sons**: [31] And if the people of the land <u>bring ware or any victuals on the sabbath day to sell</u>, that we <u>would not buy it of them on the sabbath</u>, or **ON THE HOLY DAY**: and *that we would leave the seventh year, and the exaction of every debt.* [32] Also <u>we made ordinances for us</u>, to *charge ourselves yearly with the third part of a shekel for the service of the house of our God;* [33] <u>For the shewbread, and for the continual meat offering</u>, and for <u>the continual burnt offering, of the sabbaths,</u> *of the new moons, for the set feasts, and for the holy things,* **and for the *sin offerings to make an atonement for Israel***, and **for all the work of the house of our God**. [34] And we cast the lots among the priests, the Levites, and the people, for the wood offering, to <u>bring it into the house of our God, after the houses of our fathers, at times appointed year by year,</u> to ***burn upon the altar of the LORD our God, as it is written in the LAW***: [35] And to <u>bring the firstfruits of our ground, and the firstfruits of all fruit of all trees, year by year, unto the house of the LORD</u>: [36] Also *the firstborn of our sons, and of our cattle, as it is written in the law, and the firstlings of our herds and of our flocks, to bring to the house of our God, unto the priests that minister in the house of our God*: [37] And *that we should bring the firstfruits of our dough, and our offerings, and the fruit of all manner of trees, of wine and of oil, unto the priests, to the chambers of the house of our God; and the tithes of our ground unto the Levites, that the same Levites might have the tithes in all the cities of our tillage.* [38] And *the priest the son of Aaron shall be with the Levites, when the Levites take tithes: and the Levites shall bring up the tithe of the tithes unto the house of our God, to the chambers, into the treasure house.* [39] *For the children of Israel and the children of Levi shall bring the offering of the corn, of the new wine, and the oil, unto the chambers, where are the vessels of the sanctuary, and the priests that minister, and the porters, and the singers: and we will not forsake the house of our God.*

REMEMBER, THE WORDS OF YAHUSHUA? ..**but do <u>not</u> ye after their works: *for they say, and do not.*** Matthew 23:2-4 [2] Saying The scribes and the Pharisees sit in Moses' seat:[3] <u>*All therefore whatsoever they bid you observe, that observe and do*</u>; but do not ye after their works: for they say, and do not.[4] **For they bind heavy burdens and grievous to be borne, and lay them on men's shoulders; but they themselves will not move them with one of their fingers.**

"VESTURE DIPPED IN BLOOD"

1. Do not ye after their works: for they say, and do not.
Q. Why did Jesus make this statement?

2. Now to Him that is of power to stablish you according to my gospel, and the preaching of Jesus Christ according to the revelation of the mystery.

Q. How long was the revelation of this mystery kept secret?

3. Jesus was clothed with vesture dipped in blood and His Name, is called?

4. And now also the axe is laid unto the root of the trees: therefore every tree which bringeth not forth good fruit is hewn down, and cast into the fire. Matthew 3:10

Q. Does this parable refer to believers?

"VESTURE DIPPED IN BLOOD"

1. Do not ye after their works: for they say, and do not.
Q. Why did Jesus make this statement?
A. Because, they would say but would **NOT Do, blessed is he that do!**
And they answered Joshua, saying, <u>ALL</u> THAT THOU COMMANDEST US <u>WE WILL DO</u>, AND WHITHERSOEVER <u>THOU SENDEST US, WE WILL GO.</u> Joshua 1:16

Manytimes we say the samethings, *"WE WILL GO:"*
For ye dissembled *in your hearts,* <u>**when ye sent me**</u> **unto** The LORD your God, saying, **Pray for us unto The LORD our God; and according unto all that The LORD our God shall say, so declare unto us, and** <u>**WE WILL DO IT**</u> Jeremiah 42:20

Once again, Yahushua/Jesus spoke these words,

Saying <u>The scribes</u> and <u>the Pharisees</u> sit in Moses' <u>seat:</u>
ALL THEREFORE WHATSOEVER THEY <u>BID YOU</u> observe, that observe and do; *but* do not YE *after their* <u>WORKS</u>: **for they say,** *and* <u>DO NOT</u>. MATTHEW 23:2&3

2. Now to Him that is of power to stablish you according to MY GOSPEL, and THE PREACHING OF JESUS CHRIST according to *the revelation of the mystery.*
Q. How long was the revelation of this mystery kept secret?
A. SINCE THE WORLD BEGAN. Romans 16:25
But now is made manifest, and by the scriptures of the prophets, according to the commandment of The EVERLASTING GOD, MADE *known to all nations for the obedience of faith:*
To God only wise, **be glory through Jesus Christ for ever. Amen. Romans 16:26 & 27**

3. Jesus was clothed with vesture dipped in blood and His Name is called?
A. The Word of God. Revelation 19:13

4. And now also the axe is laid unto the <u>root of the trees:</u> therefore every tree which bringeth not forth good fruit is hewn down, and cast into the fire. Matthew 3:10
Q. Does this parable refer to believers?
If so Please, use scriptures to support your answer?
A. Yes. REFERENCE FOUND IN JOHN CHAPTER 15

"VESTURE DIPPED IN BLOOD"

IF A MAN <u>ABIDE NOT</u> IN ME, HE IS <u>CAST FORTH AS A BRANCH</u>, AND <u>IS WITHERED</u>; AND MEN **gather them, and** *<u>cast them into the fire</u>,* **and they are burned.** John 15:6

HOW CAN ONE ABIDE IN A HOUSE EXCEPT HE WAS ONCE IN THE HOUSE?

Remember, one cannot abide in Jesus if he was never in Him.

READ CHAPTER 15 AND SKETCH IT OUT.

Let God be true and every man a liar including me.

EVERY BRANCH <u>IN</u> ME THAT BEARETH <u>NOT FRUIT</u> HE TAKETH AWAY: **and every branch that beareth fruit, He purgeth it, that it may bring forth more fruit.**

BEARETH, MEANING TO CONINTUE TO BEAR FRUIT, TREES CONTINUE TO BEAR FRUITS WHEN THEY ARE HEALTHY!

As therefore the tares are gathered and burned in the fire; *so shall it be in the end of this world.* THE SON OF MAN <u>SHALL</u> SEND FORTH *HIS ANGELS,* AND ***they shall gather*** OUT OF HIS KINGDOM <u>ALL</u> THINGS THAT OFFEND, **AND THEM WHICH DO INIQUITY**; *AND SHALL <u>CAST THEM INTO A FURNACE OF FIRE</u>*: THERE SHALL BE WAILING AND GNASHING OF TEETH. Matthew 13:40-42

But he that shall endure *unto the end,* the same shall be saved. Matthew 24:13

And ye **shall be hated of <u>all men</u>** FOR MY NAME'S SAKE: but **he that shall *endure unto the end*, *<u>the same shall be saved</u>*** Mark 13:13

"The Tree Of Life"

1. And when they had prayed, the place was shaken where they were assembled together; and they were <u>all filled</u> with The Holy Ghost.

    Q. What happened after the filling of The Holy Ghost?

    B. And the multitude of them that believed were of_____

2. The tree of life bared twelve manners of fruits, and yielded her fruit every month and the leaves of the tree were for what purpose?

3. The tree of life also in the midst of the garden, and_____

4. Blessed are they that do His commandments that they _____to the tree of life, and may enter in through the gates into the city.

5. Who was the first one translated according to scripture?

6. How was, this one translated?

"The Tree Of Life"

1. And when they had prayed, the place was shaken where they were assembled together; and they were <u>all filled</u> with The Holy Ghost.
Q. What happened after the filling of The Holy Ghost?
A. THEY SPAKE <u>THE WORD OF GOD WITH BOLDNESS</u>. Acts 4:31

B. And the multitude of them that believed were of_____
A. ONE HEART AND ONE SOUL. **Acts 4:32**
(Meaning, all those who believed agreed)

2. The tree of life bared twelve manners of fruits, and yielded her fruit every month and the leaves of the tree were for what purpose?

A. The **leaves** <u>of the tree</u> **were for** *the healing of the nations.*
Revelation 22:2

3. *The tree of life* also *in the midst of the garden, and* _____
A. THE TREE OF KNOWLEDGE OF GOOD AND EVIL. *Genesis 2:9*

4. Blessed are they that do His commandments, that they_____to **the tree of life**, and **may** enter in through **the gates into the city.**
A. May have right *Revelation 22:14*

"SCRIPTURES ON THE TREE OF LIFE"
The tree of life Genesis 3:22
The tree of life Genesis 3:24
The tree of life Revelation 2:7

5. Who was the first one translated according to scripture?
A. ENOCH. And Enoch walked with God: and he was not; for GOD TOOK HIM. Genesis 5:24

6. How was, this one translated?
A. By faith.
ENOCH WAS TRANSLATED *THAT HE SHOULD NOT SEE DEATH,* AND WAS **not found,** BECAUSE *GOD HAD TRANSLATED HIM.* FOR **before** his translation he *had this testimony, THAT HE PLEASED GOD.* HEBREWS 11:5

"Jesus Confessed Himself"

1. The first kings reigned over Edom; before any kings reigned over Israel true or false.

2. Who spoke these words, for God, said he, hath made me forget all my toil, and all my father's house?

3. Jesus asked His disciples this question, .Whom do men say that I The Son of man am? And they said, Some say that thou art John the Baptist: some, Elias; and others, Jeremias, or one of the prophets. He saith unto them, But whom say ye that I am? Simon Peter confessed that Jesus was The Christ, The Son of The living God. Matthew 16:13-16

Q. Who did Jesus confess Himself to be?

4. What are you saying, about Jesus if you do not confess Him before man as Peter did, will He confess you before His Father?

"Jesus Confessed Himself"

1. The first kings reigned over Edom; before any kings reigned over Israel true or false.
A. True

Now these are the kings that reigned in the land of **Edom before any king reigned over the children of Israel** 1 Chronicles 1:43

2. Who spoke these words, for God, said he, hath made me forget all my toil, and all my father's house?
A. JOSEPH GENESIS 41:51

3. Jesus asked His disciples this question, *Whom do men say that I The Son of man am*? And they said, Some say that *thou art John the Baptist*: some, *Elias; and others, Jeremias, or one of the prophets*. He saith unto them, **But whom say ye that I am**? Simon Peter confessed that Jesus was The Christ, The Son of The living God. Matthew 16:13-16
Q. Who did Jesus confess Himself to be?
A. I am The Son of God.
Say ye of Him, whom THE FATHER HATH SANCTIFIED, and sent into the world.
Thou blasphemest; because I said, I am The Son of God?
John 10:36

He trusted in God; let Him deliver Him now, IF He will have Him: FOR HE SAID, I AM THE SON OF GOD. Matthew 27:43

4. What are you saying, about Jesus if you do not confess Him before man as Peter did, will He confess you before His Father?
A. NO

Do not look over the "BIG" But word.

Whosoever therefore shall confess Me before men, him will I confess also before My Father WHICH IS IN HEAVEN BUT WHOSOEVER shall deny Me before men, Him will I also deny before My Father which is in heaven. Matthew 10:32-33

"His Abundant Mercy"

1. There were false prophets also among the people, even as there shall be _____, who privily shall bring in damnable heresies, even denying The Lord that bought them, and bring upon themselves _____

2. Blessed be The God and Father of our Lord Jesus Christ which according to His abundant mercy hath begotten us again unto a _____

3. How many years did David reign over Israel?

4. How old was Eli when he died?

B. Was Eli eyesight good or bad at the time of his death?

5. How many years did Eli judge Israel?

6. Whatever The Lord does, He does it for a purpose.

Q. Why did The Lord; established a testimony in Jacob and appointed a law in Israel?

7. If you take away the wicked from before the king how shall his throne be established?

"His Abundant Mercy"

1. There were false prophets also among the people, even as there shall be _____, who privily shall bring in damnable heresies, even denying The Lord that bought them, and bring upon themselves _____
A. **False teachers among you, Swift destruction.** 2 PETER 2:1

2. Blessed be The God and Father of our Lord Jesus Christ which according to His abundant mercy hath begotten us again unto a _____
A. LIVELY HOPE BY THE RESURRECTION OF JESUS CHRIST FROM THE DEAD.
1 Peter 1:3

3. How many years did David reign over Israel?
A. **David reign over Israel forty years.**
The days that David reigned over Israel were forty years. 1 Kings 2:11

4. How old was Eli when he died?
A. ELI WAS 98 YEARS OLD.

B. Was Eli eyesight good or bad at the time of his death?
ELI EYES WERE DIM THAT HE COULD NOT SEE. 1 SAMUEL 4:15

5. How many years did Eli judge Israel?
A. **Eli judged Israel forty years.**

6. Whatever The Lord does He does it for a purpose.
Q. Why did The Lord; established a testimony in Jacob and appointed a law in Israel?
A. **That they should be made known to their children.**
For He **established a testimony in Jacob, and appointed a law in Israel,** which *He commanded our fathers, that they should make them known to their children*: **That the generation to come might** know them, **even the children which should be born: who should arise and declare them to their children: That they might set their hope in God, and not forget the works of God,** but keep **His commandments:** And might **not** be as their fathers, a **stubborn and rebellious generation**; a generation that set *not their heart aright, and* **whose spirit was not** *stedfast* **with God.** Psalm 78:5-8

7. If you take away the wicked from before the king how shall his throne be established?
A. THE KING THRONE SHALL BE ESTABLISHED IN RIGHTEOUSNESS.
PROVERBS 25:5

PRIDE OR HONOUR"

1. The word says a man's pride shall bring him low but honour shall_____

B. When pride cometh, then cometh shame: but with the lowly is _____

C. For the sin of their mouth and the words of their lips let them even be taken in their pride:
and for _____ which they speak.

2. Paul wrote and referred to Phebe as their sister and that she was a servant of the church, that they would receive her in The Lord as becometh saints, and that they would assist her in whatsoever business she hath need of; for she hath been a succourer/helper of many including him. Romans 16:1&2

From this scripture, we can see Phebe was a woman, a servant of the church, a sister and she became a saint. Some translation says and believed she was a deaconess, a deacon, Christian sister, and some just said a friend.

I did not see one that said she was a follower of Christ but the word Christian is the name giving to the disciples those who followed Christ and His teaching. Remember, **the disciples/the followers of Jesus were** called Christians first in Antioch Acts 11:26

I heard today on a religious station that Phebe was or could have been Paul's Pastor.

Q. Was Phebe a Christian meaning, a disciple and an apostle/a follower of Jesus Christ?

3. Did Paul ever greet the women?

"PRIDE OR HONOUR"

1. The *word says a man's pride shall bring him low but honour shall* _____
     A. Honour shall uphold the humble in spirit. *Proverbs 29:23*

    B. *When pride cometh, then cometh shame: but with the lowly is* _____
       A. Wisdom. *Proverbs 11:2*

C. *For the sin of their mouth and the words of their lips let them even be taken in their pride:*
and for _____ *which they speak.*
A. Cursing and lying *Psalm 59:12*

2. Paul wrote and referred to Phebe as their sister and that she was a servant of the church, that they would receive her in The Lord as <u>becometh saints,</u> and that they would assist her in whatsoever business she hath need of; for she hath been a succourer/helper of many including him. Romans 16:1&2
From this scripture, we can see Phebe was a <u>woman,</u> <u>a servant</u> of the church, <u>a sister</u> and she became a saint. Some translation says and believed she was a deaconess, a deacon, Christian sister, and some just said a friend.
I did not see one that said she **was a follower of Christ but the word Christian is** the name giving to the **disciples those who followed Christ** and **His teaching**. Remember, the disciples/the followers of Jesus were called Christians first in Antioch Acts 11:26
I heard today on a religious station that Phebe was or could have been Paul's Pastor.
Q. Was Phebe a Christian meaning, a disciple and an apostle/a follower of Jesus Christ?
A. I believe she was.

Paul called himself many times a servant and an apostle of Jesus Christ. Romans 1:1
Paul *called to be an apostle of Jesus Christ* through **the will of God**. Unto the church of God which is at Corinth, to them that are **sanctified in Christ Jesus**, called to be saint, <u>with **all**</u> that in every place **call upon The Name of Jesus Christ our Lord**, both *their's and our's*: 1 Corinthians 1:1-2

PAUL, AN APOSTLE, (not of men, neither by man, but BY JESUS CHRIST, AND GOD THE FATHER, who raised Him from the dead;) Galatians 1:1

And ye **became followers of us, and of The Lord, having received the word in much affliction, WITH JOY OF THE HOLY GHOST.** 1 Thessalonians 1:6

"PRIDE OR HONOUR"

TEACHING QUIZZING CONTINUE

3. Did Paul ever greet the women?

A. YES.

GREET MARY, who bestowed much labour on us. Romans 16:6

Salute Rufus chosen in The Lord, **AND HIS MOTHER AND MINE.** Romans 16:13

Salute Philologus, and Julia, Nereus, **AND HIS SISTER**, and Olympas, and **all the saints which are with them**. Romans 16:15

SALUTE ONE ANOTHER WITH AN HOLY KISS. THE CHURCHES OF CHRIST/MESSIAH SALUTE YOU. Romans 16:16

Please, do not overlook this statement,

NOW I beseech you, brethren, *mark* THEM WHICH <u>CAUSE DIVISIONS AND OFFENCES CONTRARY TO THE DOCTRINE WHICH YE HAVE LEARNED</u>; AND <u>AVOID</u> THEM. **For they that are such serve *not* our Lord Jesus Christ, but their own belly; and by good words and fair speeches deceive the hearts of the simple. Romans 16:17&18**

For your **obedience is come abroad unto all men.** I am glad therefore on your behalf: *but yet I would have you wise unto that which is good,* and <u>simple concerning evil</u>. And **The God of peace** shall <u>bruise Satan</u> under <u>your feet shortly.</u> **The grace of our Lord Jesus Christ be with you.** Amen Romans 16:19 & 20

"PERFECT/COMPLETE UNDERSTANDING OF THE WORD ONE"

1. The Lord sent Moses and his brother Aaron to tell Pharaoh to let His son go, that he may serve Him: and if he refused to let him go, behold, He would slay his son, even his firstborn.

Q. Whom was The Lord referring to as Pharaoh's firstborn son?

B. Did The Lord try to kill his firstborn son?

C. If so why, please, *use scripture to support your answer*

2. How old was Moses and Aaron when The Lord sent them to speak to Pharaoh?

3. Where in scriptures can we get a perfect/complete understanding of the word one in **the Old and New Testaments?**

"PERFECT/COMPLETE UNDERSTANDING OF THE WORD ONE"

1. The Lord sent Moses and his brother Aaron to tell Pharaoh to let His son go, that he may serve Him: and if he refused to let him go, behold, He would slay his son, even his firstborn.

A. Whom was The Lord referring to as Pharaoh's firstborn son?
A. Moses
B. Did The Lord try to kill his firstborn son?
A. Yes
C. If so why please, use scripture to support your answer.
A. Because, of the circumcision.

(Moses grows up from a baby in Egypt in Pharaoh's house and not circumcised as the Israelites.)
And it came to pass by the way **in the inn, that The LORD met him, and sought to kill him.** Then Zipporah took a sharp stone, and cut off the foreskin of her son, and cast it at his feet, and said, Surely a *bloody husband art thou to me. So he let him go: then she said, A bloody husband thou art, because of the circumcision*
Exodus 4:23-26

Another translation Says, The Lord met Moses and tried to kill him.

2. **How old was Moses and Aaron when The Lord sent them to speak to Pharaoh?**
A. Moses *was* eighty years old and Aaron eighty-three years old. Exodus 7:7
3. **Where in scriptures can we get a perfect/complete understanding of the word one in the Old and New Testaments?**
A. Therefore shall a man leave his father and his mother, and shall **cleave unto his wife:** and they **shall be** one flesh. Genesis 2:24

Wherefore they are **no more twain**, but **one** flesh. Matthew 19:6

And *they twain* SHALL BE **ONE** FLESH: so then they are **no more twain, but one flesh**.
Mark 10:8

When two comes together, they are one, when the man takes a wife she takes on his name, *one name but two individuals*, if they have fifty children they all **have one name.**

ONLY THOSE WHO ARE FOLLOWERS OF CHRIST ARE, "ONE"

AND THE GLORY WHICH THOU GAVEST ME I HAVE GIVEN THEM; THAT THEY MAY BE ONE, EVEN AS WE ARE ONE: I IN THEM, AND THOU IN ME, THAT THEY MAY BE MADE PERFECT IN ONE; AND THAT THE WORLD MAY KNOW THAT THOU HAST SENT ME, AND HAST LOVED THEM, AS THOU HAST LOVED ME. JOHN 17:22 & 23

There is neither Jew nor Greek, there is neither bond nor free, there is neither **male nor female: for ye are all one IN CHRIST JESUS.** Galatians 3:28
Praise Yahweh and Yahushua for ONENESS!

"Perfect Illustration"

1. The Lord said unto Moses and Aaron, thou shalt say unto Pharaoh, Thus saith The LORD, Israel is My son, <u>even</u> My firstborn: Genesis 48:14
Q. If Jesus is God firstborn Son according to the scriptures, then how can Israel be His firstborn son?

2. And Israel stretched out his right hand, and laid it upon Ephraim's head, who was the younger, and his left hand upon Manasseh's head, guiding his hands wittingly; for Manasseh was the firstborn.
Q. Who is the father of Ephraim and Manasseh?

3. Who was Jacob's firstborn son and what benefits did he have?

4. The Lord slew/killed two of Judah sons, whom and why did The Lord take their lives?

"PERFECT ILLUSTRATION"

1. The Lord said unto Moses and Aaron, thou shalt say unto Pharaoh, Thus saith The LORD, Israel is My son, <u>even</u> My firstborn: Genesis 48:14

Q. If Jesus is God firstborn Son according to the scriptures, then how can Israel be His firstborn son?

A. For whom he did foreknow, he also did predestinate to be conformed to **the image of His Son**, that He *might be the firstborn among many brethren*. **Who is the image of The invisible God, the firstborn of <u>every creature</u>:** Romans 8:29 and & Colossians 1:15

The scripture reads, .Thus saith The LORD, Israel is My son, *even* My firstborn: **I believe it was Yahushua The Son of God, who spoke these words. NOTICE: it did not say thus saith God.**

It was The Lord The Son of God, who came down in Exodus 3:7-8

(Remember, both <u>always means two</u>, Yahweh/God The Father and Yahushua/Jesus both called Lord, this is why David said The LORD said unto my Lord.)

Please, notice LORD and Lord.

Psalm 110:1 *The LORD* said <u>unto my Lord</u>, Sit thou at My right hand, until I make *Thine enemies* Thy footstool.

Matthew 22:44 *The LORD* said <u>unto my Lord</u>, Sit thou on My right hand, till I make *Thine enemies* Thy footstool?

Luke 20:42 And David himself saith <u>in the book of Psalms</u>, *The LORD* said <u>unto my Lord</u>, Sit thou on <u>My right hand</u>,

Acts 2:34 For David <u>is not</u> <u>ascended into the heavens</u>: but he saith himself, *The Lord* said <u>unto my Lord</u>, Sit thou on my right hand,

One translation says; *THE LORD* (God) says to My Lord [The Messiah], Sit at My right hand, until I MAKE <u>Your adversaries Your footstool.</u>

And The LORD said, I have surely seen the affliction of My people which are in Egypt, and have heard their cry by reason of their taskmasters; for I know their sorrows; **AND I AM COME DOWN** to deliver them out of the **hand of the Egyptians, and to bring them up out of that land unto a good land and a large, unto a land flowing with milk and honey;** unto the place of the Canaanites, and the Hittites, and the Amorites, and the Perizzites, and the Hivites, and the Jebusites. Exodus 3:7-8.

2. And Israel stretched out his right hand, and laid it upon Ephraim's head, who was the younger, and his left hand upon Manasseh's head, guiding his hands wittingly; for Manasseh was the firstborn.

Q. Who is the father of Ephraim and Manasseh?
A. Joseph is the father of Ephraim and Manasseh.

"PERFECT ILLUSTRATION"

3. Who was Jacob's firstborn son and what benefits did he have?
A. Reuben. Reuben was his might/power, strength, the excellency of dignity, and the excellency of his power. Genesis 49:3

4. The Lord slew/killed two of Judah sons, whom and why did The Lord take their lives?
A. The two men were Er and his brother Onan.

The Lord killed these two men why

A. Er. was wicked and The Lord slew/killed him,
After The Lord took his life, His brother Onan was command by his father Judah to go in to his brother's wife and marry her and raise up seed to his brother. **Onan knew that the seed would not be his; and it came to pass, when he went in unto his brother's wife, that he spilled it on the ground,** lest that he should give seed to his brother; *and the thing which he did displeased The LORD wherefore The Lord slew him also.*
Genesis 38:7-30

MESSIAH QUIZZING

1. Jacob's firstborn son freely gave away something he should had retained for life, what was lost and who received it?

B. Why did Reuben the firstborn of Jacob, loose his birthright and who received the birthday?

2. Who was David's firstborn son?

3. Where does the word Messiah appear for the first time in the Old Testament and how many times does it appear?

4. Is the spelling of the word Messiah different in The New Testament in the (KJV)?

5. The word Messias and Messiah is being interpreted as_____

{MESSIAH QUIZZING}

1. Jacob's firstborn son freely gave away something he should had retained for life, what was lost and who received it?
A. Esau gave away his birthright and his brother Jacob received the blessing and the title Israel.

B. Why did Reuben the firstborn of Jacob, loose his birthright and who received the birthday?
A. Reuben *defiled his father's bed and his sons lost the* birthright, therefore, their birthday went to the sons of Joseph.
Now the sons of <u>Reuben</u> the <u>firstborn</u> of Israel, (for he was the firstborn; but forasmuch as he defiled his father's bed, his birthright was given unto the sons of Joseph the son of Israel: and the genealogy is not to be reckoned after the birthright. 1 Chronicles 5:1

2. Who was David's firstborn son?
A. The firstborn son of David was, Amnon. 2 Samuel 3:2

3. Where does the word Messiah appear for the first time in the Old Testament and how many times does it appear?
A. Daniel 9:25. It appears twice.
Know therefore and understand, that from the going forth of the commandment to restore and to build **JERUSALEM UNTO THE MESSIAH <u>THE PRINCE</u> SHALL BE SEVEN WEEKS**, and threescore and two weeks: the street shall be built again, and the wall, even in troublous times. Daniel 9:25
And after threescore and two weeks shall Messiah be cut off, BUT <u>NOT FOR HIMSELF</u>: *and the people of the prince that shall come shall destroy the <u>city and the sanctuary; and the end thereof shall be with a</u>* **flood,** *and unto the end of the war desolations are determined.* Daniel 9:26

4. Is the spelling of the word Messiah different in The New Testament in the (KJV)?
A. Yes. Messias

5. The word Messias and Messiah is being interpreted as_____
A. The Christ
John 1:41 *He first findeth his own brother Simon, and saith unto him, We have found **the Messias,** which is,* **BEING INTERPRETED,** *The Christ.* (KJV)
John 1:41 He first found his own brother Simon, and said to him, "*We have found The Messiah*" (which is translated, *The Christ*). (NKJV)

John 4:25 The woman saith unto Him, I know that *Messias* cometh, **which is called Christ: when He is come, He will tell us all things us** all things.

{MESSIAH QUIZZING}

REMEMBER, John 15:15 Says, Henceforth I call you not servants; *for the servant knoweth not what his lord doeth:* but I have called you friends; *for all things that I have heard of My Father I have made known unto you).*

(The word Messiah found 239 times in The Amplified Bible)

Why do the nations rage, And the people plot a vain thing? Psalm 2:1

Micah 5:2 But you, **Bethlehem** Ephrathah, *Though you are little among the thousands of Judah, Yet out of you shall come forth to Me* **The One to be Ruler in Israel, Whose goings forth are from of old, From everlasting."**

John 1:41 He first found his own brother Simon, and said to him, "We have found The Messiah" (which is translated, The Christ).

We have found The Messiah; this tells me they were **seeking for Him.**

This reminds me of tribe of Judah they turned to The Lord God of Israel and sought Him and they found Him.

I love these scriptures because, they teach us to search for Him.

Now for a **long season** Israel hath been **without The True God**, {they had many gods but not the true God} and without **a teaching priest**, and without **law.**

But when they in their trouble did turn unto the LORD God of Israel, and sought him, he was found of them. And in those times there was no peace to him that went out, *nor to him that came in,* but great vexations were upon all the inhabitants of the countries. 2 Chronicles 15:3-5

It is amazing, so many children of God have no peace at all, they take their own lives, they drink themselves drunk, use drugs as the world does, over and over deliberately breaking the commandments of God, living as they have no hope or power. In other world's, they allow Satan to control their lives and they are fight the Devil day and night, do they not believe **I will fight your battles for you** and **fight the good fight of faith not the Devil.**

What is their problem? Rejection the truth and sometimes listen to deceiving spirits.

Many times we are living as the tribe of Judah, serving everybody and everything but The True God. We are without a teaching priest, we go to church for a feeling not for a healing, The Spirit of The Lord said unto me, the churches have become like the nightclubs and If only a few people are there, they go looking for

large multitude/crowd so they can hide out in the crowd. We need to seek after The Lord and stop seeking after man. Seek The Lord early in your faith, you are no longer under the law that imputes sin, you are under grace, sin is now a choice.

And all Judah rejoiced at the oath: for they had *sworn with all their heart*, and **SOUGHT HIM WITH THEIR WHOLE DESIRE**; and he was found of them: and the LORD gave them rest round about 2 Chronicles 15:15

I love them that love Me; **and** those **that seek Me early shall find Me** Proverbs 8:17

"MYSTERY OF THE SEVEN STARS"

1. What is the mystery of the seven stars and the seven golden candlesticks, which John saw in the right hand of the one like unto the Son of man, clothed with a garment down to the foot, and girt about the paps with a golden girdle?

2. Unto the pure all things are pure: but unto them that are defiled and unbelieving is nothing pure; but even their _____

3. Do we have more than one heaven?
(Please, use scriptures to support your answer)

4. If there is more than one Heaven, how many can we see according to scriptures?

"MYSTERY OF THE SEVEN STARS AND HEAVENS"

1. What is the mystery of the seven stars and the seven golden candlesticks, which John saw in the right hand of the one like unto the Son of man, clothed with a garment down to the foot, and girt about the paps with a golden girdle?

A. The stars are the angels of the churches and the candlesticks are the churches.

.Seven stars are the angels of the seven churches: and the seven candlesticks which thou sawest are the seven churches. Revelation 1:20

2. Unto the pure all things are pure: but unto them that are defiled and unbelieving is nothing pure; but even their _____

A. Mind and conscience is defiled. Titus 1:15

3. Do we have more than one heaven?

(*Please, use scriptures to support your answer*)

A. Yes

4. If there is more than one Heaven, how many can we see according to scriptures?

A. I can see **three** *according to Paul's teaching.*

I knew a man in Christ above fourteen years ago, (*whether in the body, I cannot tell; or whether out of the body, I cannot tell: God knoweth;*) such an **one caught up to *the third heaven.*** 2 Corinthians 12:2

HERE ARE MORE SCRIPTURES ON HEAVENS FOR YOUR ACCESSIBILITY:

Joel 2:30 And I will shew wonders in the heavens and in the earth, blood, and fire, and pillars of smoke.

Joel 3:16 The LORD also shall roar out of Zion, and utter His Voice from Jerusalem; and the heavens and the earth shall shake: **BUT THE LORD WILL BE THE HOPE OF HIS PEOPLE,** *and* **the strength of the children of Israel.**

Habakkuk 3:3 **GOD CAME FROM TEMAN, and** The Holy One from mount Paran. *Selah.* **His glory covered the heavens,** *and* **the earth was full of His praise.**

Haggai 2:6 For thus saith The LORD of hosts; **Yet once, it is a little while, and I will shake the heavens,** *and the earth, and the sea, and the dry land;*

Zechariah 6:5 **And the angel answered and said unto me, These are the four spirits of the heavens,** *which go forth from standing before The LORD of all the earth.*

Matthew 3:16 And Jesus, when He was baptized, went up straightway out of the water: and, **lo, the heavens were opened unto Him,** *and he saw The Spirit of God descending like a dove, and lighting upon Him:*

Matthew 24:29 Immediately *after the tribulation* of those days shall the sun be darkened, and the moon *shall not give her light, and the stars shall fall from heaven, and the powers of the heavens* shall be shaken:

Mark 1:10 And straightway coming up out of the water, he saw the **heavens** *opened, and the Spirit like a dove descending upon Him:*

"MYSTERY OF THE SEVEN STARS AND HEAVENS"

HERE ARE MORE SCRIPTURES ON HEAVENS FOR YOUR ACCESSIBILITY:

Acts 2:34 For David is not ascended into the heavens: but he saith himself, The Lord said unto My Lord, Sit Thou on My right hand,

Acts 7:56 And said, Behold, I SEE THE HEAVENS OPENED, and THE SON OF MAN standing on the right hand of God.

This is why Stephen was stoned to death because, he testified to what he saw.
STUDY Acts 7:50-60

2 Corinthians 5:1 For we know that if our earthly house of this tabernacle were dissolved, we have a building of God, an house not made with hands,. eternal in the heavens.

Ephesians 4:10 He that descended is the same also that ascended up far above all heavens, that he might fill all things.)

Hebrews 1:10 And, Thou, Lord, in the beginning hast laid the foundation of the earth; and the heavens are the works of thine hands:

Hebrews 4:14 Seeing then that we have a Great High Priest, that is passed into the heavens, Jesus The Son of God, let us hold fast our profession.

Hebrews 8:1 Now of the things which we have spoken this is the sum: We have such an high priest, who is set on the right hand of the throne of the Majesty in the heavens;

2 Peter 3:5 For this they willingly are ignorant of, that by the word of God the heavens were of old, and the earth standing out of the water and in the water:

Ezekiel 1:1 Now it came to pass in the thirtieth year, in the fourth month, in the fifth day of the month, as I was among THE CAPTIVES by the river of Chebar, that the heavens were opened, and I saw visions of God.

Revelation 12:12 Therefore rejoice, YE HEAVENS, and ye that dwell in them. Woe to the inhabiters of the earth and of the sea! FOR THE DEVIL IS COME DOWN UNTO YOU, HAVING GREAT WRATH, because he knoweth that he hath but a short time.

REVELATION QUIZZING FROM THE OLD TESTAMENT AND THE NEW TESTAMENT

1. Who reigned in Abijam stead?
There are different spellings in this name, Abia/Abijam and Abijah

2. After Abijah died, his son Asa reigned in his stead and the land was <u>quiet ten years</u> (*The Lord gave* them rest) and he did that which was good and right in the eyes of The LORD his God.

Q What was good and right in the Eyes of The Lord his God?

3. The Spirit of God came upon Azariah and he went out to meet Asa to give them words from The Lord.

Q. What words did he give Asa, Judah and Benjamin?

4. *And he walked in all the ways of Asa his father; he turned not aside from it, doing that which was right in the eyes of The LORD: nevertheless the high places were <u>not</u> taken away; for the people offered and burnt incense yet in the high places.* 1 Kings 22:43

Q. What knowledge can we acquire from this scripture?

REVELATION QUIZZING FROM THE OLD TESTAMENT AND THE NEW TESTAMENT

1. Who reigned in Abijam stead?

There are different spellings in this name, Abia/Abijam and Abijah

A. His son Asa

And Abijam slept with his fathers; and they buried him in the city of David: and **Asa his son reigned in his stead.** Kings 15:8

2. After Abijah died, his son Asa reigned in his stead and the land was **quiet ten years** (**The Lord gave them rest)** and he did that which was good and right in the eyes of The LORD his God.

Q What was good and right in the Eyes of The Lord his God?

A. .**They sought The Lord and He gave them rest, Asa** took away the altars of the strange gods and **the high places, brake down the images, and cut down the groves: And commanded Judah to** seek The LORD God of their fathers, **and to** do the law **and** the commandment.

In addition, he took away out of **all the cities of Judah the high places and the images:** and the **kingdom was quiet** before him. **Chronicles 14:2-7**

3. The Spirit of God came upon Azariah and he went out to meet Asa to give them words from The Lord.

Q. What words did he give Asa, Judah and Benjamin?

A. .**Hear ye me, Asa,** and all Judah and Benjamin; *The LORD is with you,* while ye be with Him; **and if** ye *seek* Him, He will *be found* of you; *but* IF ye forsake Him, He **will** forsake you.

2 Chronicles 15:2

4. And he walked in all the ways of Asa his father; he turned not aside from it, doing that which was right in the eyes of The LORD: nevertheless the high places were not taken away; for the people offered and burnt incense yet in the high places. 1 Kings 22:43

Q. What knowledge can we acquire from this scripture?

A. *THEY* DID NOT *HAVE THE* KNOWLEDGE *NOR* UNDERSTANDING *THAT BURNT INCENSE AND THE HIGH PLACES WAS NO LONGER REQUIRED OF THE LORD; SHOULD THEY HAVE BEEN DEMOLISHED? YES.*

Sacrifice and offering *thou didst not desire;* **mine** *ears hast thou* opened: burnt offering and sin offering hast thou not required. **Psalm 40:6**

And now, Israel, WHAT DOTH THE LORD THY GOD REQUIRE OF THEE, **but** to fear The LORD thy God, to walk in all His ways, and to love Him, and to serve The LORD thy God with all thy heart and with all thy soul. **Deuteronomy 10:12**

THIS IS WHAT REQUIRED EVEN TODAY FROM THE PEOPLE OF YAHWEH

REVELATION QUIZZING FROM THE OLD TESTAMENT AND THE NEW TESTAMENT

For I spake **NOT** unto your fathers, nor commanded them in the day that I brought them out of the land of Egypt, concerning burnt offerings or sacrifices: But *this thing commanded I them, saying,* **OBEY MY VOICE,** and *I will be your God, and ye shall be My people*: and walk ye in all the ways that I have commanded you, that it may be well unto you. **But** they hearkened n**OT**, nor **inclined their ear, BUT** *walked in the counsels and in the imagination of their evil heart,* AND WENT BACKWARD, and. NOT FORWARD *Since the day that your fathers came forth out of the land of Egypt unto this day I have even sent unto you all My servants the prophets, daily rising up early and sending them:* **Yet they hearkened not unto Me,** *nor inclined their ear, but hardened their neck: they did worse than their fathers. Therefore, thou shalt speak all these words unto them; but they will not hearken to thee: thou shalt also call unto them; but they will not answer thee. But thou shalt say unto them,* This is a ***nation that obeyeth not The Voice of The LORD their God,*** *nor receiveth correction:* ***truth is perished, and is cut off from their mouth.*** Jeremiah 7:22-28

2 Kings 10:27 **And they brake down the image of Baal,** and **brake down the house of Baal,** and made it a draught house unto this day.
2 Kings 11:18 And all the people of the land went into *the house of Baal*, and brake it down; his altars and his images brake they in pieces thoroughly, and slew Mattan the priest of Baal before the altars. And the priest appointed officers over the house of The LORD.

"MORE SCRIPTURES ON BRAKE DOWN THE IMAGES AND CUTTING DOWN THE GROVES"

2 Kings 18:4 **He removed the high places, and brake the images, and cut down the groves,** and brake in pieces the brasen serpent that Moses had made: for unto those days the children of Israel did burn incense to it: and he called it Nehushtan.
2 Kings 23:7 **And he brake down the houses of the sodomites,** that were by the house of The LORD, where the women wove hangings for the grove.
2 Kings 23:8 **And he brought all the priests out of the cities of Judah,** and **defiled the high places where the priests had burned incense,** from Geba to Beersheba, and brake down the high places of the gates that were in the entering in of the gate of Joshua the governor of the city, which were on a man's left hand at the gate of the city.
2 Kings 23:12 And the altars that were on the top of the upper chamber of Ahaz, **which the kings of Judah had made, and the altars which Manasseh had made in the two courts of the house of The LORD,** did the **king beat down**, and brake them down from thence, and cast the dust of them into the brook Kidron.
2 Kings 23:14 **And he brake in pieces the images, and cut down the groves, and filled their places with the bones of men.**

174

REVELATION QUIZZING FROM THE OLD TESTAMENT AND THE NEW TESTAMENT

MORE SCRIPTURES ON BRAKE DOWN THE IMAGES AND CUTTING DOWN THE GROVES"

2 Kings 23:15 Moreover the altar that was at Bethel, and the high place which Jeroboam the son of Nebat, who made Israel to sin, had made, both that altar and the high place he brake down, and burned the high place, and stamped it small to powder, and burned the grove.

2 Chronicles 14:3 For he took away the altars of the strange gods, and the high places, and brake down the images, and cut down the groves:

2 Chronicles 23:17 Then all the people went to the house of Baal, and brake it down, and brake his altars and his images in pieces, and slew Mattan the priest of Baal before the altars.

2 Chronicles 31:1 Now when all this was finished, **all Israel that were present went out to the cities of Judah, and brake the images in pieces, and cut down the groves, and threw down the high places and the altars out of all Judah and Benjamin, in Ephraim also and Manasseh, until they had utterly destroyed them all**.

Then all the children of Israel returned, every man to his possession, into their own cities.

2 Chronicles 34:4 **And they brake down the altars of Baalim in his presence; and the images, that were on high above them, he cut down; and the groves, and the carved images, and the molten images, he brake in pieces, and made dust of them, and strowed it upon the graves of them that had sacrificed unto them.**

FOR IT IS NOT POSSIBLE THAT THE BLOOD OF BULLS AND OF GOATS SHOULD TAKE AWAY SINS. Wherefore when **He cometh into the world,** He saith, **Sacrifice and offering Thou** _wouldest not,_ but **a Body hast Thou prepared Me:** In burnt offerings and sacrifices for sin Thou hast had _no_ pleasure. Hebrews 10:4-6

Then said I, Lo, I come (in the volume of the book it is written of Me,) to **do Thy will, O God.** Above when He said, Sacrifice and offering and burnt offerings and offering for sin Thou wouldest not, neither hadst pleasure therein; **which are offered by the law;** _Then said He, Lo, I come to do Thy will,_ O God. He taketh away the first that He may establish the second Hebrews 10:7-9

He took away the first blood covernant and established the SECOND BLOOD COVERNANT that was Yahushua /Jesus body. "Not Ten Commandments" This is the word covernant, read Psalm 78

Luke 22:20 Likewise also the cup after supper, saying, This cup is _the new testament in My blood,_ which is _shed for you._

1 Corinthians 11:25 After the same manner also He took the cup, when He had supped, saying, this cup is the new testament in My blood: this do ye, as oft as ye drink it, in remembrance of me.

"RACHEL AND LEAH"

1. Therefore are they before <u>the throne of God</u>, and <u>serve Him day and night in His temple:</u> and He that sitteth <u>on the throne</u> shall dwell among them. Revelation 7:15
A woman prophetess departed not from the temple and served God day and night with fastings and prayers.
Q. What is the Prophetess name and what tribe did she come from?

2. Is the spelling of Jacob's son Aser spelled different in the Old Testament?

3. How many years did Jacob served Laban for his two daughters, Rachel and Leah?

4. This phrase used in our Churches bulletin many times, "The LORD watch between me and thee, when we are absent one from another.
Q. Is this phrase scriptural, if so who spoke these words?

If yes, please give book, chapter and verse to support your answer.

"RACHEL AND LEAH"

1. Therefore are they before <u>the throne of God</u>, and <u>serve Him day and night in His temple:</u> and He that sitteth <u>on the throne</u> shall dwell among them. Revelation 7:15

A woman prophetess that departed not from the temple, and <u>served God day and night with fastings and prayers</u>.

Q. What is the Prophetess name and what tribe did she come from?

A. *The Prophetess name is Anna from the tribe of Aser.* Luke 2:36 & 38

And there was *one <u>Anna, a prophetess</u>, the daughter of Phanuel*, of the tribe of Aser: she was of a **GREAT AGE, AND HAD LIVED WITH AN HUSBAND SEVEN YEARS FROM HER VIRGINITY;** And <u>she was a **WIDOW**</u> of about fourscore and four years, **which departed not from the temple, but served God with fastings and prayers night and day. And she coming in that instant gave thanks likewise unto <u>The Lord</u>,** and *spake of Him to all them that looked for redemption in Jerusalem.*

2. Is the spelling of Jacob's son Aser spelled different in the Old Testament?

A. Yes. Asher. And Leah said, Happy am I, for <u>the daughters will call me blessed</u>: and she called his name Asher. **See the sons of Jacob/Israel Genesis chapter 49 and the name Asher in 49:20**

3. How many years did Jacob served Laban for his two daughters, Rachel and Leah?

A. Jacob served fourteen years for his two wives. Gen. 31:41

4. This phrase used in our Churches bulletin many times, "*The LORD watch between me and thee*, when we are absent one from another.

Q. Is this phrase scriptural, if so who spoke these words?

If yes, Please give book, chapter and verse to support your answer.

A. Yes. Genesis 31:49. I believe it was Laban.

Please, read 43-55 *And Laban answered and said unto Jacob, **These daughters are my daughters**, and these **children are my children**, and these cattle are my cattle, and all that thou seest is mine: and what can I do this day unto these my daughters, or unto their children which they have born? Now therefore come thou, let us make a covenant, I and thou; and let it be for* **a witness between me and thee.** *And **Jacob took a stone**, and set it up for a pillar. And Jacob said unto his brethren, Gather stones; and they took stones, and made an heap: and they did eat there upon the <u>heap</u>. And Laban called it Jegarsahadutha: but Jacob called it Galeed.* **And Laban said, This heap is a *witness between me and thee this day. Therefore was the name of it called Galeed; And Mizpah; for he said, The LORD watch between me and thee, when we are absent one from another.***

***If thou <u>shalt afflict my daughters</u>, or* if** thou <u>shalt take other wives beside my daughters</u>, no man is with us; see, <u>God is witness betwixt me and thee</u>. *And Laban said to Jacob, Behold <u>this heap</u>, and behold <u>this pillar</u>, which I have cast betwixt me and thee: <u>This heap be witness</u>, and this <u>pillar be witness</u>, that I will not pass over this heap to thee, and that thou shalt not pass over this heap and this pillar unto me, <u>for harm</u>. The God of Abraham, and The God of Nahor, The God of their father, judge betwixt us. And Jacob sware by the <u>**fear**</u> of his father Isaac. Then Jacob offered sacrifice upon the mount, and called his brethren to eat bread: and they did eat bread, and tarried all night in the mount. And early in the morning Laban rose up, and <u>kissed his sons</u> and <u>his daughters, and blessed them</u>: and Laban departed, and returned unto his place.*

"A COMMANDMENT TO BLESS THE PEOPLE"

1. How did The Lord command Aaron and his sons to bless the people?

2. Wherewith the mower filleth not his hand; nor he that bindeth sheaves his bosom.

Neither do they which go by say, _____ we bless you in The Name
of The LORD.

3. I call heaven and earth to record this day against you, that I have set before you life
and death, blessing and cursing: therefore _____ that both thou and
thy seed may live: That thou mayest love The Lord thy God, and that thou mayest
obey His voice, and that thou mayest cleave unto Him: for He is thy life, and the
length of thy days: that thou mayest dwell in the land which The Lord sware unto thy
fathers, to Abraham, to Isaac, and to Jacob, to give them.

4. Who was Abram's father?

B. Who were Abram's brothers?

C. Who was Lot's father?

5. According to scriptures, if we take instruction at the first and do not let it slip will it
preserve our lives?

6. Jesus is the only way to The Father; if we do not believe He is not His Father but He
is the only way to His Father, do we have the truth and life?

"A COMMANDMENT TO BLESS THE PEOPLE"

1. How did The Lord command Aaron and his sons to bless the people?
A. And The LORD spake unto Moses, saying, Speak unto Aaron and unto his sons, saying, On this wise ye <u>shall bless the children of Israel</u>, saying unto them, The LORD bless thee, and keep thee: The LORD make His Face shine upon thee, and be gracious unto thee: The LORD lift up His countenance upon thee, and give thee peace. And they shall put My Name <u>upon the children of Israel, and I will bless them.</u> Numbers 6:20-27

2. Wherewith the mower filleth not his hand; nor he that bindeth sheaves his bosom. Neither do they which go by say, _____ <u>we bless you in The Name of The LORD</u>.
A. The blessing of The LORD be <u>upon</u> you: Psalm 129:7-8

3. I call heaven and earth to record this day against you, that I have set before you life and death, blessing and cursing: therefore_____that both thou and thy seed may live: That thou mayest love The Lord thy God, and that thou mayest obey His voice, and that thou mayest cleave unto Him: for He is thy life, and the length of thy days: that thou mayest dwell in the land which The Lord sware unto thy fathers, to Abraham, to Isaac, and to Jacob, to give them.
A. Choose life. Deuteronomy 30:19 &20

4. Who was Abram's father?
A. Terah. Genesis 11:27

B. Who were Abram's brothers?
A. HARAN AND Nahor. GENESIS 11:27

C. Who was Lot's father?
A. Haran. Genesis 11:27

5. According to scriptures, if we take instruction <u>at the first</u> and do not let it slip will it preserve our lives?
A. Yes.
Take _fast hold of instruction_; let her _not go_; keep her; for she is thy life.
Proverbs 4:13

6. Jesus is the <u>only way to The Father</u>; if we do not believe He is not His Father but He is the only way to His Father, do we have the truth and life?
A. No
Jesus saith unto him, I AM THE way, THE truth, AND THE life: no man cometh <u>unto</u> The Father, <u>but</u> _by Me_. John 14:6

IDENTICAL MESSAGE PREACHED"

1. There were three messages preached by different ones that were the same, from the beginning of their ministry.
Q. What was the message?

B. Who preached the same message?

2. Where in scriptures can we find the first examples of what the kingdom of heaven is like?

3. Where in scriptures can we find two powerful examples, of what the kingdom of Heaven is like?

4. Did you know the kingdom of God, is not teaching one how to be adopted into the family of God?

You answer yes or no.

"IDENTICAL MESSAGE PREACHED"

1. There were three messages preached by different ones that were the same, from the beginning of their ministry.

Q. What was the message?

A. Repent ye for the kingdom of heaven is at hand.

B. Who preached the same message?

A. John, Jesus and He commanded His disciples to go and preach the kingdom of heaven is at hand.
And saying, Repent ye: for the kingdom of heaven is at hand. Matthew 3:2

From that time Jesus began to preach, and to say, Repent: for the kingdom of heaven is at hand. Matthew 4:17

And AS YE GO, PREACH, SAYING, THE KINGDOM OF HEAVEN IS AT HAND. MATTHEW 10:7

2. Where in scriptures can we find the first examples of what the kingdom of heaven is like?
A. MATTHEW 13:31-53

Another parable put He forth unto them, saying, **The kingdom of heaven is like to a grain of mustard seed,** *which a man took, and sowed in his field:*

Another parable spake He unto them; The kingdom of heaven is like unto leaven, which a woman took, and hid in three measures of meal, till the whole was leavened.

Again, the kingdom of heaven is like unto treasure hid in a field; the which when a man hath found, he hideth, and for joy thereof goeth and selleth all that he hath, and buyeth that field.

Again, the kingdom of heaven is like **unto a merchant man, seeking goodly pearls:**

Again, the kingdom of heaven is like unto a net, that was cast into the sea, and gathered of every kind:

Then said He unto them, Therefore every scribe which is instructed unto the kingdom of heaven is like unto a man that is an householder, which bringeth forth out of his treasure things new and old.

3. **Where in scriptures can we find two powerful examples, of what the kingdom of Heaven is like?**
A. Matthew chapter 20 & chapter 25.

4. **Did you know the kingdom of God, is not teaching one how to be adopted into the family of God?**
You answer yes or no. **I say yes!**

Matthew chapter 25 Then shall the kingdom of heaven be likened unto <u>ten virgins</u>, *which took their lamps, and went forth to* meet the bridegroom. *And* **five of them were wise, and five were foolish**. *They that were* **foolish took their lamps**, *and took* <u>no oil</u> *with them:* **But the <u>wise took oil in their vessels with their lamps.</u>** *While the bridegroom tarried, they all* <u>slumbered and slept</u>. *And at midnight there was a cry made, Behold, The Bridegroom cometh; go ye out to meet Him. Then* <u>all those virgins arose</u>, *and* <u>trimmed their lamps</u>. *And* <u>the foolish said unto the wise</u>, <u>Give us of your oil; for our lamps are gone out.</u> *But the wise answered, saying,* <u>Not so; lest there be not enough for us and you: but go ye rather to them that sell, and buy for yourselves.</u> *And* **while they went to buy, the bridegroom came**; *and they that were ready went in with him to the marriage:* and <u>the door was shut</u>. *Afterward came also the other virgins, saying, Lord, Lord, open to us.* **But he answered and said, Verily I say unto you, I <u>know you not</u>.** <u>Watch therefore</u>, *for ye know neither the day nor the hour wherein* **The Son of Man** *cometh.*

"WHAT THE KINGDOM OF HEAVEN IS LIKE" PLEASE READ

For the kingdom of heaven is as a man travelling into a far country, who called his own servants, and delivered unto them his goods. [15]And unto one he gave five talents, to another two, and to another one; to every man according to his several ability; and straightway took his journey. Then he that had received the five talents went and traded with the same, and made them other five talents. And likewise he that had received two, he also <u>gained other two</u>. But he that had received one went and digged in the earth, and <u>hid his lord's money</u>. After a long time the lord of those servants cometh, and reckoneth with them. And so he that had <u>received five talents came and brought other five talents</u>, saying, Lord, thou deliveredst unto me five talents: behold, I have gained beside them five talents <u>more</u>. His lord said unto him, Well done, thou <u>good and faithful</u> servant: thou hast been faithful over a few things, I will make thee <u>ruler over many things</u>: enter thou into <u>the joy of thy lord.</u> He also that had received two talents came and said, <u>Lord, thou deliveredst unto me two talents</u>: behold, I have gained <u>two other talents beside them</u>. His lord said unto him, <u>Well done, good and faithful servant;</u> thou hast been <u>faithful over a few things,</u> I will make thee <u>ruler over many things</u>: enter thou into <u>the joy of thy lord.</u> Then he which had received the one talent came and said, Lord, I knew thee that thou art an hard man, reaping where thou hast not sown, and gathering where thou hast not strawed: And I was afraid, and went and hid thy talent in the earth: lo, there thou hast that is thine. His lord answered and said unto him, Thou wicked and slothful servant, thou knewest that I reap where I sowed not, and gather where I have not strawed: Thou oughtest therefore to have put my money to the exchangers, and then at my coming I should have received mine own with usury. <u>Take therefore the talent from him, and give it unto him which hath ten talents.</u> For unto every one that hath shall be given, and he shall have <u>abundance:</u> but from him that hath not shall <u>be taken away even that which he hath.</u> And cast ye the unprofitable servant into <u>outer darkness</u>: there shall be <u>weeping and gnashing of teeth.</u> 𝒲hen the 𝒮on of man shall come in 𝐻is glory, and all *the holy angels with 𝐻im,* then shall 𝐻e sit upon *the throne of 𝐻is glory:* And before 𝐻im shall be gathered all nations: and *𝐻e shall separate them one from another,* as a shepherd divideth his sheep from the goats: And 𝐻e shall set the sheep on 𝐻is right hand, but *the goats on the left.* **Then shall The King say unto them on <u>His right hand,</u>** Come, ye **blessed of <u>My Father,</u> <u>inherit the kingdom</u> <u>prepared</u> for you from <u>the foundation of the world</u>**: For I was an hungred, and **ye gave Me meat**: I was thirsty, and **ye gave Me drink**: I was a stranger, and *ye took Me in:* Naked, and **ye clothed Me:** I was sick, and **ye visited Me:** I was in prison, and **ye came unto Me**. *Then shall the righteous answer Him, saying, <u>Lord,</u> when saw we thee an hungred, and fed Thee? or thirsty, and gave Thee drink? When saw we thee a stranger, and took Thee in? or naked, and clothed Thee? Or when saw we thee sick, or in prison, and came unto Thee? And The King shall answer and say unto them, 𝒱erily 𝐼 say unto you, 𝐼nasmuch as ye have done it unto one of the least of these 𝑀y brethren, ye have done it unto 𝑀e.* **Then shall He say also unto them on the left hand, Depart from <u>Me, ye cursed</u>,** *<u>into everlasting fire, prepared for the devil and his angels</u>*: For I was an hungred, and ye gave Me **no** meat: I was thirsty, and ye gave Me **no** drink: I was a stranger, and ye took Me **<u>not</u> in:** naked, and ye clothed Me **not**: sick, and in prison, and ye visited Me **not. Then shall they also answer Him, saying, <u>Lord, when saw we Thee an hungred, or athirst, or a stranger, or naked, or sick, or in prison, and did not minister unto Thee?</u>** Then shall He answer them, saying, Verily I say unto you, Inasmuch as ye <u>did it not to one of the least of these</u>, ye did it <u>not </u>to me. **And these <u>shall go</u> away into <u>everlasting punishment</u>: but <u>the righteous into life eternal.</u>**
INASMUCH AS YE HAVE DONE IT UNTO ONE OF THE LEAST OF THESE MY BRETHREN, YE HAVE DONE IT UNTO ME.

"Commanded to Preach and Do"

1. For unto you it is given in the behalf of Christ, not only to believe on Him, **but** also to **suffer for His sake.** Sometimes we suffer for Christ sake, but many times for our mistakes.

Q. We should not; suffer as whom?

2. Christ suffered for us thereby leaving us? _____

3. What did Jesus give His disciples when He called them to Himself, that in order for us to overcome we must have the same?

4. Where did Jesus send His disciples and what did He command them to preach and do?

5. Jesus, confessed I am sent to whom_____

6. Jesus departed into the coasts of Tyre and Sidon and behold, a woman of Canaan came out of the same coasts, and cried unto Him, saying, Have mercy on me, O Lord, thou son of David; my daughter is grievously vexed with a devil.

Q. How did the woman worship Jesus?

"COMMANDED TO PREACH AND DO"

1. For unto you it is given in the behalf of Christ, not only to believe on Him, **but** also to **suffer for His sake;** Philippians 1:29
Sometimes we do suffer for Christ sake but sometimes repeatedly for our mistakes.
Q. We should not; suffer as whom?
A. Murderer, thief, evildoer and busybody in other men's matters.

Yet if any man suffer as a Christian, *let him not be ashamed;* but LET HIM **glorify God on this behalf.** For the *time is come that judgment must begin at the house of God*: AND IF IT FIRST BEGIN AT US, **WHAT SHALL THE END BE OF THEM THAT OBEY NOT** THE GOSPEL OF GOD? But let none of you suffer as a murderer, or as a thief, or as an evildoer, or as a busybody in other men's matters. 1 Peter 4:15-17

2. Christ suffered for us; thereby leaving us what?
A. An example that we should follow is *His steps*.
For even hereunto were ye called: because Christ also suffered for us, leaving us an example, that ye should follow His steps: Who **did no sin,** *neither was guile found in His mouth:* Who, when He was reviled, reviled **not again**; when He suffered, He threatened not; but **committed himself to him** that **judgeth righteously: Who His Own Self bare our sins in His own body on the tree,** that we, being *dead to sins*, should live *unto righteousness*: by whose stripes ye WERE healed. 1 Peter 2:21-24

3. What did Jesus give His disciples when He called them to Himself, that in order for us to overcome; we must have the same?
A. Power against unclean spirits.
He gave them power against unclean spirits, to cast them out, and to heal all manner of sickness and all manner of disease. Matthew 10:1

4. Where did Jesus send His disciples and what did He command them to preach and do?
A. To the *lost sheep of the house of Israel*, to preach the kingdom of heaven is at hand, to heal the sick, to cleanse the lepers, to raise the dead and cast out devils. Freely they had received and freely they were to give.
Matthew 10:6-8 Amen!

5. Jesus, confessed I am sent to whom_____
A. Jesus answered and said, **I am not sent but unto the lost sheep** of the house of Israel **But He answered her not a word.** And His disciples came and besought Him, saying, Send her away; for **she crieth after us. But He answered and said, I am not sent but unto the lost sheep of the house of Israel. Matthew 15:23-24**

"COMMANDED TO PREACH AND DO"

6. Jesus departed into the coasts of Tyre and Sidon and behold, a woman of Canaan came out of the same coasts, and **cried unto Him**, saying, **Have mercy on me, O LORD, thou son of David**; my daughter is grievously vexed with a devil.
Q. How did the woman worship Jesus?

A. She cried unto Him, saying, Have mercy on me, O Lord, she called Him Lord and said help me.

THEN CAME SHE AND WORSHIPPED HIM, SAYING, LORD, HELP ME. Matthew 15:25

"Mystery of the Kingdom"

1. And this gospel of the kingdom shall be preached in all the world for a witness unto all nations; and then shall the end come.

    Q. What did Jesus teach before He made this statement and what gospel was He speaking of?

2. **And the apostles, when they were returned, told Him all that they had done. And He took them, and went aside privately into a desert place belonging to the city called Bethsaida. And the people, when they knew it did what?**

3. Jesus disciples asked Him, saying, what might this parable be?

    Q. How did Jesus respond to their question?

4. **If a seed fall by the way side, the fowls of the air will devour it, if the word fall by the way side, what will happen to it?**

5. **How Can God take away one in Jesus, if he was never in Him?**

6. When Jesus taught them these words "with what measure ye mete, it shall be measured to you: and unto you _____ shall more be given.

    Q Was, Jesus teaching them about finances?

"MYSTERY OF THE KINGDOM"

1. And this gospel of the kingdom shall be preached in all the world for a witness unto all nations; and then shall the end come.

Q. What did Jesus teach before He made this statement and what gospel was he speaking of?

A. HE THAT SHALL <u>ENDURE UNTO THE END</u>, <u>THE SAME</u> SHALL BE SAVED.

But he that shall endure unto the end, the same shall be saved. And this gospel of the kingdom shall be preached in all the world for a witness unto all nations; and then shall the end come.
Matthew 24:13-14

2. And the apostles, when they were returned, told Him all that they had done. And He took them, and went aside <u>privately into a desert place</u> belonging to the city called Bethsaida. And the people, when they knew it did what?

A. They followed Him.

They **FOLLOWED** Him **AND *HE RECEIVED*** them, and spake unto them of ***the kingdom of God, and healed them that had need of healing.*** Luke 9:10-11

3. Jesus disciples asked Him, saying, what might this parable be?

Q. How did Jesus respond to their question?

A. And He said, **Unto you it is given to know *the mysteries of the kingdom of God*: BUT to others in parables; *that seeing* they <u>might not see,</u> and hearing they might not understand. Luke 8:9-10**

"Quizzing #62 focused on the kingdom of heaven and what the kingdom was like"

"What the kingdom of God is like" Study Mark Chapter 4 and Luke chapter 8 for a better revelation and understanding.

Mark 4:1 &2 And He began again to teach by the sea side: and there was <u>gathered unto Him a great multitude</u>, so that he entered into a ship, and sat in the sea; and the whole multitude was by the sea on the land. ²*And He taught them many <u>things by parables</u>*, and said unto them in **HIS DOCTRINE,**

If we did not understand the meaning, or the word doctrine, this should clarify its meaning; doctrine is a teaching not just the death, burial and resurrection of Yahushua Messiah/Jesus Christ.

Another translation says, And He taught them many things in **parables illustrations or comparisons** *and in* **His teaching** *He said to them:)*

4. If a seed fall by the way side, the fowls of the air will devour it, if the word fall by the way side, what will happen to it?

A. It will not prosper it will withered away.

Hearken; Behold, there went out a <u>sower to sow</u>: And it came to pass, as he sowed, some fell by the way side, and the fowls of the air came and devoured it up. And some fell on stony ground, where it had not much earth; and immediately it sprang up, because it had no depth of earth:

187

"MYSTERY OF THE KINGDOM"

My Father is The Husbandman. Every branch in Me that beareth not fruit He taketh away: *and every branch that beareth fruit, He purgeth it, that it may bring forth more fruit.)*

Remember, In Me not out of Me. John 15:1-2
Yahweh is The Husbandman, Yahushua is The Vine and we are the branches.
Yahweh/God is the Head of the Messiah/Christ and Yahushua/Jesus is the Head of every man as said in,
1 Corinthians 11:3 But I would have you know, that **the head of every man is Christ**; and **the head of the woman** is the **man**; and the head of **Christ is God.**

But when the sun was up, it **was scorched**; and because it had **no root**, it **withered away**. And some fell among thorns, and the thorns grew up, and **choked it,** and it **yielded no fruit**. And other *fell on good ground, and did yield fruit that sprang up and increased; and brought forth,* some thirty, and some sixty, and some an hundred. Mark 4:3-4:8

5. How Can God take away one in Jesus, if he was never in Him?
A. Impossible He cannot.

Mark 4:9 And He said unto them, *he that hath ears to hear,* **let him hear.** 10And when He was alone, they that were about Him with the **twelve asked of Him the parable.** 11And He said unto them, **Unto you it is given to know the mystery of the kingdom** of God: **but** *unto them that are without, all these things* ***at any time they should be converted, and their sins should be forgiven them***. 13And He said unto them, **Know ye not this parable**? and how then will ye **know all parables?** 14The *are done in parables:* 12*That seeing they may see, and not perceive; and hearing they may hear, and not understand;*
14 *The sower soweth the word.* 15And these are they by **the way side, WHERE THE WORD IS SOWN; BUT** when they **have heard, Satan cometh immediately, AND TAKETH AWAY THE WORD** *THAT WAS SOWN* **IN THEIR HEARTS.**

Here we can see the word was in their hearts but Satan took it away from them remember, he came for that purpose to takeaway.

16 And these are they likewise which are sown on stony ground; who, when, *they have heard the word immediately receive it with gladness;* 17And have *no root in themselves, and so endure but for a time:* afterward, when *affliction or persecution* ariseth *for the word's sake,* immediately they are offended.

REMEMBER, AND BLESSED IS HE, WHOSOEVER SHALL NOT BE OFFENDED IN ME.
Matthew 11:6 & Luke 7:23

"MYSTERY OF THE KINGDOM"

18 And these are they which are sown among thorns; such as hear the word, 19And the cares of this world, and the deceitfulness of riches, and the lusts of other things entering in, choke the word, and it *becometh unfruitful.*

20And these are they which are sown on *good ground; such as hear the word, and receive it, and bring forth fruit, some thirtyfold, some sixty, and some an hundred.*

21And He said unto them, Is a candle brought to be put under a bushel, or under a bed? and not to be set on a candlestick? 22 For there is nothing hid, which shall not be manifested; neither was any thing kept secret, but that it should come abroad. 23IF ANY MAN HAVE EARS TO HEAR, let him hear.

6. When Jesus taught them these words "with what measure ye mete, it shall be measured to you: and unto you _____ shall more be given.

Q Was, Jesus teaching them about finances?

A. No

Jesus was teaching them to take heed/pay attention or take notice to what they were hearing.

AND HE SAID UNTO THEM, Take heed what ye hear: WITH WHAT MEASURE YE METE, IT SHALL BE MEASURED TO YOU: AND UNTO you that hear SHALL MORE BE GIVEN.

For he that hath, to him shall be given: and he that hath NOT, FROM HIM SHALL BE TAKEN EVEN THAT WHICH HE HATH. Mark 4:24 & 25

Here is wisdom again; Satan cannot take away what Jesus never had. "The Truth is in the Word"

Remember, And He said unto them that stood by, Take from him the pound, and give it to him that hath ten pounds. For I say unto you, That unto every one which hath shall be given; and from him that hath not, even that he hath shall be TAKEN AWAY FROM HIM. 27But those mine enemies, which would not that I should reign over them, bring hither, and slay them before Me. Luke 19:24-27

Mark 4:26 And He said, So is the kingdom of God, as if a man should cast seed into the ground; And should sleep, and rise night and day, and the seed should spring and grow up, he knoweth not how. 28For the earth bringeth forth fruit of herself; first the blade, then the ear, after that the full corn in the ear. 29But when the fruit is brought forth, immediately he putteth in the sickle, because the harvest is come. 30And He said, Whereunto shall we liken the kingdom of God? or with what comparison shall we compare it? 31It is like a grain of mustard seed, which, when it is sown in the earth, is LESS than all the seeds that be in the earth: 32But when it is sown, it groweth up, and becometh greater than all herbs, and shooteth out great branches; so that the fowls of the air may lodge under the shadow of it. 29But when the fruit is brought forth, immediately he putteth in the sickle, because the *harvest is come.*

We should be able to see and understand that life is a process, the blade, the ear, after that the full corn in the ear.

"Scriptures on the process of time"

Genesis 4:3 And in process of time it came to pass . . . , Genesis 38:12 And in process of time . . .

Exodus 2:23 And it came to pass in process of time, that the king of Egypt died..

Judges 11:4 And it came to pass in process of time, that the children of Ammon made war against Israel. 2 Chronicles 21:19 And it came to pass, that in process of time, after the end of two years, his bowels fell out by reason of his sickness: so he died of sore diseases..)

"REVELATION AND MANIFESTATION QUIZ"

1. Who spoke these words? "Not by <u>might</u>, nor by <u>power,</u> but by <u>My Spirit?</u>

2. Then the angel that talked with me answered and said unto me, Knowest thou not what these be? And I said, No, <u>my lord</u>.
Q. How did the angel his lord answer this question?

3. The Branch, is this another Name for Yahushua The Messiah/The Lord Jesus Christ?

REVELATION AND MANIFESTATION QUIZ

1. Who spoke these words? "Not by <u>might</u>, nor by <u>power,</u> but by <u>My Spirit?</u>

A. The LORD of hosts

The LORD is The Angel/Yahushua and He is The Son of God, the things that He did were not **by His <u>might</u> nor by His <u>power</u> but by The Spirit that was in Him.**

The Spirit of His Father, Yahweh The Living and everlasting Father.

Then answered Jesus and said unto them, Verily, verily, I say unto you, **The Son can do nothing of Himself,** but what He *seeth The Father do:* for what *things soever He doeth,* these also *DOETH THE SON LIKEWISE.* John 5:19

<u>YAHUSHUA/JESUS</u> the Messiah/Christ is the **power** of God, and **the wisdom** of God.

1 Corinthians 1:24

2. Then <u>the angel that talked with me</u> answered and said unto me, Knowest thou not what these be? And I said, No, <u>my lord.</u>

Q. How did the <u>ANGEL HIS LORD</u> answer this question?

A. Then he answered and spake unto me, saying, THIS IS THE <u>WORD OF</u> THE LORD unto Zerubbabel, saying, **Not by might, nor by power, but by My Spirit, saith The LORD of hosts** Zechariah 4:5-7

Zechariah 2:8-11 and verse 13. **For thus saith The LORD of hosts;** After *THE GLORY HATH HE SENT ME* unto **the nations** which spoiled you: **for he that toucheth you toucheth the apple of His eye.** [9]**For, behold, I will shake Mine hand upon them, and they shall be a spoil to their servants: and ye <u>shall know</u> that The LORD of hosts hath sent Me.** [10]Sing and rejoice, O daughter of Zion: for, lo, I come, and I will dwell in the midst of thee, saith The LORD. [11]**And many nations shall be joined to The LORD in that day,** and **shall** *be My people:* and **I will dwell in the midst of thee,** and thou **shalt know that The LORD of hosts hath sent Me unto thee.**[13]Be silent, O all flesh, BEFORE THE LORD: FOR *He is raised up out of His holy habitation*.

And he shewed me *Joshua the high priest standing before* The angel of The LORD, *and Satan standing at his right hand to resist him.* [2]And **The LORD said unto** Satan, The LORD rebuke thee, O Satan; EVEN THE LORD THAT HATH CHOSEN JERUSALEM REBUKE THEE: *is not this a brand plucked out of the fire? Zechariah 3:1-2*

IF WE READ CHAPTER 1-8 WE SHOULD BE ABLE TO SEE THIS IS YAHUSHUA/THE SON OF GOD

Footnotes from Amplified Bible:

Zechariah 1:8 The Angel of the Lord of Zech. 1:11.

Zechariah 1:9 The interpreting angel, mentioned in Zech. 1:9, 13-14; 2:3; 4:1, 4-5; 5:5, 10; 6:4-5, not to be confused with the Man of Zech. 1:8 or the Angel of the Lord of Zech. 1:11. Zechariah 1:11 **That the Angel of the Lord is an uncreated angel distinguished from other angels,** *and in many places identified with the Lord God, is* **undeniable.** *On the other hand, there are passages in which* He seems to be distinguished <u>from</u> God the Father.

Praise you Yahweh in The Name of your Son Yahushua The Messiah, for revealing to me that this Angel is Your Son before I read this information. Read John 14:21 . . . I will love him, and will *manifest myself* to him.

"REVELATION AND MANIFESTATION QUIZ"

The simplest way of reconciling THESE TWO CLASSES IS TO ADOPT THE OLD VIEW THAT THIS ANGEL IS CHRIST, the second person of The Godhead, EVEN At that early period appearing as The Revealer of The Father (Johan P. Lange, A Commentary). See also footnote on Gen. 16:7.

I Prophetess Neal would say The Angel throughout Genesis 16, but in this verse especially 16:13. And she called The Name of The LORD that spake unto her, Thou God seest me: for she said, Have I also here looked after him that seeth me?

If He answered her question; it is not, recorded in scripture. Read Genesis Chapter 28.

Genesis 32:24-30 24And Jacob was left alone; and there wrestled a man with him until the breaking of the day. 25AND WHEN HE SAW THAT HE PREVAILED NOT AGAINST HIM, he touched the hollow of his thigh; and the hollow of Jacob's thigh was out of joint, as he wrestled with him. 26And he said, Let me go, for the day breaketh. And he said, I will not let thee go, except thou bless me.27And he said unto him, What is thy name? And he said, Jacob. 28AND HE SAID, THY NAME SHALL BE CALLED NO MORE JACOB, BUT ISRAEL: FOR AS A PRINCE HAST THOU POWER WITH GOD AND WITH MEN, AND HAST PREVAILED. 29And Jacob asked him, and said, TELL ME, I PRAY THEE, THY NAME. And he said, Wherefore is it that thou dost ask after my name? And he blessed him there. 30And Jacob called the name of the place Peniel: for I have seen God face to face, and my life is preserved.

This is the third one as far as I can see asked for His name; here it says he blessed him there. Did He make himself known to Jacob? I BELIEVE He did.

Read John chapter 5 and focus on 5:19-47.

John 1:18 No man hath seen God at any time, the only begotten Son, which is in the bosom of The Father, He hath declared Him.

John 6:46 Not that any man hath seen The Father, save He which is of God, He hath seen The Father. Read John 6:45-47

1 John 4:12 No man hath seen God at any time. If we love one another, God dwelleth in us, and His love is perfected in us. Read 1 John 4:11-13

1 John 4:20 If a man say, I love God, AND hateth his brother, he is a liar: for he that loveth not his brother whom he hath seen, how can he love God whom he hath not seen?

3. The Branch, is this another Name for YahushuaThe Messiah/ The Lord Jesus Christ?

A. Yes

And speak unto him, saying, Thus speaketh The LORD of hosts, saying, Behold The Man whose Name is The BRANCH; and He shall grow up out of His place, and He shall build the temple of The LORD: Zechariah 6:12

REVELATION AND MANIFESTATION QUIZ

And there shall come forth **a rod out of the stem of Jesse,** and **a Branch shall grow out of his roots**: Isaiah 11:1

Behold, the days come, saith The LORD, **that I will raise unto David a righteous Branch,** and **A KING SHALL REIGN AND PROSPER, AND SHALL EXECUTE JUDGMENT AND JUSTICE IN THE EARTH.** Jeremiah 23:5

In those days, and at that time, will I cause **THE BRANCH OF RIGHTEOUSNESS TO GROW UP UNTO DAVID; AND HE SHALL EXECUTE JUDGMENT AND RIGHTEOUSNESS IN THE LAND.**
Jeremiah 33:15

Hear now, O Joshua the high priest, thou, and thy fellows that sit before thee: for they are men wondered at: for, behold, **I will bring forth My servant The BRANCH**. Zechariah 3:8

SOMETIME, BOTH YAHWEH AND YAHSUHUA ARE CALL GOD AND LORD. Please, notice LORD and Lord again.

The LORD said unto *My Lord,* Sit thou at My right hand, until I make Thine enemies Thy footstool. Psalm 110:1

The LORD said unto *My Lord,* Sit thou on My right hand, till I make Thine enemies Thy footstool? Matthew 22:44

And David himself saith in the book of Psalms, The LORD said unto *My Lord,* Sit Thou on My right hand, [43] Till I make Thine enemies Thy footstool.[44] David therefore calleth **Him Lord, how is He then his son?** [45] **Then in the audience of all the people He said unto His disciples, Luke 20:42-44**

For David is *not ascended into the heavens*: but he saith himself, **THE LORD** said unto *My Lord,* Sit thou on My right hand, Until I make Thy foes Thy footstool.

Therefore let all the house of Israel know assuredly, that God hath made The same Jesus, whom ye have crucified, both Lord and Christ. Acts 2:34-36

"Remember, His disciples' confession"

His disciples said unto him, Lo, now speakest thou **plainly,** and **speakest no proverb. Now are we sure** that thou **knowest all things,** and needest not that any man should ask thee: by **THIS WE BELIEVE** *that thou* **camest forth from God**.[31] *JESUS ANSWERED THEM, DO YE NOW BELIEVE?* John 16:29-31

"RIGHTLY DIVIDING THE WORD OF TRUTH"

1. And the children of Israel did evil again in the sight of The LORD; and The LORD delivered them into the hand of the Philistines forty years. And there was a certain man of Zorah, of the family of the Danites, whose name was Manoah; and his wife was barren, and bare not. And The Angel of The LORD appeared unto the woman, and said unto her, Behold now, thou art barren, and bearest not: but thou shalt conceive, and bear a son.
Q. What instructions did The Angel Give Her?

Answer found in the book of Judges

2. Did The Angel appear first to Manoah or his wife?

Answer found in the book of Judges

3. Who did Manoah believe The Angel was?

Answer found in the book of Judges

4. Who do you believe this Angel was?

"RIGHTLY DIVIDING THE WORD OF TRUTH"

1. And the children of Israel did evil again in the sight of The LORD; and The LORD delivered them into the hand of the Philistines forty years. And there was a certain man of Zorah, of the family of the Danites, whose name was Manoah; and his wife was barren, and bare not. And The Angel of The LORD appeared unto the woman, and said unto her, Behold now, thou art barren, and bearest not: but thou shalt conceive, and bear a son.

Q. What instructions did The Angel Give Her?

A. **Drink not wine nor strong drink,** and **eat not any unclean thing**: For, lo, thou shalt conceive, and bear a son; and no razor shall come on his head: for the child shall be **a Nazarite** unto **God from the womb**: and **he shall begin to deliver Israel** out of the hand of the Philistines. Judges 13:4 & 5

2. Did The Angel appear first to Manoah or his wife?

A. The Angel appeared unto the woman twice before He appeared to Manoah. Then Manoah intreated The LORD, and said, **O my Lord**, let the man of God which thou didst send come again unto us, and **teach us what we shall do unto the child that shall be born.** And God hearkened to the voice of Manoah; and The Angel of God came again unto the woman as she sat in the field: but Manoah her husband was not with her. And the woman made haste, and ran, and shewed her husband, and said unto him, Behold, the man hath appeared unto me, that came unto me the other day. And Manoah arose, and **went after his wife,** and **came to the man, and said unto him, Art thou the man that spakest unto the woman?** And **He said I am.** 12And Manoah said, Now *let thy words come to pass. How shall we order the child, and how shall we do unto him?* And The Angel of The LORD said *unto Manoah,* OF ALL THAT *I SAID UNTO THE WOMAN let her beware. She may not eat of any thing that cometh of the vine,* neither let her drink wine or strong drink, nor *eat any unclean thing*: **all that I commanded** her LET HER OBSERVE. Judges13:8-14 . . . Remember, Matthew 28:20 TEACHING *them* to **OBSERVE ALL THINGS whatsoever** I **have commanded you:** and, lo, *I am with you always,* **even unto the end of the world.** Amen.

And Manoah said unto **The Angel** of The LORD, I pray thee, **let us detain thee,** until we shall have made *ready a kid for Thee.* 13:15 **(This verse reminds me of Genesis chapter 18 &19)**

3. Who did Manoah believe The Angel was?

A. **God.** He believed that He had SEEN THE FACE OF GOD . . . FOR HE SAID; we shall surely die, because we have seen God. Judges 13:22 AND THE ANGEL OF THE LORD said unto Manoah, Though thou **DETAIN ME**, I *will* **not** *eat of thy bread: and if thou wilt offer a burnt offering,* THOU MUST OFFER IT UNTO THE LORD. For Manoah knew **not** that He WAS AN ANGEL OF THE LORD. And Manoah said unto *The Angel of The LORD*, WHAT IS THY NAME, THAT WHEN THY SAYINGS COME TO PASS WE MAY DO THEE HONOUR?

195

"RIGHTLY DIVIDING THE WORD OF TRUTH"

AND THE <u>ANGEL</u> OF THE LORD SAID UNTO HIM, *WHY ASKEST THOU THUS AFTER MY NAME*, SEEING IT IS SECRET?

It is the glory of God to conceal a thing; but the honour of kings is to search out a matter.
Proverbs 25:2

THE SECRET THINGS BELONG UNTO THE LORD OUR GOD; but those things which are revealed belong unto us and to our children FOR EVER, that we *may do all the words of this law*. Deuteronomy 29:29

[5] That your faith **SHOULD NOT STAND IN THE WISDOM OF MEN,** but **in the power of God.** [6] Howbeit we **SPEAK WISDOM AMONG THEM THAT ARE perfect**: yet not the wisdom of this world, nor of the princes of this world, that come to <u>nought</u>: [7] **But we speak the wisdom of God in a mystery**, even the **hidden wisdom**, *which God ordained before the world unto our glory:* [8] **Which none of the princes of this world knew: for had they <u>known</u> it, they would not have <u>CRUCIFIED</u> the Lord of glory.** [9] But as it is written, Eye hath not seen, nor ear heard, neither have entered into the heart of man, the things which God hath prepared for them that love him. 1 Corinthians 2:5-9

CONTINUING IN JUDGES 13

So Manoah took a kid with a meat offering, and *offered it upon a rock* unto *The LORD*: and The Angel did wonderously; and Manoah and his wife <u>looked on</u>. For it came to pass, when the <u>flame went up toward heaven from off the altar</u>, that <u>The Angel of The LORD ascended in the flame of the altar</u>. And Manoah and his wife looked on it, and <u>fell on their faces to the ground.</u> But <u>The Angel of The LORD did no more appear to Manoah and to his wife.</u> Then Manoah *knew* **THAT HE WAS AN <u>ANGEL</u> OF THE LORD**. [22] *And Manoah* said unto his wife, **WE SHALL <u>SURELY DIE</u>, BECAUSE WE HAVE <u>SEEN GOD</u>**. [23] But his wife said unto him, *If The LORD were <u>pleased to kill us</u>, He would not have <u>received a burnt offering</u> and a <u>meat offering at our hands</u>, neither would He have <u>shewed us all these things</u>, nor would as at this time have told us such things as these.*

4. Who do you believe this Angel was?
A. I SAY AGAIN, HE IS YAHUSHUA THE MESSIAH THE SON OF GOD.
Exodus 33:2 **AND I WILL SEND AN ANGEL** before thee . . .
Exodus 23:20 Behold, **I send an Angel before thee,** to **keep thee in the way**, and to *bring thee into the place which I have prepared.*
Exodus 23:23 **FOR MINE ANGEL SHALL GO BEFORE THEE,** and bring thee in unto the Amorites, and the Hittites, and the Perizzites, and the Canaanites, the Hivites, and the Jebusites: and **I will cut them off.**

"RIGHTLY DIVIDING THE WORD OF TRUTH"

Daniel 2:22 HE REVEALETH THE <u>DEEP AND SECRET THINGS</u>: **He knoweth what is in the darkness, and the light dwelleth with Him.**

Matthew 13:35 THAT IT MIGHT BE FULFILLED WHICH WAS SPOKEN BY THE PROPHET, SAYING, I WILL OPEN MY MOUTH IN PARABLES; I WILL UTTER THINGS WHICH HAVE BEEN **kept secret** from *the foundation of the world.*

Deuteronomy 29:29 THE SECRET THINGS BELONG UNTO THE LORD OUR GOD: **but those things which are revealed belong unto us and to our children** <u>FOR EVER.</u> THAT WE MAY DO ALL THE WORDS OF THIS LAW.

Genesis 24:40 **And He said unto me, The LORD, before <u>whom I walk,</u> will <u>send His angel</u> with thee, and prosper thy way; and thou shalt take a wife for my son of my kindred, and of my father's house:**

Faith cometh by hearing and hearing, the word of God, therefore, these are added again. These scriptures were in last week quizzing but they are references to this one also.

The Angel throughout Genesis chapter 16 and in this verse 16:13 especially. And she called The Name of The LORD that spake unto her, Thou God seest me: for she said, *Have I also here looked after him that seeth me?*

He did not answer her. Read Gen. Chapter 28.

Genesis 32:24-30, 24And Jacob was left alone; and there wrestled a man with him until the breaking of the day. ²⁵And when he saw that he prevailed not against him, he touched the hollow of his thigh; and the hollow of Jacob's thigh was out of joint, as he wrestled with him. ²⁶And he said, Let me go, for the day breaketh. And he said, I will not let thee go, except thou bless me.²⁷And he said unto him, What is thy name? And he said, Jacob. ²⁸And he said, Thy name shall be called no more Jacob, but Israel: for as a prince hast thou power with God and with men, and hast prevailed. ²⁹And Jacob asked him, and said, Tell me, I pray thee, thy name. And he said, Wherefore is it that thou dost ask after my name? And he blessed him there. ³⁰And Jacob called the name of the place Peniel: for I have seen God face to face, and my life is preserved.

Read John chapter 5 and focus on 5:19-47.

John 1:18 No man hath seen God at any time, the only begotten Son, which is in the bosom of The Father, he hath declared Him.

John 6:46 Not that any man hath seen The Father, save He which is of God, He hath seen The John 6:45-47

1 John 4:12 No man hath seen God at any time. If we love one another, God dwelleth in us, and His love is perfected in us. Read 1 John 4:11-13

"After The Holy Ghost Come upon You"

1. The people <u>pressed</u> upon Jesus to <u>hear The Word of God</u> as He stood by the lake of Gennesaret, there were two ships standing by the lake, the fishermen were gone out of the ships and Jesus entered into one of the ships.
Q. Who ship did Jesus enter into?

2. Jesus said unto His disciples, it is not for you to know the times or the seasons, which The Father hath put in <u>His own power.</u> But ye shall <u>receive power,</u> <u>after that The Holy Ghost is come upon you.</u>
Q. What did Jesus teach would happen after The Holy Ghost came upon them?

3. There was a man taken with palsy, when Jesus saw their faith, He said unto him, Man, <u>thy sins</u> are <u>forgiven thee</u>, the scribes and the Pharisees began to reason, saying, Who is this which speaketh blasphemies?
Q Why did the scribes and Pharisees believe the words of Jesus were blaspheming?

"AFTER THE HOLY GHOST COME UPON YOU"

1. The people <u>pressed</u> upon Jesus to <u>hear The Word of God</u> as He stood by the lake of Gennesaret, there were two ships standing by the lake, the fishermen were gone out of the ships and Jesus entered into one of the ships.

Q. Who ship did Jesus enter into?

A. *Jesus entered into Simon's ship.* Luke 5:3

2. Jesus said unto His disciples, it is not for you to know the times or the seasons, which The Father hath put in <u>His own power.</u> But ye shall <u>receive power,</u> <u>after that The Holy Ghost is come upon you.</u>

Q. What did Jesus teach would happen after The Holy Ghost came upon them?

A. YE SHALL BE WITNESSES UNTO ME . . .

<u>both in Jerusalem, and in all Judaea, and in Samaria, and unto the uttermost part of the earth</u>. Acts 1:7&8

But when The Comforter is come, **whom <u>I will send</u> unto you from The Father, <u>even</u> The Spirit of <u>truth,</u>** *which proceedeth from The Father,* <u>*HE SHALL TESTIFY OF ME:*</u> *And ye also shall <u>bear witness,</u> because ye have been with Me from the beginning.* John 15:26-27

3. There was a man taken with palsy, when Jesus saw their faith, He said unto him, Man, <u>thy sins</u> are <u>forgiven thee</u>, the scribes and the Pharisees began to reason, saying, *Who is this which speaketh blasphemies?*

Q Why did the scribes and Pharisees believe the words of Jesus were blaspheming?

A. THEY BELIEVED THAT ONLY GOD COULD FORGIVE SINS. WHO CAN FORGIVE SINS, BUT GOD ALONE THEY SAID.

But when Jesus perceived their thoughts, He answering said unto them, **What reason ye in your hearts?** Whether is easier, to say, **Thy sins be forgiven thee**; or to say, **Rise up and walk**? But that **ye <u>may know</u>** that **The Son of Man hath <u>power</u> upon earth to <u>forgive sins,</u>** (he said unto the sick of the palsy,) I say unto thee, *Arise, and take up thy couch, and go into thine house.* **Luke 5:21&24**

"REJECTING THE COUNSEL OF GOD"

1. When the people complained, it displeased The LORD: and The LORD heard it; and His anger was kindled; and the fire of The LORD burnt among them, and consumed them that were in the uttermost parts of the camp. The people cried unto Moses; and when Moses prayed unto The LORD, the fire was quenched. And the mixt multitude that was among them fell a lusting: and the children of Israel also wept again, and said, Who shall give us flesh to eat?

After the children of Israel came out of Egypt, they turned back to Egypt in their hearts; did they remember the hard bondage or something else?

Q. What did the children of Israel remember?

2. Manna was as coriander seed; the people would gather and ground it in mills or beat it in a mortar and bake and made cakes of it.

What did Manna taste like?

3. If we teach baptism does not save anyone, is this scriptural, additional are we rejecting the counsel of God just like the Pharisees and the lawyers?

4. Why should, we be baptized?

"Rejecting the Counsel of God"

1. When the people complained, it displeased The LORD: and The LORD heard it; and His anger was kindled; and the fire of The LORD burnt among them, and consumed them that were in the uttermost parts of the camp. The people cried unto Moses; and when Moses prayed unto The LORD, the fire was quenched. And the mixt multitude that was among them fell a lusting: and the children of Israel also wept again, and said, Who shall give us flesh to eat?

After the children of Israel came out of Egypt, they turned back to Egypt in their hearts; did they remember the hard bondage or something else?

Q. What did the children of Israel remember?

A. They remembered *the fish they had freely consumed in Egypt, the cucumbers, the melons, the leeks, the onions, and the garlick.* Numbers 11:4&5

2. Manna was as coriander seed; the people would gather and ground it in mills or beat it in a mortar and bake and made cakes of it.

Q. What did Manna taste like?

A. *Manna had the taste of fresh oil.* Numbers 11:8 3

3. If we teach baptism does not save anyone, is this scriptural, additional are we rejecting the counsel of God just like the Pharisees and the lawyers?

A. THIS IS NOT BIBLICAL AND WE ARE REJECTING THE COUNSEL OF GOD, as did the **Pharisees and the lawyers.**

And all the people that heard Him, and the publicans, **justified God**, BEING BAPTIZED WITH THE BAPTISM OF JOHN. BUT the <u>Pharisees</u> and <u>lawyers</u> <u>rejected the counsel of God against themselves</u>, being <u>not</u> baptized of him. Luke 7:29-30

4. Why should, we be baptized?

A. BECAUSE, WE ARE TO FULFILL ALL RIGHTEOUSNESS AS JESUS DID AND TAUGHT IN MATTHEW CHAPTER 3.

IF WE ARE, BAPTIZED WE ARE DYING TO THE OLD AND BECOMING A NEW MAN.

Why does many believe baptism is not a requiremen be, saved?

Could it be we do not have a perfect/complete understanding of this word saved? The ungodly is justified by faith; once he is justified, there are other requiements.

Examples, If I am baptized, I am saved from being <u>**not**</u>-baptized, <u>if</u> I stop lying, then I am saved from lying, <u>If</u> I <u>was</u> in a car accident but not harmed, I <u>was</u> saved from injury but this does not promise me it will never happen again and the next time I could lose my life. *You answer right or wrong.*

However, it does not change that I was, <u>saved the first time</u> but not the <u>last time.</u>

Then cometh Jesus from Galilee to Jordan unto John, to **be baptized of him.** But John forbad Him, saying, I have **need to be baptized of Thee**, and comest thou to me? <u>**Remember, John baptized with water which is man's baptism**</u> *BUT Jesus baptizes with The Holy Ghost)* And Jesus answering said unto him, Suffer it to **be so now: <u>for thus it becometh us to fulfil all righteousness.</u> Then he suffered Him. And**

"REJECTING THE COUNSEL OF GOD"

Jesus, when He was baptized, went up straightway <u>out of the</u> water: and, lo, the heavens were opened unto Him, and He SAW THE SPIRIT OF GOD **descending like a dove,** and *<u>LIGHTING UPON HIM</u>:* AND **lo A voice <u>from heaven</u>, saying,** This is My beloved Son, in whom I am well pleased. *Please, read Matthew 3:13-18.*

When we are baptized this is pleasing in God sight because, **WE HAVE FULFILL HIS RIGHTEOUSNESS.** *We should be able to see and understand baptism was a requirement in the book of Exodus, when the people were <u>baptized unto Moses</u> as said in* 1 Corinthians 10:1-5, *please read this chapter.*

Moreover, brethren, I would not that ye should be ignorant, how that all our fathers were under the cloud, and all passed through the sea; And were all baptized unto Moses in the cloud and in the sea; And did all eat the *same spiritual meat, And did all drink the same spiritual drink:* for they drank of that Spiritual Rock that followed them: and that Rock *was <u>Christ</u>* But with many of them <u>God was not well pleased</u>: for they were overthrown in the wilderness.

If we could not see before that Christ <u>was</u> that rock that <u>follow them,</u> here it is, Exodus 14:19 And The **Angel of God**, which <u>went</u> **before the camp** of Israel, **removed and went behind** <u>them;</u> and the *pillar of the cloud <u>went from before their face,</u> and <u>stood behind</u>* them.

In this verse, we can see it was The Lord: *And The <u>LORD went before them</u> by day in a pillar of a cloud, to <u>lead them the way</u>; and by night <u>in a pillar of fire</u>, to give them light; to go by day and night:* **Exodus 13:21**

Fear and dread shall fall upon them; by the greatness of thine arm they shall be as still as a stone; till <u>Thy people pass over</u>, O LORD, till the people pass over, which **THOU HAST PURCHASED.** Exodus 15:16

MORE SCRIPTURES ON BAPTISM:

Jesus answered, Verily, verily, I say unto thee, Except a man be born of <u>water</u> and of <u>the</u> Spirit, he cannot enter **<u>into the</u> <u>kingdom of God.</u>** John 3:5

He that <u>believeth</u> and is baptized SHALL BE SAVED; BUT **he that *<u>BELIEVETH NOT SHALL BE DAMNED.</u>*** Mark 16:16

For it is better, **<u>if</u>** the <u>will</u> of God be so, **that ye suffer for well doing, than for evil doing.** For Christ also hath once suffered for sins, the just for the unjust, that He might bring us to God, **being put to death in the flesh, but quickened by the Spirit:** By which also He went and preached unto the <u>spirits</u> in prison;

"REJECTING THE COUNSEL OF GOD"

Which sometime were <u>disobedient,</u> when once the <u>longsuffering of God waited</u> in the days of Noah, while the ark was a <u>preparing</u>, wherein few, that is, EIGHT SOULS WERE SAVED BY WATER. *The <u>like figure</u> whereunto even baptism doth also now save us (not the putting away of the filth of the flesh, but the answer of a good conscience **toward God**,) by the resurrection of Jesus Christ: 1 Peter 3:17-21*

Having a <u>good conscience</u>; that, whereas they <u>speak evil of you</u>, as of <u>evildoers,</u> they may be ashamed that falsely accuse your <u>good conversation in Christ</u>. 1 Peter 3:6.
Go ye therefore, and *teach all nations, baptizing them in The Name of The Father, and of The Son, and of The Holy Ghost.* Matthew 28:19
*And as they went on their way, they came unto **A CERTAIN <u>WATER:</u>** and the eunuch said, **SEE, HERE IS <u>WATER:</u> WHAT DOTH HINDER ME TO BE BAPTIZED?** And Philip said, If thou believest with all thine heart, thou mayest. And he answered and said, <u>I believe that Jesus Christ is The Son of God</u>.* And he commanded the chariot to stand still: and **they went down both into the water,** both Philip and the eunuch; and HE BAPTIZED HIM. *Acts 8: 36 & 38*
In whom also ye are circumcised with the circumcision <u>made without hands</u>, in putting <u>off</u> the body of the <u>sins</u> of <u>the flesh</u> by the circumcision of Christ: BURIED WITH HIM IN BAPTISM, Colossians 2:11-13
If ye then be *<u>risen</u>* with Christ, <u>SEEK</u> THOSE <u>THINGS</u> which <u>are</u> above, where Christ *<u>sitteth</u>* on the right hand of God. Colossians 3:1 1
Else what <u>shall they do</u> which are BAPTIZED FOR THE DEAD, IF THE DEAD RISE NOT at all? why are they then BAPTIZED FOR THE DEAD? 1 Corinthians 15:29
Know ye not, that <u>so many</u> of us as **were baptized into Jesus Christ** were **baptized into His death?** Therefore we are <u>buried</u> with Him <u>by</u> baptism into <u>death</u>: that <u>like</u> as Christ was <u>raised up</u> from the dead by <u>the glory of The Father,</u> EVEN SO WE ALSO SHOULD WALK IN NEWNESS OF LIFE. For <u>if</u> we have been <u>planted</u> together in the **likeness** of His death, we ***shall b*e** also in **the likeness** of His resurrection: Knowing this, that our **old man** is **crucified with Him**, *that the **body of sin might be destroyed**,* that henceforth <u>we should</u> **not serve sin.** For he that is DEAD IS FREED FROM SIN. Now **if** we be **dead** with Christ, we <u>believe</u> that we <u>shall</u> also <u>live</u> with Him: Knowing that Christ <u>being raised</u> from the dead DIETH NO MORE; DEATH HATH NO MORE DOMINION OVER HIM.
IF WE ARE <u>DEAD</u> *SIN SHOULD NO LONGER HAVE* <u>DOMINION</u> over us! *Let <u>not sin</u> therefore <u>reign</u> in your mortal body,* that ye ***should obey*** it in the *<u>lusts</u> thereof.* <u>Neither</u> yield ye your members as instruments of unrighteousness unto sin: BUT <u>yield</u> <u>yourselves unto God</u>, as those that are ALIVE FROM THE DEAD, AND YOUR MEMBERS AS INSTRUMENTS OF RIGHTEOUSNESS UNTO GOD. Please, Read Romans 6:1-16

"DESCENDED FIRST INTO THE EARTH"

1. Where can we find the first place in scriptures where The Lord descended first into the earth and we can see that it was, The Son of The living and everlasting God?

2. Where can we find scriptures in the New Testament that supports this belief?

3. When the cloudy pillar descended and stood at the door of the tabernacle, who talked with Moses?

4. The Lord Jesus, The Son of God came down in clouds in Moses's days.

Q. How was The Lord Jesus, The Son of God received into heaven and how will He return?

"DESCENDED FIRST INTO THE EARTH"

1. Where can we find the first place in scriptures where The Lord descended first into the earth and we can see that it was, The Son of The living and everlasting God?

A. Exodus 19:17-19 The LORD descended, God answered him by A VOICE.

And Moses brought forth the people out of the camp to meet with God; and they stood at the nether part of the mount. And mount Sinai was altogether on a smoke, because **The LORD descended upon it in fire:** and the smoke thereof ascended <u>as</u> the smoke of a furnace, and the whole mount quaked greatly. And when the voice of the trumpet sounded long, and waxed louder and louder, Moses spake, and, **GOD ANSWERED HIM BY A VOICE**

2. Where can we find scriptures in the New Testament that supports this belief?

A. Ephesians 4:8-10, **HE ALSO DESCENDED FIRST INTO THE LOWER PARTS OF THE EARTH.**

Wherefore He saith, When He ascended up on high, He led captivity captive, and gave <u>gifts</u> unto men. (Now that **HE ASCENDED,** what is it but that He *also* **DESCENDED FIRST** *into the lower parts of the earth?* He that <u>descended is</u> <u>the same</u> <u>also</u> that a<u>scended</u> up **far above** <u>all</u> <u>heavens</u>, that **He might** <u>**fill all things.**</u>)

And no man hath ascended up to heaven, but He that came down from heaven, even The Son of man which is in heaven. John 3:13

3. When the cloudy pillar descended and stood at the door of the tabernacle, who talked with Moses?

A. *The Lord talked with Moses.*

And it came to pass, when Moses went out unto the tabernacle, that all the people rose up, and stood every man at his tent door, and **looked after Moses,** until he was gone into the tabernacle. And it came to pass, as **Moses entered into the tabernacle**, the, <u>cloudy pillar descended</u> and stood at the door of the tabernacle, and *The Lord talked with Moses.* And all <u>the people</u> **SAW THE CLOUDY** PILLAR stand at the tabernacle door: **and all the people rose up and worshipped, every man in his tent door.**

Exodus 33:8-10

I saw in the <u>**night visions**</u>**, and, behold,** <u>**one like the Son of**</u> Ancient of days, and they brought him near before him. **And there was given Him** <u>**dominion, and** *glory, and a kingdom,*</u> that **all** *people, nations, and languages, should serve Him*: His <u>dominion is an</u> <u>everlasting dominion,</u> which shall not pass away, and <u>**man**</u> **came with the** *clouds of heaven,* and came to the **His kingdom that which shall not be destroyed.** Daniel 7:13-14

(IF WE READ FROM THE AMPLIFIED BIBLE, WE CAN SEE THIS IS THE SON OF GOD

Daniel 7:13-14.

I saw in the night visions, and behold on the clouds of the heavens *CAME ONE LIKE A SON OF MAN,* **a**nd He came to the **Ancient of Days and was presented before** Him. And there was <u>given</u> Him **[THE MESSIAH]** *dominion and glory and kingdom, THAT ALL PEOPLES,* nations, and *languages should serve Him. His dominion is an everlasting dominion which shall not pass away, and His kingdom is one which shall not be destroyed.)*

DESCENDED FIRST INTO THE EARTH

4. The Lord Jesus, The Son of God came down in clouds in Morse's days.
Q. How was The Lord Jesus, The Son of God received into heaven and how will He return?

A. A cloud received Him, He will return in the clouds of heaven.
And when He had spoken these things, while they beheld, He was taken up; and a cloud received Him out of their sight. And while they looked stedfastly toward heaven as He went up, behold, two men stood by them in white apparel; Which also said, **YE MEN OF GALILEE, WHY STAND YE GAZING UP INTO HEAVEN?**

this same Jesus, which is _taken_ up from you _into heaven_, shall so come in like manner as ye have seen Him go into heaven. Acts 1:9-11

And then shall appear the *sign of The Son of man in heaven*: and then shall all the *tribes of the earth mourn*, and *they shall see The Son of man coming in the clouds of heaven with power and great glory*. Matthew 24:30

Jesus saith unto him, Thou hast said: nevertheless I say unto you, Hereafter shall ye see The Son of man sitting on *the right* hand **OF POWER**, and coming in the clouds of heaven.
Matthew 26:64

AND JESUS SAID I AM: AND YE SHALL *SEE THE SON OF MAN SITTING* ON THE *RIGHT HAND OF POWER, AND COMING IN THE CLOUDS OF HEAVEN.*
MARK 14:62

THESE VERSES ADDED TO SHOW WHAT HAPPENED BEFORE AND AFTER YAHUSHUA MADE THE STATEMENT IN MARK 14:62, "YE SHALL *SEE THE SON OF MAN SITTING* ON THE _right hand of power_,
And the high priest stood up in the midst, **and asked Jesus, saying,** Answerest thou *nothing?* what is it which these witness against thee? But **He held his peace, and answered nothing**. Again the high priest asked Him, AND SAID UNTO HIM, Art thou The Christ, The Son of The Blessed? Mark 14:60 &61 61

Yahushua/Jesus confessed Himself when He voiced these words, "JESUS SAID, I AM"
THEN the *high priest* **rent his clothes, and saith**, *WHAT NEED WE ANY FURTHER WITNESSES?* YE HAVE HEARD *THE BLASPHEMY*: what think ye? And they all *condemned him to be guilty of death*. Mark 14:63 &64
HE CONFESSED THE TRUTH Art thou The Christ, The Son of The Blessed? I AM!

WHAT IS HIS NAME, <u>AND</u> WHAT IS HIS SON'S NAME?

1. I neither learned wisdom, nor have the knowledge of the **holy**.
Who <u>hath ascended up into heaven</u>, or <u>descended</u>? who hath gathered the wind in His fists? who hath bound the waters in a garment? who hath established all the ends of the earth?

What is His Name, and what is His Son's Name, if thou canst tell? Every word of God is _____ He is a shield unto them that put their trust in Him.

2. Beware therefore, lest that come upon you, which is spoken of in the prophets; Behold, ye despisers, and <u>wonder</u>, <u>and perish</u>: for I work a work in your days, a work which ye shall in no wise believe, though a man declare it unto you. Acts 13:40-41

Q. Where can we find a cross-reference to this scripture?

3. What is the fear of The Lord and what does He hate?

WHAT IS HIS NAME, AND WHAT IS HIS SON'S NAME?

1. I neither learned wisdom, nor HAVE THE KNOWLEDGE OF THE HOLY. WHO HATH ASCENDED UP INTO HEAVEN, OR DESCENDED? who hath gathered the wind in His fists? who hath bound the waters in a garment? who hath established all the ends of the earth?
What is His Name, and what is His *Son's Name*, if thou canst tell?
Every word of God is _____ He is a shield unto them that put their trust in Him.
A. UNPOLLUTED: PROVERBS 30:3-5

2. Beware therefore, lest that come upon you, which is spoken of in the prophets; Behold, ye despisers, and wonder, and perish: for I work a work in your days, a work which ye shall in no wise believe, though a man declare it unto you. Acts 13:40-41
Q. Where can we find a cross-reference to this scripture?
A. HABAKKUK 1:5
Behold ye among the heathen, and regard, and wonder marvelously: for I will work a work in your days which ye will not believe, *though it be* told you.

3. What is the fear of The Lord and what does He hate?
A. The **FEAR** of The LORD is to *hate evil: pride, and arrogancy, and the evil way, and the froward mouth,* do I hate. Counsel is Mine, and sound wisdom: I am understanding; I have strength. Proverbs 8:13-14

Through Thy precepts I get understanding: therefore **I hate every false way.** Thy word is a lamp unto my feet, and a light unto my path. Psalm 119:104-105

Therefore I love Thy commandments above gold; yea, above fine gold.
Therefore I esteem *all Thy precepts concerning all things to be right;* and *I hate every false way.*
Thy testimonies are wonderful: therefore doth my soul keep them. Psalm 119:127-128

Yahweh, grant those whom you has justified by faith, wisdom, knowledge and above all understanding in The Name of Yahushua The Messiah.

1. The foundations of the wall of the city were garnished with all manner of precious stones.
Q. How many foundations and precious stones did the City have?

2. The twelve gates were twelve pearls: every several gate was of one pearl: and the street of the city was pure gold, as it <u>were</u> transparent glass. And I saw no temple therein: for The Lord God Almighty <u>and</u> The Lamb are the temple of it. And the city <u>had no need of the sun, neither of the moon,</u> to <u>shine in it</u>: for The <u>Glory</u> of God did lighten it, <u>and</u> The Lamb is the light thereof. And the nations of them which are *saved* shall <u>walk in the light</u> of it: and <u>the kings of the earth do bring their glory and honour</u> into it. And the <u>gates of it shall not be shut</u> at all by day: for there shall be <u>no night</u> there. And they shall bring the <u>glory and honour</u> of the nations into it.
The twelve gates were twelve pearls and the street of the city was pure gold.
Q. Who shall in no wise, enter into this beautiful and glorious City?

3. According to the Holy Scriptures, who shall have their part in the lake which burneth with fire and brimstone?

4. And I saw a great white throne, and Him that sat on it, from whose face the earth and the heaven fled away; and there was found no place for them.
Q. Who was standing before God?

Yahweh, grant those whom you has justified by faith, wisdom, knowledge and above all understanding in The Name of Yahushua The Messiah.

1. The foundations of the wall of the city were garnished with all manner of precious stones.
Q. How many foundations and precious stones did the City have?
A. The wall of the city had **twelve foundations,** and in them **the Names of the twelve apostles of The Lamb.**
The city had <u>twelve stones</u> the first foundation was jasper; the second, sapphire; the third, a chalcedony; the fourth, an emerald; the fifth, sardonyx; the sixth, sardius; the seventh, chrysolyte; the eighth, beryl; the ninth, a topaz; the tenth, a chrysoprasus; the eleventh, a jacinth; the twelfth, an amethyst.
Revelation 21:14 & 21:19-20

2. The twelve gates were twelve pearls: every several gate was of one pearl: and the street of the city was pure gold, as it <u>were</u> transparent glass. And I saw no temple therein: for THE LORD GOD ALMIGHTY **and The Lamb** are the temple of it. And the city <u>had no need of the sun, neither of the moon,</u> to <u>shine in it</u>: for The <u>Glory</u> of God did lighten it, **and The Lamb is the light thereof.** And the **nations of them which are** *<u>saved</u>* shall <u>walk in the light</u> of it: and <u>the kings of the earth do bring **their** glory and honour</u> into it. And the <u>gates of it shall not be shut</u> at all by day: for there shall be **no night** there. And they shall **bring the glory and honour of the nations into it.** Revelation 21:21-26

The twelve gates were twelve pearls and the street of the city was pure gold.
Q. Who shall in <u>no wise enter</u> into this beautiful and glorious City?
A. AND THERE SHALL **in no wise enter** INTO IT **any thing that defileth, neither** <u>**whatsoever**</u> **worketh abomination, or** *maketh a lie*: but they which *ARE WRITTEN IN The LAMB'S BOOK OF LIFE.* Revelation 21:27

3. According to the Holy Scriptures, who shall have their part in the lake which burneth with fire and brimstone?
A. Those that <u>DO NOT</u> overcome these things until the end; *WILL DIE TWICE*, this is THE <u>SECOND DEATH</u>.
THESE THINGS ARE: *the fearful, and unbelieving, and the abominable, and murderers, and whoremongers, and sorcerers, and idolaters, and <u>all liars</u>,* **shall** have their part in *the lake which burneth with fire and brimstone:* which is the **second death.** *Revelation 21:7-8*
Revelation 2:17 **He that hath an ear, let him hear what The Spirit saith unto the churches; To him that overcometh will I give to eat of the hidden manna,** and will **give him a white stone,** and in **the stone a New Name written, which** *<u>no</u>* **man knoweth saving** *he* **that receiveth it.**

Yahweh, grant those whom you has justified by faith, wisdom, knowledge and above all understanding in The Name of Yahushua The Messiah.

Revelation 2:26 **And he that overcometh, and keepeth My works unto the end, to him will I give power over the nations:**
Revelation 3:5 **He that overcometh,** the same **shall be clothed in white raiment;** *and* <u>I will not blot out his name out of the book of life,</u> **but** <u>I will</u> <u>confess his name before</u> <u>MY</u> **Father,** and before **His angels**

Here is wisdom:
*Please, do not overlook he that <u>overcometh</u> shall <u>be clothed</u> in <u>white raiment</u> and He will not <u>blot</u> that **overcomer out of the book of life** <u>BUT,</u> what about **the ones that does not continue to overcome unto the end?** You answer.*

And to her <u>WAS GRANTED</u> that she should be arrayed in fine linen, clean and white: for the fine linen is the righteousness of saints. Revelation 19:8

Revelation 3:12 **Him that overcometh will I make a pillar in the temple of My God,** and he shall go no more out: and **I will write upon him The Name of My God,** and **the name of the city of My God,** which is **New Jerusalem, which cometh down out of heaven from My God**: and *I WILL WRITE UPON HIM MY NEW NAME.*
Revelation 3:21 **To him that overcometh will I grant to sit with Me in My throne, even as I also overcame, and am set down with My Father in His throne.**
Revelation 21:7 **He that overcometh shall inherit all things; and I will be his God, and he shall be My son.**

Yahushua/Jesus overcame <u>and inherited *all things*.</u>

<u>*All things*</u> are delivered unto Me of My Father: and no man <u>knoweth The Son</u>, but The Father; neither knoweth any man The Father, <u>save</u> The Son, and <u>he</u> to *whomsoever <u>The Son will reveal Him.</u>* Matthew 11:27

Whom did Jesus manifest His Father's Name?
[6] I have **manifested Thy Name unto the men which Thou gavest Me out of the world**: Thine they were, and **Thou gavest them Me**; and **they have kept Thy word.** [7] Now they **have known that all things** whatsoever Thou hast given Me are of Thee. [8] **For I have given unto them the words which Thou gavest Me**; and **they have received them,** and **have known surely that I came out from thee,** and **they have believed that thou didst send Me.**
[9] **I pray for them**: I pray *not for the world,* **but** for them **which thou hast given me;** for they are Thine. John 17:6-9

Yahweh, grant those whom you has justified by faith, wisdom, knowledge and above all understanding in The Name of Yahushua The Messiah.

FOR THE FATHER JUDGETH NO MAN, BUT HATH COMMITTED ALL JUDGMENT UNTO THE SON: JOHN 5:22

4. And I saw a great white throne, and Him that sat on it, from whose face the earth and the heaven fled away; and there was found no place for them.
Q. Who was standing before God?
A. The dead small and great

And I saw **the dead, small and great**, stand before God; and the **books** were opened: and **another book** was opened, **which is the book of life**: and the <u>dead were judged</u> out of those things which were written in the books, **according to their works**. And *the sea gave up the dead* which were in it; and DEATH AND HELL DELIVERED UP THE DEAD WHICH WERE IN THEM: <u>and they were judged every man according to their works.</u>
Revelation 20:11-13
DECEIVING SPIRITS WILL SAY OUR WORKS DO NOT COUNT, I CAN ONLY SAY LORD HAVE MERCY ON THESE DISBELIEVER IN YOUR WORD.

Here is the patience of the saints: *here are they that <u>keep the commandments of God, <u>and</u> the <u>faith of Jesus</u>.*

{Yahushua believed every word that came from the mouth of Yahweh}
And I heard a voice from heaven saying unto me, Write,
Blessed are the dead <u>WHICH DIE</u> in The Lord from henceforth: Yea, saith The Spirit, that they may rest from their labours; **and their works do follow them.** And I looked, and behold a white cloud, and upon the cloud one sat like unto The Son of man, having on His head a golden crown, and in His hand a *sharp sickle.* Revelation 14:12-14

WHO WILL BE, BLESSED?
Blessed are the dead <u>which die</u> in The Lord

In The Lord

LAME MAN RECEIVED STRENGTH

1. Elijah prophesied saying, As The LORD God of Israel liveth, before whom I stand, there shall not be dew nor rain these years, except according to my word. It came to pass the brook dried up, because there had been no rain in the land. The Lord commanded a widow woman to sustain/provide for Elijah. And it came to pass after these things that the son of the woman the mistress of the house, fell sick; and his sickness was so sore, that there was no breath left in him.
Q How did Elijah revive the child?

2. A certain man lame from his mother's womb was carried into temple called Beautiful, to ask alms from those who entered into the temple. He, seeing Peter and John about to go into the temple, asked for alms. And Peter, fastening his eyes upon him with John, said, "Look on us." And he gave heed unto them, expecting to receive something from them. Peter said, "Silver and gold have I none, but such as I have, I give thee: in The Name of Jesus Christ of Nazareth, rise up and walk." And he took him by the right hand and lifted him up, and <u>immediately his feet and ankle bones received strength.</u>
Sometimes we need a little help in order to become strong.
Q. After the lame man received his strength what things was he able to achieve?

3. John warned many of the Pharisees and Sadducees that came to his baptism, he said unto them,
O generation of vipers, <u>who hath warned you to flee from the wrath to come</u>?
Jesus warned His decuples saying, Take heed and beware of the leaven of the Pharisees and of the Sadducees.
Q. Why did Jesus warn them and why does He warn us?

LAME MAN RECEIVED STRENGTH

1. Elijah prophesied saying, "As The LORD God of Israel liveth, before whom I stand, there shall not be dew nor rain these years, except according to my word." It came to pass the brook dried up, because there had been no rain in the land. The Lord commanded a widow woman to sustain/provide for Elijah. And it came to pass after these things that the son of the woman the mistress of the house, fell sick; and his sickness was so sore, that there was no breath left in him.

Q How did Elijah revive the child?

A. *Elijah stretched himself upon the child three times, and cried unto The LORD, and said, O LORD my God, I pray thee, let this child's soul come into him again.*
And The LORD heard the voice of Elijah; and the soul of the child came into him again, and he revived.

And Elijah took the child, and brought him down out of the chamber into the house, and delivered him unto his mother: and Elijah said, **SEE, THY SON LIVETH.**
And the woman said to Elijah, **Now by this I know that thou art a man of God**, and that the word of *The LORD* in thy mouth is truth. 1 Kings 17:21-24

Remember, the word says *whosoever shall call upon The Name of The Lord shall be saved.* Romans 10:13
Then they cried unto The LORD in their trouble, and He saved them out of their distresses. Psalm 107:13

2. A certain man lame from his mother's womb was carried into temple called Beautiful, to ask alms from those who entered into the temple. He, seeing Peter and John about to go into the temple, asked for alms. And **Peter, fastening his eyes upon him with John, said, "Look on us."** And he gave heed unto them, expecting to receive something from them. Peter said, *"Silver and gold have I none, but such as I have, I give thee: in The Name of Jesus Christ of Nazareth, rise up and walk."* And he took him by the right hand and lifted him up, and immediately **his feet and ankle bones received strength**.

Sometimes we need a little help in order to become strong.

Q. **After the lame man received his strength what things was he able to achieve?**

A. **The first thing he was able to accomplish he leaped up,** then he was **able to stand up**, and then he was able to **walk and entered with the disciples into the temple walking and leaping and did not forget to praise God!** And all the people **saw him walking and praising God.** Acts 3:2-9

LAME MAN RECEIVED STRENGTH

3. John warned many of the Pharisees and Sadducees that came to his baptism, he said unto them, O generation of vipers, **who hath warned you to flee from the wrath to come?**
Jesus warned His decuples saying, "**Take heed and *beware of the leaven of the Pharisees and of the Sadducees.*"**
Q. Why did Jesus warn them and why does He warn us?
A. Because, **He did not want them to be deceived by false doctrine/false teaching**.
Yahushua/Jesus said unto them, .How is it that ye do not understand that I spoke it **not t**o you concerning bread, **but** that ye should beware of the leaven of the Pharisees and the Sadducees?"
Then *understood* they how that He bade them *not* beware
of the LEAVEN OF BREAD, **BUT** of *the <u>doctrine</u>* of the
Pharisees and of the Sadducees. Matthew 16:11-12

What Questions Did Yahushua/Jesus Ask His Disciples After He Warn Them?

<u>Answer found in Matthew 16:13-20</u>
When Jesus came into the coasts of Caesarea Philippi,
He asked His disciples, saying, **Whom do men say that I The Son of Man am?**
[14] AND THEY SAID, *Some say that thou art John the Baptist: some, Elias; and others, Jeremias, or one of the prophets.*
[15] HE SAITH UNTO THEM, BUT <u>whom say ye that I am?</u>
[16] And Simon Peter answered *<u>and said</u>*, THOU ART THE CHRIST, THE SON OF THE LIVING GOD.

Hear is WISDON and Revelation:

Peter was _the only one that confessed_ who Jesus was and Jesus only confessed him. [17] **And Jesus answered and said unto _him_**, Blessed art thou, Simon Barjona: **for _flesh and blood_ hath not revealed it unto thee, but My Father which is in heaven.** [18] And I say also unto thee, That thou art Peter, **and upon this** rock **I will build My church; and the gates of hell shall not prevail against it.**, 19 And I will give unto thee the keys of the kingdom of heaven: and whatsoever thou shalt bind on earth shall be bound in heaven: and whatsoever thou shalt loose on earth shall be loosed in heaven. [20] **Then charged He His disciples that they should tell no man that He was Jesus The Christ.**

I hope we can understand why Jesus only confessed the one who confessed Him when we read these verses. Yahushua/Jesus made known Yahweh/The Father God, to His decuples **BUT** Yahweh/God made know the revelation to Peter who Yahushua was, Jesus said I know Mine and they know Me! Peter had Rock faith, sound and hard as a rock; hard rocks are unbreakable engraved in one's heart. Praise The Lord! I can truly say He confessed Me and I did hear His Voice!

Whosoever shall confess Me before men, him shall The Son of Man also confess before the angels of God: BUT He that _denieth Me before men shall be denied before the angels of God._ Luke 12:7-9

Whosoever therefore shall confess Me before men, him will **I confess also before My Father which is in heaven.** But whosoever shall deny Me before men, him will **I** also deny before My Father which is in heaven. **THINK NOT THAT I AM COME TO SEND PEACE ON EARTH: I** came not to _send peace,_ **but a sword. Matthew 10:32-34**

But a sword, what is this sword? The sword of His Mouth is the word from God.

Found in Revelation 2:15-17. So hast thou also them that hold the doctrine _of the Nicolaitanes,_ which **thing I hate. Repent; or else I will come _unto thee quickly._ and will fight against them with the sword of My Mouth.** _He that hath an ear, let him hear what the Spirit saith unto the churches_; **To him that overcometh will I give to eat of the hidden manna,** and _will give him a white stone, and in the stone a new name written, which no man knoweth saving he that receiveth it._

216

ILLUMINATING QUIZ "THEY HATED ME WITHOUT A CAUSE"

1. Now the chief priests, and elders, and all the council, sought <u>false witness against Jesus</u>, to put Him to death; But found none: yea, <u>though many false witnesses came</u>, yet <u>found they none</u>. At the last came two false witnesses, And said, This fellow said, I am able to destroy the temple of God, and to build it in three days. And the high priest arose, and said unto him, Answerest thou nothing? <u>what is it which these witness against thee</u>? But <u>Jesus held His peace</u>, And the high priest answered and said unto Him, I adjure Thee by The living God, that Thou tell us whether Thou be The Christ, The Son of God. Jesus saith unto him, Thou hast said: nevertheless I say unto you, Hereafter shall ye <u>see</u> The Son of man <u>sitting on the right hand</u> of power, and coming in the clouds of heaven. Then the high priest <u>rent his clothes</u>, saying, He *hath spoken blasphemy; <u>what further</u>* need have we of *witnesses*? Behold, now <u>ye</u> have <u>heard</u> *His blasphemy*. Matthew 26:59-65
Q. Why did they need two, three or more witnesses or two false witnesses?

2. What two things are essential, to be saved?
*(**Please, notice I did not say justified**)*

3. If I had not done among them the works which none other man did, they had not had sin: but now have they both seen and hated both Me and My Father. But this cometh to pass, that the word might be fulfilled that is written in their law, <u>They hated Me without a cause</u>. But when The Comforter is come, whom I will send unto you from The Father, even The Spirit of truth, which proceedeth from The Father, He shall testify of Me:
John 15:24-26
Q. **Where can we discover other scriptures that read without a cause?**

ILLUMINATING QUIZ "THEY HATED ME WITHOUT A CAUSE"

1. Now the chief priests, and elders, and all the council, sought <u>false witness against Jesus,</u> to put Him to death; But found none: yea, <u>though many false witnesses came,</u> yet <u>found they none</u>. At the last came two false witnesses, And said, This fellow said, I am able to destroy the temple of God, and to build it in three days. And the high priest arose, and said unto him, Answerest thou nothing? <u>what is it which these witness against thee?</u> But <u>Jesus held His peace,</u> And the high priest answered and said unto Him, I adjure, **Thee by The living God** that Thou tell us whether ***THOU BE THE CHRIST, THE SON OF GOD.*** Jesus saith unto him, **Thou hast said:** nevertheless I say unto you, Hereafter shall ye <u>see</u> 𝔗he Son of man sitting on the right hand of power, and coming in the clouds of heaven. Then the high priest **rent his clothes**, saying, He hath spoken **blasphemy;** *what further* need have we of witnesses? Behold, now <u>ye</u> have <u>heard</u> **His blasphemy**. Matthew **26:59-65**

Q. Why did they need two, three or more witnesses or two false witnesses?

A. Because, it is recorded in the scriptures at the mouth of two witnesses, or at the mouth of three witnesses, shall the matter be established.

At the mouth of **two witnesses, or three witnesses**, shall he that is *worthy of death* be put to death; ***but*** at the mouth of ONE WITNESS HE SHALL NOT BE PUT TO DEATH. Deuteronomy 17:6

One witness shall **not rise** up against a man for any iniquity, or for any sin, in any sin that he sinneth: at **the mouth of two witnesses, or at the mouth of three witnesses, shall the matter be established.** Deuteronomy 19:15

HE THAT DESPISED MOSES' LAW DIED WITHOUT MERCY UNDER TWO OR THREE WITNESSES:
Hebrews 10:28

But if he will not hear thee, then ***take with thee one or two more, that in the mouth of two or three witnesses every word may be established.*** Matthew 18:16

And I will give power unto My two witnesses, and they shall prophesy a thousand two hundred and threescore days, clothed in sackcloth. Revelation 11:3

Against an elder receive not an accusation, but **before two or three witnesses.**
1Timothy 5:19

2. What two things are essential, to be saved?
(Please, notice I did not say *justified*)

A. OUR CONFESSION/SPOKEN WORDS AND OUR HEARTS NEED TO AGREE WITH THE WORD OF GOD.

That <u>if</u> thou shalt confess with thy mouth The Lord Jesus, <u>and</u> shalt believe in thine heart that God hath raised Him/JESUS FROM THE DEAD, thou *SHALT* BE SAVED. Romans 10:9

Other words, if you <u>do</u> and believe in your heart this will be done.
But, notice the word is shalt not shall or should

ILLUMINATING QUIZ "THEY HATED ME WITHOUT A CAUSE"

We having the same spirit of faith, according as it is written, I believed, and therefore have I spoken; WE ALSO BELIEVE, AND THEREFORE SPEAK; **Knowing** that <u>He</u> which raised up The Lord Jesus shall raise up us also <u>BY</u> **Jesus,** and shall present us with you.
2 Corinthians 4:13-15

3. **If I had not** done among them **the works which none other man did, they had not had sin:** BUT now have **they both seen** and <u>hated *BOTH*</u> **Me** AND **My Father.** But this cometh to pass, that the **word might be fulfilled** that is **written in their law, <u>They hated Me without a cause.</u>** But when **The Comforter is come,** whom I will <u>**send unto you** **from The Father,**</u> EVEN **The Spirit of truth, which proceedeth from The Father, He** <u>**shall testify of Me**</u>: John 15:24-26

Q. Where can we discover other scriptures that read without a cause?
A. Princes have persecuted me without a cause: but my heart standeth in awe of Thy word.
Psalm 119:161

They compassed me about also with **words of hatred; and fought against me without a cause.** Psalm 109:3

Let the **proud be ashamed; for they dealt perversely with me without a cause:** but I will meditate in Thy precepts. Psalm 119:78

Let not them that are mine enemies wrongfully rejoice over me: neither let them wink with t**he eye that hate me without a cause.** Psalm 35:19

They that hate me without a cause are more than the hairs of mine head: they that would destroy me, being mine enemies wrongfully, are mighty: then I restored that which I took not away.
Psalm 69:4

"EDIFYING QUIZ"
"THAT HOLY THING DID A GOOD THING"

1. Every year we honour the Friday before Easter Sunday and calls it Good Friday, I can understand why because, That Holy Thing did a Good Thing.
(Yes, The Son of God was to be called; That Holy Thing).
(And the angel answered and said unto her, The Holy Ghost shall come upon thee, and the power of The Highest shall overshadow thee: therefore also That Holy Thing which shall be born of thee shall be called The Son of God).
However, for this study is Good Friday scriptural in the King James Version?

2. We celebrate the resurrection of our Lord and Savor Jesus Christ, The Son of The Living God every year on what many call Easter Sunday and Resurrection Sunday.
Q. For this study only, is Easter a Biblical word in the King James Version?

3. And he saith unto them, Be not affrighted: Ye seek Jesus of Nazareth, which was crucified: He is risen; He is not here: behold the place where they laid Him. But go your way, tell His disciples and_____ that He goeth before you into Galilee: there shall ye see Him, as He said unto you.
Mark 16:6 &7

4. If the answer is yes on #2, according to scriptures does Easter have anything to do with the resurrection of our Lord Jesus Christ?
(*If so please, use scripture to support your answer*).

"Edifying Quiz"
"That Holy Thing did a Good Thing"

1. Every year we **honour the Friday before Easter Sunday and calls it Good Friday,** I can understand why because, **That Holy Thing did a Good Thing.**
(Yes, The Son of God was to be called; That Holy Thing).
(And the angel answered and said unto her, The Holy Ghost shall come upon thee, **and** the power of The Highest shall overshadow thee: therefore also **That Holy Thing which shall be born of thee shall be called The Son of God).**
However, for this study is Good Friday scriptural in the King James Version?
A. No

2. We celebrate the resurrection of our Lord and Savor Jesus Christ, The Son of The Living God every year on what many call Easter Sunday and Resurrection Sunday**.**
Q. For this study only, is Easter a Biblical word in the King James Version?
A. Yes

3. And he saith unto them, Be not affrighted: Ye seek Jesus of Nazareth, which was crucified: He is risen; He is not here: behold the place where they laid Him. **But go your way, tell His disciples and**_____that He goeth before you into Galilee: there shall ye see Him, as He said unto you. Mark 16:6 &7
A. Peter

4. If the answer is yes on #2, according to scriptures does Easter have anything to do with the resurrection of our Lord Jesus Christ?
(*If so please, use scripture to support your answer*)
A. No

Please, read Acts chapter 11 & 12, the revelation I am getting is; it relates to unleavened bread [the Passover week].
Amplified Bible: reads, .purposing <u>after</u> the Passover to bring him forth to the people. Acts 12:4

King James Version: **Reads**, .Now about that time Herod the king stretched forth his hands to vex certain of the church.. **And he killed James the brother of John with the sword And because he saw it pleased the Jews, he proceeded further to take Peter also. (Then were the days of <u>*unleavened bread*</u>.)** And when he had apprehended him, he put him in prison, and delivered him to four quaternions of soldiers to keep him; INTENDING **after Easter** TO BRING HIM FORTH TO THE PEOPLE.

And thus shall ye eat it; with your loins girded, your shoes on your feet, and your staff in your hand; and ye shall eat it in haste: it is The LORD's **Passove**r. Exodus 12:11
Luke 22:1 Now the feast of <u>**unleavened bread**</u> drew nigh, which is **called the Passover.**
Luke 22:7 Then came the day of <u>unleavened bread</u>, when the Passover must be killed. Passover noted
1 Corinthians 5:7 <u>**PURGE OUT**</u> therefore **THE OLD LEAVEN**, that ye **may be** <u>a new lump, as ye are unleavened</u>. For *<u>even Christ our Passover is sacrificed for us:</u>*
Hebrews 11:28 Through faith he **kept the Passover,** <u>and</u> the sprinkling of blood, lest he that **destroyed the firstborn** should touch them.
Passover noted in Scriptures seventy two times (72) as far as I can see.

"GOD'S COMPLETE PLAN AND PURPOSE"

1. When God raised Jesus from the dead, He sent Him back to earth to His people first.
Q. What was the whole plan and purpose for Jesus returning to His own people first?

2. How did God plan to bless His People?
(Those who are in Christ Jesus are His people)

3. The disciples spoke to the people, the priests, the captain of the temple and the Sadducees came upon them grieved that they taught the people and preached <u>through Jesus the resurrection from the dead.</u> However, many of them which heard the word believed, the number of the men was about five thousand. When they had set them in the midst, they asked, by what power, or by what name, have ye done this?
Q. Who answered this question?

B. What was the abundant that this one had?

4. How did the one that answered in answer #3 respond to their grief?

GOD'S COMPLETE PLAN AND PURPOSE

1. When God raised Jesus from the dead, He sent Him back to earth to His people first.
Q. What was the whole plan and purpose for Jesus returning to His own people first?
A. His plan and purpose was to bless them. Acts 3:26

2. How did God plan to bless His People?
(Those who are in Christ Jesus are His people).

A. By sending **His Son Jesus to bless them** *in turning* them from their iniquities. Acts 3:26
UNTO YOU FIRST GOD, HAVING RAISED UP HIS SON JESUS, SENT HIM TO BLESS YOU, *IN TURNING AWAY EVERY ONE OF YOU FROM HIS INIQUITIES.* ACTS 3:26

3. The disciples spoke to the people, the priests, the captain of the temple and the Sadducees came upon them grieved that they taught the people and preached ***through Jesus the resurrection from the dead.*** *However, many of them which heard the word believed,* the number of the men was **about five thousand. When they had set them in the midst, they asked, by what power, or by what name, have ye done this?**
Q. Who answered this question?
A. Peter. Acts 4:6
B. What was the abundant that this one had?
A. PETER WAS FILLED WITH, THE HOLY GHOST. ACTS 4:6

4. How did the one that answered in #3 respond to their grief?
A. Then Peter, **FILLED WITH THE HOLY GHOST, SAID UNTO THEM,** Ye **rulers of the people, and elders of Israel,** If we this day are examined about the good deed done to the infirm man, and by what means **he is made whole, known unto you all and to all the people of Israel,** THAT BY THE NAME OF JESUS CHRIST OF NAZARETH, WHOM YE CRUCIFIED AND WHOM GOD RAISED FROM THE DEAD, **even** by HIM DOTH THIS MAN STAND HERE BEFORE YOU WHOLE. This is the *stone which was set at nought by you builders and which has become the head of the corner.'* **Neither is there salvation in any other, for there is no other name under** heaven **given among men whereby we must be saved."** **Now** when they saw the **boldness of Peter and John, and perceived** that they were **unlearned and ignorant** men, they marveled; and they TOOK NOTE concerning them THAT THEY HAD BEEN WITH **Jesus.**
Acts 4:6-13

"MANIFESTATION TIME IS NOW"

1. There are seven spirits in Revelation chapter 5 and seven spirits in Revelation chapter 7.
Q. What is the different between these two?

2. According to the book of Revelation, who shall wipe away all tears from their eyes?

3. Who is sitting on the throne?

4. Does Jesus made His followers worthy to receive SEVEN SPIRITS. Yes or No_____

5. How many chapters is this statement noted, The Father of our Lord Jesus Christ?

"MANIFESTATION TIME IS NOW"

1. There are seven spirits in Revelation chapter 5 and seven spirits in Revelation chapter 7.
Q. What is the different between these two?
The Lamb of God <u>is worthy</u> to <u>take the book</u>, and to open the seals thereof,
A. The Lamb is in <u>the midst of the throne</u> and He is <u>worthy to receive</u> these seven Spirits.
Revelation 5:12.
Might and thanksgiving are **not** in chapter 5 **but** they are in chapter 7.
After all the tribes were sealed there were a great multitude *which no man could number* giving
honour to <u>both</u> The Lamb and God, saying, **Salvation to our God which sitteth upon
the throne**, AND unto **The Lamb**. Revelation 7:9-10
And all **the angels** stood round about the throne, and about the **elders and the four beasts**, and
fell before the throne on their faces, and **worshipped God,**
Saying, Amen: **Blessing, and glory, and wisdom, and thanksgiving, and honour, and
power, and might, be unto our God** for ever and ever. Amen. Revelation 7:11&12
(*Remember, and is in addition*)

**The Lamb was worthy to RECEIVE these but God <u>always</u> had them; be unto our
God for ever and ever.**

2. According to the book of Revelation, who shall wipe away all tears from their eyes?
A. God shall wipe away all tears from their eyes
for The lamb which is in the midst of the throne shall feed them, and shall <u>lead them</u> <u>unto
living fountains of waters:</u> *and* GOD SHALL WIPE AWAY ALL TEARS FROM THEIR
EYES. Revelation 7:17
And God <u>shall wipe away</u> <u>all tears from their eyes</u>; and **there shall be no more death, neither
sorrow, nor crying, neither shall there be any more pain: for the former things are passed away**.
Revelation 21:4

3. Who is sitting on the throne?
A. God The Father of our Lord Jesus Christ.
Therefore are they **before the throne of God,** and **serve Him day and night in His
temple**: and He THAT SITTETH ON THE THRONE shall dwell among them. Revelation 7:15
And when he had opened the seventh seal, there was silence in heaven about the space of half an
hour.
And I saw the seven angels which **stood before God**; and to them were given seven trumpets.
AND another ANGEL CAME AND STOOD AT THE ALTAR, having a golden censer; and
there was given unto **Him much incense, that he should offer it with the *prayers of all
saints*** upon the golden altar which was before the throne. And the smoke of the incense, **which
came with the prayers of the saints, ascended up before God OUT OF THE *ANGEL'S*
HAND.** And the angel took the censer, and filled it with fire of the altar, and cast it into the earth:
and there were voices, and thunderings, and lightnings, and an earthquake. Revelation 8:1-5

"MANIFESTATION TIME IS NOW"

"Men to be saved and to come unto the knowledge of the truth"

I EXHORT THEREFORE, THAT, FIRST OF ALL, supplications, prayers, intercessions, and giving of thanks, be made for _ALL MEN_; **For kings, and for all that are in authority;** that we **may lead a quiet** and **peaceable life in all** _godliness and honesty_. For this is _good and acceptable in_ **the sight of God our Saviour, Who** WILL HAVE ALL MEN TO BE SAVED, _and_ TO COME UNTO THE KNOWLEDGE OF THE TRUTH. _For there is_ ONE _God_, AND One mediator BETWEEN GOD AND MEN, The Man Christ Jesus; Who gave Himself a ransom for all,

TO BE TESTIFIED IN DUE TIME. 1 TIMOTHY2:1-6.

It is due time for manifestation and confirming the word of God.

Thank You Yahweh for manifesting Your Son in me and knowing that your will is, to have all men to be saved, and to come unto the knowledge of the truth. For there is One True God, and One Mediator between You and men and that Man is Your Son, The Man Yahushua the Messiah/Jesus The Christ; Who gave **Himself** a ransom **for all**, to **be testified in due time**. 1Timothy 2:4-6

(I will say it again, it is due time for manifestation and affirming the word of God
Thanks again Father for manifesting your Son in me!

Wow! Hefty Revelation: Remembering the words of Paul in Galatians 1:12-18
For I neither **received it of man**, neither was I taught it, but by **the revelation of Jesus Christ.**
For ye have heard of my conversation in time past in the Jews' religion, how that beyond measure _I persecuted the church of God, and wasted it:_
And profited in the Jews' religion above many my equals in mine own nation, being more exceedingly zealous of the traditions of my fathers.
But when it pleased God, who separated me from my mother's womb, and called me by His grace,
To **reveal His Son in me**, that I might preach him among the _heathen_, immediately I conferred not with flesh and blood:
Neither went I up to Jerusalem to them _which were apostles before me_; but I went into Arabia, and returned again unto Damascus.
Then **after three years** I went up to **Jerusalem to see Peter, and abode with him fifteen days.**

4. Does **Jesus made His followers worthy to receive SEVEN SPIRITS. Yes or No____**
   A. YES. Power, riches, wisdom, strength, honour, glory, and blessing. **Alleluia!**

"MANIFESTATION TIME IS NOW"

5. How many chapters is this statement noted, The Father of our Lord Jesus Christ?

A. I discover seven.

Ephesians 3:14 For this cause I bow my knees **unto The Father of our Lord Jesus Christ,**

Romans 15:6 That ye may **with one mind** and **one mouth glorify God, EVEN The Father of our Lord Jesus Christ.**

Colossians 1:3 We give thanks to God and The Father **of our Lord Jesus Christ,** praying always for you,

2 Corinthians 11:31 The **God and Father** OF **our Lord Jesus Christ, which is blessed for evermore, knoweth that I lie not.**

Ephesians 1:3 BLESSED BE THE GOD AND FATHER OF OUR LORD JESUS CHRIST, WHO HATH BLESSED US WITH ALL SPIRITUAL BLESSINGS IN HEAVENLY PLACES IN CHRIST:

2 Corinthians 1:3 **Blessed be God, even The Father of our Lord Jesus Christ,** *THE FATHER OF MERCIES, AND THE GOD OF ALL COMFORT;*

1 Peter 1:3 Blessed be **The God and Father of our Lord Jesus Christ,** which according to His ABUNDANT MERCY hath **begotten us again unto a lively hope** by THE RESURRECTION OF JESUS CHRIST FROM THE DEAD.

Seven Is Completions

"ELI JUDGED ISRAEL"
&
"REPROVE ONE THAT HATH UNDERSTANDING"

1. How old was Eli when he died?

B. Was Eli eyesight good or bad when he breathed his last breath?

2. How many years did Eli judge Israel?

3. Whatever The Lord does He does it for a purpose.
Q. Why did The Lord; established a testimony in Jacob and appointed a law in Israel?

4. If you take away the wicked from before the king how shall his throne be established?

5. Let the righteous smite me; it shall be a kindness: and let him reprove me; it shall be_____, which shall not break my head: for yet my prayer also shall be in their calamities.

6. Reprove one that hath understanding, and he will_____

7. Preach the word; be instant in season, out of season; _____ with all longsuffering and doctrine.

"ELI JUDGED ISRAEL"
&
"REPROVE ONE THAT HATH UNDERSTANDING"

1. How old was Eli when he died?
A. Eli was 98 years old.

B. Was Eli eyesight good or bad when he breathed his last breath?

A. Eli eyes were dim that he could not see. 1 Samuel 4:15

2. How many years did Eli judge Israel?
A. Eli judged Israel forty years.

3. Whatever The Lord does He does it for a purpose.
Q. Why did The Lord; established a testimony in Jacob and appointed a law in Israel?
A. That they should be made known to their children...,
For He **established a testimony in Jacob**, and **appointed a law in Israel**, *which He COMMANDED our fathers,* that THEY *SHOULD* make them **known to their children**: That the **generation to come might** know them, even the children which *should* be born; who should **arise** AND DECLARE THEM TO THEIR CHILDREN: That they *might* set their hope in God, and not forget the works of God, but **keep His commandments**: And *might NOT* BE AS THEIR FATHERS, a **stubborn and rebellious generation**; a generation that set **not their heart aright, and** *whose spirit was not stedfast with God.* Psalm 78:5-8

4. If you take away the wicked from before the king how shall his throne be established?
A. The king throne shall be **established in righteousness.** Proverbs 25:5

5. Let the **righteous smite me**; it shall **be a kindness**: and let **him reprove me**; it shall **be_____,** which shall **not break my head**: for yet my prayer also shall be in their calamities.
A. AN Excellent oil. Psalm 141:5

6. Reprove one that <u>hath understanding</u>, and he will_____
A. Understand knowledge.
Smite a scorner, and THE SIMPLE WILL BEWARE: <u>**and reprove**</u> **one that** HATH **understanding, and he will understand knowledge.** Proverbs 19:25

7. Preach the word; be instant in season, out of season; _____ with all longsuffering and doctrine.
A. REPROVE, REBUKE, EXHORT. 2 TIMOTHY 4:2 (**Exhort:** urge, press, push, encourage, insist, pressure)

"THE WILL OF GOD"

1. The scriptures admonish and teach us not to be deceived with vain words, for because of these things cometh the wrath of God upon <u>the children of disobedience</u>.

For ye were sometimes darkness, but now are ye light in The Lord: walk as children of light:

(For the fruit of the Spirit is in all _____and _____and _____ ;)

B. We are encouraged, not to have fellowship with what?

C. Whom should we reprove and what should we prove?

2. Things, made manifest by the light, what things?

3. Who has the right and the authority to manifest, things that are true?

4. What is the perfect will of God?'

5. Who will abide forever?

6. How many scriptures can you find on the will of God?

"THE WILL OF GOD"

1. The scriptures admonish and teach us not to be deceived with vain words, for because of these things cometh the wrath of God upon <u>the children of disobedience</u>.
For ye were sometimes darkness, but now are ye light in The Lord: walk as children of light:
(For the fruit of the Spirit is in all _____ and _____ and _____ ;)

A. Goodness, righteousness, truth.

B. We are encouraged, not to have fellowship with what?
A. The unfruitful works of darkness

C. Whom should we reprove and what should we prove?
A. We are to reprove _the works of darkness_ as said in Ephesians 5:1-12 and we are to _prove what is acceptable unto The Lord._
And to have _no fellowship with the unfruitful works of darkness,_ but rather reprove them.
We are to reprove that, fornication, and all uncleanness, or covetousness, neither filthiness, nor foolish talking, nor jesting..

For this ye know, that no whoremonger, nor unclean person, nor covetous man, who is an idolater, hath any inheritance in the kingdom of Christ and of God.

Please, Read Ephesians 5:1-12
According to this teaching, someone is being deceitful.
Remember, Revelation 21:7&8
He that overcometh shall <u>inherit all things</u>; and I will be His God, and He shall be My Son.
But the **fearful**, and **unbelieving**, and the **abominable**, and **murderers**, and **whoremongers**, and sorcerers, <u>and idolaters, and all liars</u>, **shall have their part in the lake which burneth with fire and brimstone: which is the second death**

2. Things, made manifest by the light, what things?
A. _All things_ that _are reproved_ are made manifest by the light.
But all things that are reproved are made manifest by the light: for whatsoever doth make manifest is light. Ephesians 5:13
3. Who has the right and the authority to manifest, things that are true?
A. Only the ones in the light and continue to walk in the light.
WHEREFORE HE SAITH, <u>Awake thou that sleepest</u>, <u>and</u> arise from the dead, and Christ <u>shall</u> give _thee light_. See then that ye <u>walk circumspectly</u>, not as fools, but as wise,
Redeeming the time, because the days are evil.
(Circumspectly: _cautiously, watchfully, carefully, vigilantly, suspiciously_)
Wherefore be ye <u>not unwise</u>, **but** <u>understanding</u> _what <u>the will of The Lord is.</u>_
Ephesians 5:14-17

"THE WILL OF GOD"

4. What is the perfect will of God?
A. **The perfect will of God is,** that we change the way we believe and think because, so a man thinketh so is he . . . , and Be **not conformed to this world: but** be ye **transformed by the renewing of your mind**, that ye **may prove** what is **that good, and acceptable, and perfect, will of God.** Romans 12:2

5. Who will abide forever?
A. THE ONES THAT DOES THE WILL OF YAHWEH/GOD
And the world passeth away, and the lust thereof: BUT he that DOETH the will of God abideth
FOR EVER. 1 JOHN 2:17
(ABIDETH: MEANING, A CONTINUATION . . . . UNTIL THE END.

6. How many scriptures can you find on the will of God?
Yahweh has more than one will and He has a perfect will as we acknowledged in #4.

A. SCRIPTURES I FOUND ON THE WILL OF GOD:
Mark 3:35 For whosoever shall **do the will of God,** the same is My brother, and My sister, and mother.
Acts 13:36 For David, after he had served his own generation **by the will of God**, fell on sleep, and was laid unto his fathers, and saw corruption:
Romans 1:10 Making request, if by any means now at length I might have a prosperous journey **by the will of God** to come unto you.
Romans 8:27 And He that searcheth the hearts knoweth what is the mind of the Spirit, because *He maketh intercession for the saints according* **to the will of God**.
Romans 15:32 That I may come unto you with joy **by the will of God**, and may with you be refreshed.

1 Corinthians 1:1 Paul called to be an apostle of Jesus Christ through **the will of God**, and Sosthenes our brother,
2 Corinthians 1:1 Paul, an apostle of Jesus Christ **by the will of God.** and Timothy our brother, unto the church of God which is at Corinth, with all the saints which are in all Achaia:
2 Corinthians 8:5 And this they did, not as we hoped, but first gave their own selves to The Lord, and unto us **by the will of God.**
Galatians 1:4 Who gave Himself for our sins, that He might *deliver us from this present evil world, according to* **the will of God** *and our Father:*
Ephesians 1:1 Paul, an apostle of Jesus Christ by the will of God, to the saints which are at Ephesus, and to the faithful in Christ Jesus:
Ephesians 6:6 Not with eyeservice, as menpleasers; but as the servants of Christ, doing the will of God from the heart;
Colossians 1:1 Paul, an apostle of Jesus Christ by the will of God, and Timotheus our brother,
Colossians 4:12 Epaphras, who is one of you, a servant of Christ, saluteth you, always labouring fervently for you in prayers, that ye **MAY STAND PERFECT AND COMPLETE IN ALL THE WILL OF GOD.**
1 Thessalonians 4:3 For this is **the will of God**, *even* your sanctification, that *ye should* abstain *from fornication*.
1 Thessalonians 5:18 In every thing give thanks: for this is **the will of God in Christ Jesus** concerning you.
2 Timothy 1:1 Paul, **an apostle of Jesus Christ by the will of God.** according to the promise of life which is **in** Christ Jesus.
Hebrews 10:36 For ye have need of patience, that, **after ye have done the will of God**, ye **MIGHT RECEIVE THE PROMISE.**
1 Peter 2:15 **For so is the will of God**, that with well doing ye may put to silence the ignorance of foolish men:
1 Peter 3:17 For it is better, **if the will of God be so, that ye suffer for well doing**, than for evil doing.
1 Peter 4:2 That he no longer should live the rest of his time in the flesh to **the lusts of men, but to the will of God**.
1 Peter 4:19 Wherefore let them **that suffer according to the will of God commit the keeping of their souls** to him in well doing, as unto a faithful Creator.

"The Lord Overthrow"

1. What is a wellspring of life?

2. These things also belong to the wise; it is not good to have respect of persons in what?

3. Who words does The Lord Overthrow and continues to overthrow?

4. What is the highway of the upright?

THE LORD OVERTHROW

1. What is a wellspring of life?
A. Understanding. Proverbs 16:22
Understanding is a <u>wellspring of life unto him that hath it</u>: but the instruction of fools is folly.
The <u>words of a man's mouth</u> are as <u>deep waters</u>, and the <u>wellspring of wisdom as a flowing brook</u>. **Proverbs 18:4**

But WHOSOEVER DRINKETH OF THE WATER THAT I SHALL <u>GIVE HIM</u> SHALL NEVER THIRST; but the water that I shall give him shall be IN HIM A WELL OF WATER SPRINGING UP INTO EVERLASTING LIFE. JOHN 4:14

THAT HE MIGHT *<u>SANCTIFY AND CLEANSE IT WITH THE WASHING OF WATER BY THE WORD</u>*, EPHESIANS 5:26

For it is sanctified by the word of God and prayer. 1 Timothy 4:5
For every one that USETH MILK IS <u>UNSKILFUL IN THE WORD OF RIGHTEOUSNESS</u>: **for he is a babe. Hebrews 5:13**

<u>Being born again</u>, not of <u>corruptible seed,</u> but of incorruptible, by the <u>WORD OF GOD</u>, which <u>liveth and abideth for ever</u>. 1 Peter 1:23

2. These things also belong to the wise; it is not good to have respect of persons in what?
A. Judgment. Proverbs 24:23

3. Who words does The Lord Overthrow and continues to overthrow?
A. THE WORDS OF THE TRANSGRESSOR
THE EYES OF THE LORD PRESERVE KNOWLEDGE, AND HE <u>OVERTHROWETH</u> THE WORDS OF THE TRANSGRESSOR. PROVERBS 22:12

4. WHAT IS THE HIGHWAY OF THE UPRIGHT?
A. To depart from evil Proverbs 16:17

LET US ADD LEARNING TO OUR LIPS!

1. Can a Man preserve his own soul?

2. The heart of the wise, continue to teach his mouth by doing so he does what?

3. He that saith unto the wicked, Thou are righteous; him shall the people curse, nations shall do what?

4. What is an abomination to kings?

"LET US ADD LEARNING TO OUR LIPS"

1. Can a Man preserve his own soul?

A. Yes.

PRESERVETH HIS SOUL PROVERBS 16:17

He that continues to keep his way will continue to preserve his soul.

2. The heart of the wise, continue to teach his mouth by doing so he does what?
A. CONTINUES TO ADD LEARNING TO HIS LIP. PROVERBS 16:23
The heart of the wise teacheth his mouth, and addeth learning to his lips.

3. He that saith unto the <u>wicked</u>, Thou are <u>righteous</u>; him <u>shall the people curse</u>, nations shall do what?
A. Abhor him. Proverbs 24:24
THE LORD HATH MADE US KINGS AND PRIESTS UNTO GOD AND HIS FATHER; TO HIM BE GLORY AND DOMINION FOREVER AND EVER. AMEN. REVELATION 1:5&6.

4. What is an abomination to kings?
A. **It is an abomination to kings to commit wickedness: for the throne is established by righteousness. Proverbs 16:12**

ALLELUIA PRAISE THE LORD!

I PRAISE THEM <u>BOTH</u> YAHWEH/GOD THE EVERLASTING FATHER AND YAHUSHUA THE MESSIAH/JESUS THE CHRIST, THE SON OF THE TRUE AND LIVING GOD. ALLELUIA! PRAISE YAH. YAHWEH AND YAHUSHUA.

Luke 14:15 And when one of them that sat at meat with him heard these things, he said unto him, Blessed is he that shall eat bread in the kingdom of God.
Revelation 1:3 Blessed is he that readeth, and they that hear the words of this prophecy, and keep those things which are written therein: for the time is at hand.
Revelation 16:15 Behold, I come as a thief. Blessed is he that watcheth, and keepeth his garments, lest he walk naked, and they see his shame.
Revelation 22:7 Behold, I come quickly: blessed is he that keepeth the sayings of the prophecy of this book.
Speak unto Aaron and unto his sons, saying, On this wise ye <u>shall bless **the children of Israel**,</u> *saying unto them, The LORD bless thee, and keep thee:*[25] *The LORD make His Face shine upon thee, and be gracious unto thee:* Numbers 6:23-25

"A Wealth of Information"

"A Wealth of Information"

Things we need to know to transform our live and help us to overcome that O Devil.

A Charge for you and your children to *Arise and Declare*

Arise and Bless the World that she might become a Great Nation

We will never be Holy if we reject what makes one Holy

What can Nations and people do to inherit, the blessings?

If we are sick, we seek for a physician/doctor.

Steps required after we are declared the righteousness of God/Yahweh

For God so loved the world, that He gave

Sanctified through the truth The Word of Yahweh is truth.
<u>Being born again *by the word* of God</u>

Let us look at what KNOWLEDGE NICODEMUS DID HAVE. John 3:1-4.

What Did Paul Declared Unto His Brethren, "<u>Not T</u>he Ungodly"

I know what man is saying about Me but,
Whom do you say that I the Son of man am?

Simon Peter was born again.

Baptism took place in what man call The Old Testament in the book of Exodus

One thing *should hinder one from being; baptized in water.*

Certificate on Baptism

Neither Known Him

How do we know that we know Him?

Testing time

Highlighting Romans 6

'The conclusion of the matter"

What Did Yahweh give Israel *after* they came out of Egypt &
What dose Yahweh gives His children <u>after</u> they come out of the world?

What do we owe each other?

What do we need to <u>do</u> to have eternal life?

How Did Yahushua response to this question?

What Is The Love Of God?

What will we receive in this life and how will we receive them?

What did Yahushua say eternal Life was?

Who will go away into everlasting punishment and who will go away into life eternal?

Master, what shall I <u>do</u> to inherit eternal life? Paraphrasing and Summarizing

It seemed good in His sight. Why

Master, what shall I do to inherit eternal life?
Continuing in Luke chapter 10

Conclusion: The whole duty of man.

Why did The Lord; established a testimony in Jacob and appointed a law in Israel?
That they **should** be made known to their children.

For He established a testimony in Jacob, and appointed a law in Israel, which *He commanded our fathers,*
that they should make them known to their children:
That the generation to come <u>might</u> know them,
even the children which should *be born;*
who should arise and declare them to their children:
That they might set their hope in God,
and not forget the works of God,
but keep His commandments:
And might not be as their <u>fathers</u>, a stubborn and rebellious generation;
a generation that set <u>*not their heart aright,*</u>
<u>*and*</u> whose spirit was not *stedfast* with God.
Psalm 78:5–8

"Arise and Bless the World that she might become a Great Nation"

Stand on The Word from our creator. Yahweh gave them to Yahushua and He gives them to us. Hang them where all that come in will see them and say what a nation so blessed!

Keep therefore and do them; for this is your wisdom and your understanding in the sight of the nations, which shall hear all these statutes, and say, Surely this great nation is a wise and understanding people.
For what nation is there so great, who hath God so nigh unto them, as The LORD our God is in all things that we call upon Him for?

And what nation is there so great, that hath statutes and judgments so righteous as all this law, which I set before you this day
Deuteronomy 46-8

"We will never be Holy if we reject what makes one Holy"
The law of The Lord is perfect, converting the soul: the testimony of The Lord is sure, making wise the simple. The statutes of The Lord are right, rejoicing the heart: the commandment of The Lord is pure, enlightening the eyes. The fear of The Lord is clean, enduring for ever: the judgments of The Lord are true and righteous altogether. Psalm 19:7-9

Wherefore the law is holy, and the commandment holy, and just, and good.
Romans 7:12

What can Nations and people do to inherit, the blessings? Obey My Voice said The Lord!

²² **For I spake _not_ unto your fathers, _nor_ commanded them in the day that I brought them out of the land of Egypt, concerning _burnt offerings or sacrifices:_**

²³ **But this thing commanded I them, saying, Obey My voice, and I will be your God, and ye shall be My people: AND walk ye in all the ways that I have commanded you, that it may be well unto you.**

²⁴ **B**ut they hearkened not, nor inclined their ear, but walked in the counsels and in the imagination of their evil heart, and went backward, and not forward.

²⁵ Since the day that your _fathers came forth out of the land of Egypt unto this day I have even_ **sent unto you all my servants the prophets, daily rising up early and sending them:**

²⁶ **Yet they hearkened not unto me, nor inclined their ear, but hardened their neck: they did worse than their fathers.**

²⁷ Therefore thou shalt speak all these words unto them; but they will not hearken to thee: thou shalt also call unto them; but they will not answer thee.

²⁸ **But thou shalt say unto them**, **This is** a nation that obeyeth not the voice of the LORD their God, nor receiveth correction: truth is perished, and is cut off from their mouth.
Jeremiah 7:22-28

For I earnestly protested unto your fathers in the day that I brought them up out of the land of Egypt, even unto this day, rising early and protesting, saying, **Obey my voice.** Jeremiah 11:7

If we are sick, we seek for a physician/doctor.

We were all born sin sick, ungodly because, of the first Adams Mr. and Mss. Adam, both names Adam Gen. 5:1-3

If we need healing we need to do something, sometimes we go see the doctor. Because, of the first Adam all was born in sin before they sinned, Why because, sin was imputed upon every man; by the same example, because, of The second Adam, The Lord from Heaven, righteousness is imputed upon everyman before he do any righteousness/what is wright.

How is one declared, righteous? The same, as our father Abraham he believed God and it was, counted to him for righteousness before he was tried; and made perfect. He put work with his faith and that made him perfect.

Romans 4:11 And he received the sign of circumcision, a seal of the **righteousness of the faith** which he had yet being **UNCIRCUMCISED**: that he might be the **father of all them that believe**, though they be **not circumcised**; *that righteousness might be imputed unto them also*: Romans 4:22-24 And therefore it **was imputed** to him for righteousness. **Now it was not written for his sake alone, that it was imputed to him**; But for us also, to whom it shall be imputed,

HOW IS RIGHTEOUSNESS, IMPUTED UPON THE UNGODLY?

If we believe on HIM GOD/YAHWEH *THAT RAISED UP* **Jesus/Yahushua our Lord from the dead**;

Romans 5:13 **(For until the law** <u>sin was in the world</u>: but sin *IS NOT IMPUTED WHEN THERE IS NO LAW.*

Meaning, there is no law to impute sin upon the righteous he is justified by his faith.

This is how the ungodly is justified.

For sin shall not have *dominion over you*: **for ye are not** <u>under the law</u>, **but** <u>under grace</u>. **Romans 6:14 &15⁵**

James 2:23 **And the scripture was** <u>fulfilled</u> **which saith, Abraham** <u>believed God</u>, **and it was imputed unto him for righteousness: and he was** *called the Friend of God*.

"Steps required after we are declared the righteousness of God/Yahweh"

Let us look at some steps that are required from us after we are; declared the righteousness of God/Yahweh.

I was in **the past** ungodly/without Yahweh/God in my life but now I have been justified I am no longer without God in my life. Remember, Romans 4:22-24

People that have been justified by faith many of them starts out believing John 3:16 The spirit said unto me **John 3:16 does not say that we are, saved but** it says for God so love **the world . . .**

God loves everyone in the "World" GOD IS LOVE!

For God so loved the world, that He gave His only begotten Son, that **whosoever believeth in Him should not perish, but have everlasting life. John 3:16**

243

Many say this but no longer believe Yahweh/God gave **"not he came"** His only begotten Son, we are saying and teaching God wrapped Himself in flesh died and rose Himself from the dead. Yahweh/God never died but Yahushua /Jesus did die. Yahweh is from everlasting to everlasting. If Yahweh had died there, would have been no one in control or in authority for three days. Read 1 John chapter 5 and Revelation chapter five this should help and clarify the difficulty.

Furthermore, It said whosoever believeth in Him should *not* perish, but have everlasting life. Here we need to focus on three phrases; a. believeth b. *in Him* and c. *should* not perish. {Believeth is to continue in Him as if you abide in Me}

*This is the one **in Him** "not out of Him" Why because he is not condemned, if he sin he can confess and repent/turn away from sin.* For God sent not His Son into the world to condemn the world; but that the world **through Him might be saved.**[18] He that BELIEVETH **on** HIM IS NOT CONDEMNED: but he that **believeth not is condemned already**, because he **hath not believed in The name of The only begotten Son of God.** [19] And **this is the condemnation, that light is come into the world, and men loved darkness rather than light**, BECAUSE their *deeds were evil.* [20] For every one that *doeth evil hateth the light,* neither **cometh to the light**, lest **his deeds should be reproved**.[21] **But he that doeth truth** COMETH TO THE LIGHT, THAT HIS DEEDS MAY BE MADE MANIFEST, THAT THEY ARE WROUGHT IN GOD. [22] After these things came Jesus and His disciples into the land of Judaea; and there **He tarried** with them, and BAPTIZED.

Now cross-reference this with John chapter 15 and sketch it out, focus on, verses 2, 6 & 7 **Every branch in Me** that beareth not fruit He taketh away: and **every branch that beareth fruit,** He purgeth it, that it may bring forth more fruit. 15:26-7 **If** a man **abide not *IN ME*, he is** cast forth as a branch, and is withered; and men gather them, and **cast them into the fire, and they are burned.** [7] **If** ye **abide in Me, and My words abide in you**, ye *shall ask what ye will, and it shall be done unto you.*

"Sanctified through the truth" The Word of Yahweh is truth.
Being born again by the word of God
Sanctify them through thy truth: thy word is truth As Thou hast sent Me into the world, even so have I also sent them into the world. And for their sakes I sanctify Myself, that they also *might be sanctified through the truth.* John 17:17-19

Being born again, not of corruptible seed, but of incorruptible, *by the word* of God, which liveth and abideth for ever. 1 Peter 1:23

Let us look at what knowledge Nicodemus did have. John 3:1-4.
NICODEMUS WAS A RULER OF THE JEWS, HE CALLED YAHUSHUA **RABBI** AND HE SAID WE KNOW THAT THOU **ART A TEACHER COME FROM GOD:** FOR **no man can do these miracles that thou doest, except God be with him.** JESUS ANSWERED AND SAID UNTO HIM, VERILY, VERILY, I SAY UNTO THEE, EXCEPT A MAN BE **BORN AGAIN**, HE **CANNOT SEE THE KINGDOM** OF GOD.

Notice: Except a man be **born again**, he **cannot see** the kingdom of God, in additional,
Except a man be born of **water and of the Spirit**, he **cannot** *enter into the kingdom of God.* Read John 3:3-5.
We must be born *again* by the **water and the Spirit**, man baptizes with water so did John but *Yahushua baptizes with The Holy Ghost. Remember, born again BY THE* WORD OF GOD WHICH **LIVETH AND ABIDETH FOR EVER.**

We are trying to bring people to God and convert The Jews and the Muslim but we need to be converted. Many believe Yahweh/God sent Yahushua The Messiah/Jesus the Christ but when we are saying one thing and turn around and say Yahweh/God came and died for your sins this is puzzling and incorrect. However, we know we cannot show what we cannot see.

Paul could not teach what he could not see but once he received his spiritual sight, he went straightway and preached Christ/The Messiah in the synagogues, that He is The Son of God. Acts 9:20

What Did Paul Declared Unto His Brethren, "Not The Ungodly"

MOREOVER, BRETHREN, I declare unto you the **gospel which I preached unto you**, which also ye have **received**, and **wherein ye stand**; By which **also ye are SAVED, If ye keep in memory** what I preached unto you:, **unless ye have believed in vain.** For **I delivered unto you first of all that which I also received**, how **that Christ died for our sins according to the scriptures**; And **that He was buried, and that He rose again the third day** according to the scriptures 1 Corinthians 15:1-4

I KNOW WHAT MAN IS SAYING ABOUT ME BUT, WHOM DO YOU SAY THAT I THE SON OF MAN AM?

Remember, Yahushua asked His disciples, **Whom do men say that I the Son of man am?** they said, Some say that thou art John the Baptist: some, Elias; and others, Jeremias, or one of the prophets. **He saith unto them, But whom say ye that I am?** Only one confessed and He only confess him, [16] **And Simon Peter answered and said, Thou art The Christ, The Son of The living God.** [17] **And Jesus answered and said unto him, Blessed art thou, Simon Barjona: for** flesh and blood hath *not* revealed it unto thee, *but* **My Father which is in heaven. Matthew 16:13-17.**

Peter had a revelation that the others did not have. Solid as a rock, hard rocks do *not breakdown they stand! The others did not confess Him and He did not confess them Why, Because, of what He said in Matthew 10:32 &33.*

Whosoever therefore **shall confess Me before men**, him will I confess also **before My Father** which is in heaven, **But** whosoever shall **deny Me before men**, him will I also deny before My Father which is in heaven.

Simon Peter was born again, how could I be sure?
1 John 5:1. Whosoever believeth that Jesus is The Christ is born of God: and every one that loveth *Him that begat loveth Him also that is begotten of Him.*

In other words, if we love Yahweh/God, we love His Son Yahushua/Jesus in additional, we love one another.

If someone said unto you, you do not need to be baptized you should look up all the scriptures on baptism. **Baptism took place in what man call The Old Testament in the book of Exodus.** How can I be sure?

Moreover, brethren, I would not that ye **should be ignorant**, *how that all our fathers were under the cloud, and all passed through the sea;* **And were all baptized unto Moses in the cloud and in the sea**; And did all eat the same spiritual meat; And did all drink the same spiritual drink: **for they drank of that spiritual Rock that followed them: and that Rock was Christ. 1 Corinthians 10:1-4**

Also Read chapter 10, You SHOULD SEE, it was Yahushua The Messiah that followed them and how Yahweh was not well pleased with them, . . . But with many of them God **was not well pleased:** for **they were overthrown in the wilderness.** 10:5

Now there is one thing *should hinder one from being; baptized in water*.

And as they went on their way, they came **unto a certain water: and the eunuch said, See, here is water; what doth** *hinder me to be baptized*? And Philip said, **If** thou believest with all thine heart, thou mayest. Acts chapter 8:36-39.

If one do not believe with all his heart, he should not, be baptized.
What scriptures support this belief? Romans 10:9-10

That **if** thou shalt *confess with thy mouth* The Lord Jesus, **and** shalt believe *in thine heart that God* hath **raised Him from the dead, thou shalt be saved**. For with **the heart man believeth** *unto* **righteousness; and with the mouth** *confession is made unto salvation*. **What did he confess? And he answered and said**, **I believe that Jesus Christ is The Son of God**. After he confessed, what he believed Philip commanded the chariot to stand still: and they went down both **into the water**, **both** Philip and the eunuch; and he baptized him. And when they were come up out of the water, the Spirit of The Lord caught away Philip, that the eunuch saw him no more: and he went on his way rejoicing.

Please, see The Certificate on Baptism:

If you did not see the Certificate on Baptism please, do so it is a wealth of information on this subject. Years, ago The Spirit of The Lord had me to write to a well-known Christian International Broadcasting Network because, they would say, over and over again "just say the sinner prayer and you will be saved"

After I sent them, Romans10:9-10, 10:13, Mark 16:16 and Acts 2:21 Plus some other information and expounded on the word, I did not hear that teaching from the company owner nor other teaches as much. But many are continuing to preach and teach the so called "sinners prayer"

The word of God do not teach a sinner prayer but I would say we should teach the sinners to repent and believe the word of God and when and if they sin, (Yes, all will sin sometimes but we do not or should not sin everyday as some deceitful spirit teaches.) I John 1:9 Confess you sins meaning to agree with Yahweh that sin is sin. If someone says, we do sin every day the only thing I can say I do not. Is this scriptural that we sin every day? No. Let us look at what the word says, not man.

1 John 3:6 **Whosoever abided in Him sonnet not:** whosoever **sonnet hath not seen Him,** **neither known Him.**
1 John 5:18 **We know that whosoever is born of God sinneth not;** but he that is begotten of God **keepeth himself, and** *that wicked one toucheth him not.*

He will not continue to sin deliberately and if he does he confess and repent/ turn away from sin.

2 Chronicles 7:14 If My people, which ARE CALLED BY MY NAME, shall humble themselves, and pray, and seek My Face, and turn from their wicked ways; *then* **will I hear from Neither Known Him:**

How do we know that we know Him?
AND HEREBY WE do know that we know Him, if we keep his commandments. He that saith, I know Him, and *keepeth not His commandments, is a liar,* and the truth is *not* in him. 1 John 2:3 & 4 Read 1 John chapter 2

There are two groups in Psalm.1:5 and 1 Peter 4:18 THE UNGODLY in addition the sinners.

Therefore the ungodly shall *NOT STAND IN THE JUDGMENT*, nor sinners in the congregation of the righteous. And if the righteous scarcely be saved, where shall the UNGODLY and the sinner appear?

What can we see? If you cannot see the door, how can you inter into it?
READ ALL THE PARABLES ON THE KINGDOM, WHAT THE KINGDOM IS LIKE, THE KINGDOM OF HEAVEN AND THE KINGDOM OF GOD IT WILL BLESS YOU. AND HE WILL GATHER OUT OF HIS KINGDOM, YOU CANNOT TAKE MY CAR IF I DO NOT HAVE ONE.

Matthew 13:40-42 AS THEREFORE THE TARES ARE GATHERED AND BURNED IN THE FIRE; SO SHALL IT BE IN THE END OF THIS WORLD. THE SON OF MAN SHALL SEND FORTH HIS ANGELS, AND THEY SHALL GATHER OUT OF HIS KINGDOM ALL THINGS THAT OFFEND, AND THEM WHICH DO INIQUITY; AND SHALL CAST THEM INTO A FURNACE OF FIRE: THERE SHALL BE WAILING AND GNASHING OF TEETH. CROSS-REFERENCE WITH JOHN 15.

Should not perish, how can one know the different? Judas was, called chosen and anointed but he was lost so the scripture would be filfulled, this is an example that the same can happen if we do not overcome the world, everything written is for our ensample and example.
Read the book of Ezekiel, The Lord said warn, My people from Me. **The righteous and the wicked, focus chapters 2,3,18, 33-36.**
2 Chronicles 19:10 And what cause soever shall come to you of your brethren that dwell in your cities, between **blood and blood, between law and commandment, statutes and judgments**, ye shall **even warn them that they trespass not against The LORD,** and so wrath come upon you, and upon your brethren: this do, and ye shall not trespass.

Ezekiel 3:18-19 When I say unto the **wicked,** Thou **shalt surely die;** and thou givest him not warning, nor speakest to warn the wicked from his wicked way, **to save his life;** the same wicked man **shall die in his iniquity**; but his **blood will I require at thine hand.** Yet if thou warn the wicked, and he turn not from his wickedness, nor from his wicked way, he shall die in his iniquity; but thou hast delivered thy soul.

Ezekiel 3:21 **Nevertheless if thou warn the righteous man**, that the **righteous sin not,** and he doth not sin, he shall surely live, because he is warned; also thou hast delivered thy soul.

Ezekiel 33:3 If when he seeth the sword come upon the land, **he blow the trumpet**, and

warn the people;

Ezekiel 33:7-9 So thou, O son of man, I have set thee a watchman unto the house of Israel; therefore thou shalt **HEAR THE WORD AT <u>MY MOUTH</u>, AND <u>WARN THEM FROM ME</u>**. When I say unto the wicked, O wicked man, thou shalt surely die; if thou dost not speak to warn the wicked from his way, that wicked man shall die in his iniquity; but his blood will I require at thine hand. Nevertheless, *if thou warn the wicked of his way to turn from it; if he do not turn from his way, he shall die in his iniquity; but thou hast delivered thy soul.*

Acts 20:31 Therefore watch, and remember, that by the space of three years I ceased not **to warn every one night and day with tears.**
heaven, and will forgive their sin, and will heal their land.

Testing time: But according to *Romans 10:13, Acts 2:21 and Joel 2:32* Yes, I can be delivered and become an overcomer. Praise Yah.
For whosoever shall <u>call</u> upon The Name of The Lord shall be saved.Romans 10:13
And it *shall* come to pass, that *whosoever* <u>shall call</u> on The Name of The Lord shall be saved Acts 2:21
And it shall come to pass, that whosoever shall call on The Name of The **LORD shall be delivered**: for in mount Zion and in Jerusalem **SHALL BE DELIVERANCE**, as **The LORD hath said**, and in the remnant whom **The Lord shall call**. Joel 2:32
If we did not know saved in these verses is to be, delivered.
Man begin to walk with God when he begain to call upon The Name of the lord
Genesis 4:26 And to Seth, to him also there was born a son; and he called his name Enos: then began men to **call upon the name of the LORD.**
Psalm 116:13 I will take the cup of salvation, and call upon The Name of The LORD.
Psalm 116:17 I will offer to thee **the sacrifice of thanksgiving**, and will call upon The Name of The LORD.

Zephaniah 3:9 For then will I turn to the people **a pure language**, that they may all call upon The Name of The LORD, **to serve him with one consent..**
Yes, I will sin and come short of the glory of God but I should not sin willfully According to Hebrews 10:26-27. For **if we sin willfully after that we have received the knowledge of the truth, there remaineth no more sacrifice for sins,** But a *certain fearful looking for of judgment and fiery indignation, which shall devour the adversaries.*
If we confess/agree with God that sin is sin, the blood of The Messiah will clean us as it did when we were first **justified.** As said in 1 John 1:8-10, ***<u>He is faithful and just to forgive us our sins, and to cleanse us from all unrighteousness)</u>***
[8] **IF** we say that **we have no sin, we deceive ourselves**, and **the truth is not in us.** [9] **If we confess our sins, He is faithful and just to forgive us our sins, and to cleanse us from all unrighteousness.**[10] **If we say that we have not sinned, we make him a liar, and his word is not in us.**

Highlighting Romans 6

6:1 <u>What shall we say then? Shall we continue in sin, that grace may abound?</u> ² God forbid. **How shall we, that are dead to sin**, live any **longer therein**? ³ Know ye not, that <u>so many of us as were baptized into Jesus Christ were baptized into His death?</u> ⁴ Therefore we are ***buried with him by baptism into death***: that **like as Christ** was raised up from the dead by the glory of the Father, even so we also should <u>***walk in newness of life***</u>. ⁵ For IF we have been planted together in the likeness of His death, we shall be also **in the likeness of His resurrection**:⁶ KNOWING THIS, THAT OUR <u>OLD MAN IS CRUCIFIED WITH HIM</u>, THAT THE *BODY OF SIN* <u>*MIGHT*</u> BE DESTROYED,

that **henceforth we** <u>***should not***</u> **serve sin.** ⁷ For he that is **dead** is freed from sin. ⁸ **Now if** we be **dead with Christ**, <u>*we believe that we shall also live with Him*</u>: ⁹ **Knowing that Christ being raised from the dead dieth <u>no</u> more**; death hath no more <u>dominion</u> over Him. ¹⁰ **For in that He died, He died unto sin** *once*: **but** in that **He liveth, He liveth unto God.** ¹¹ **Likewise** <u>*RECKON YE ALSO YOURSELVES TO BE DEAD INDEED UNTO SIN*</u>, but **alive unto God through Jesus Christ our Lord**.

Here is knowledge, wisdom and understand if we can receive and obey

¹² **Let not sin therefore reign in your mortal body**, that **ye should obey it in the lusts thereof.**¹³ NEITHER YIELD YE YOUR MEMBERS AS INSTRUMENTS OF UNRIGHTEOUSNESS UNTO SIN: but YIELD YOURSELVES UNTO GOD, AS THOSE THAT ARE ALIVE FROM THE DEAD, and **your members as instruments of righteousness unto God**. ¹⁴ **For sin shall not have dominion over you: for ye are not under the law, but under grace.** ¹⁵ WHAT THEN? SHALL WE SIN, BECAUSE WE ARE NOT UNDER THE LAW, BUT UNDER GRACE? GOD FORBID. ¹⁶ **Know ye not, that to <u>whom ye yield yourselves servants to obey</u>, his servants ye are to** <u>***whom ye obey***</u>; **whether of** *sin unto death*, or of <u>OBEDIENCE UNTO RIGHTEOUSNESS</u>?

ROMANS 10:9 , SAYS, *THAT IF THOU SHALT CONFESS WITH THY MOUTH THE LORD JESUS, AND SHALT BELIEVE IN THINE HEART THAT GOD HATH RAISED HIM FROM THE DEAD,* <u>*THOU SHALT BE SAVED.*</u>¹⁰ FOR WITH THE HEART MAN BELIEVETH <u>UNTO RIGHTEOUSNESS</u>; AND *WITH THE MOUTH CONFESSION IS MADE UNTO SALVATION.*

¹⁷ **But God be thanked,** that ye <u>**were the servants of sin**</u>, but ye have <u>**obeyed from the heart**</u> that **form of doctrine which was delivered you.** ¹⁸ **Being then made free from sin,** <u>***ye became***</u> <u>the servants of righteousness</u>. ¹⁹ **I speak after the manner of men because of** the infirmity of your flesh: for **as <u>ye have</u> yielded your *members servants to uncleanness and to iniquity unto iniquity; even so now yield your members servants to righteousness unto holiness*.** ²⁰ **For when ye were the servants of <u>sin</u>, ye were <u>free from righteousness</u>**. ²¹ What fruit had ye then in those things whereof ye are now ashamed? for the end of those things is death. ²² **But now being made free from sin,** and **become servants to God, ye have your fruit unto holiness, and the** <u>***end everlasting life.***</u> ²³ <u>**For the wages of sin is death**</u>; <u>**but the gift of God**</u> *is eternal life through Jesus Christ our Lord.*

The conclusion of the matter is, if we *sin until death* the payment FOR SIN is death but if WE LIVE UNTO RIGHTEOUSNESS UNTIL DEATH, THE **gift is eternal life** AND WE CAN ONLY HAVE IT **through** JESUS CHRIST OUR LORD/YAHUSHUA THE MESSIAH.

Did we notice the end everlasting life?

WHATEVER THE LORD DOES, HE DOES IT FOR A PURPOSE.
WHAT WAS AND IS HIS PURPOSE?
PSALM 78:5-8
Why did The Lord; established a testimony in Jacob and appointed a law in Israel?

That they should be made known to their children
For He established a testimony in **Jacob,** and appointed a **law in Israel**,
which He *commanded our fathers*,
that they **SHOULD MAKE THEM KNOWN TO THEIR CHILDREN:**
That the **generation to come might know them**,
even **the children which should** *be born;*
who should arise and declare them to their children*:*
That they might **set** *their hope in God,*
and **not forget the** *works* **of God,**
but KEEP HIS COMMANDMENTS:
And might not be as their fathers, a **stubborn and rebellious** generation;
a generation that set **not their heart aright,**
and **whose spirit was not** *stedfast* **with God.** *Psalm 78:5-8*

'The conclusion of the matter"

The conclusion of the matter is, if we *sin until death* the payment FOR SIN is death but if WE LIVE UNTO RIGHTEOUSNESS UNTIL DEATH, THE **gift is eternal life** AND WE CAN ONLY HAVE IT **through** JESUS CHRIST OUR LORD/ YAHUSHUA THE MESSIAH.
Did we notice the end everlasting life?

WHAT DID YAHWEH GIVE ISRAEL *AFTER* THEY CAME OUT OF EGYPT
&
What dose Yahweh gives His children <u>after</u> they come out of the world?

A. Deuteronomy 4

4 Now therefore hearken, O Israel, unto the statutes and unto the judgments, which I teach you, for to do them, that ye may live, and go in and possess the land which the LORD God of your fathers giveth you.

2 Ye shall not add unto the word which I command you, neither shall ye diminish ought from it, that ye may keep the commandments of the LORD your God which I command you.

3 Your eyes have seen what the LORD did because of Baalpeor: for all the men that followed Baalpeor, the LORD thy God hath destroyed them from among you.

4 But ye that did cleave unto the LORD your God are alive every one of you this day.

5 Behold, I have taught you statutes and judgments, even as the LORD my God commanded me, that ye should do so in the land whither ye go to possess it.

6 Keep therefore and do them; for this is your wisdom and your understanding in the sight of the nations, which shall hear all these statutes, and say, Surely this great nation is a wise and understanding people.

7 For what nation is there so great, who hath God so nigh unto them, as the LORD our God is in all things that we call upon him for?

8 And what nation is there so great, that hath statutes and judgments so righteous as all this law, which I set before you this day?

9 Only take heed to thyself, and keep thy soul diligently, lest thou forget the things which thine eyes have seen, and lest they depart from thy heart all the days of thy life: but teach them thy sons, and thy sons' sons;

10 Specially the day that thou stoodest before the LORD thy God in Horeb, when the LORD said unto me, Gather me the people together, and I will make them hear my words, that they may learn to fear me all the days that they shall live upon the earth, and that they may teach their children.

11 And ye came near and stood under the mountain; and the mountain burned with fire unto the midst of heaven, with darkness, clouds, and thick darkness.

12 And the LORD spake unto you out of the midst of the fire: ye heard the voice of the words, but saw no similitude; only ye heard a voice.

13 And he declared unto you his covenant, which he commanded you to perform, even ten commandments; and he wrote them upon two tables of stone.

14 And the LORD commanded me at that time to teach you statutes and judgments, that ye might do them in the land whither ye go over to possess it.

15 Take ye therefore good heed unto yourselves; for ye saw no manner of similitude on the day that the LORD spake unto you in Horeb out of the midst of the fire:

16 Lest ye corrupt yourselves, and make you a graven image, the similitude of any figure, the likeness of male or female,

17 The likeness of any beast that is on the earth, the likeness of any winged fowl that flieth in the air,

18 The likeness of any thing that creepeth on the ground, the likeness of any fish that is in the waters beneath the earth:

¹⁹ And lest thou lift up thine eyes unto heaven, and when thou seest the sun, and the moon, and the stars, even all the host of heaven, shouldest be driven to worship them, and serve them, which the Lord thy God hath divided unto all nations under the whole heaven.

²⁰ But the Lord hath taken you, and brought you forth out of the iron furnace, even out of Egypt, to be unto him a people of inheritance, as ye are this day.

²¹ Furthermore the Lord was angry with me for your sakes, and sware that I should not go over Jordan, and that I should not go in unto that good land, which the Lord thy God giveth thee for an inheritance:

²² But I must die in this land, I must not go over Jordan: but ye shall go over, and possess that good land.

²³ Take heed unto yourselves, lest ye forget the covenant of the Lord your God, which he made with you, and make you a graven image, or the likeness of any thing, which the Lord thy God hath forbidden thee.

²⁴ For the Lord thy God is a consuming fire, even a jealous God.

²⁵ When thou shalt beget children, and children's children, and ye shall have remained long in the land, and shall corrupt yourselves, and make a graven image, or the likeness of any thing, and shall do evil in the sight of the Lord thy God, to provoke him to anger:

²⁶ I call heaven and earth to witness against you this day, that ye shall soon utterly perish from off the land whereunto ye go over Jordan to possess it; ye shall not prolong your days upon it, but shall utterly be destroyed.

²⁷ And the Lord shall scatter you among the nations, and ye shall be left few in number among the heathen, whither the Lord shall lead you.

²⁸ And there ye shall serve gods, the work of men's hands, wood and stone, which neither see, nor hear, nor eat, nor smell.

²⁹ But if from thence thou shalt seek the Lord thy God, thou shalt find him, if thou seek him with all thy heart and with all thy soul.

³⁰ When thou art in tribulation, and all these things are come upon thee, even in the latter days, if thou turn to the Lord thy God, and shalt be obedient unto his voice;

³¹ (For the Lord thy God is a merciful God;) he will not forsake thee, neither destroy thee, nor forget the covenant of thy fathers which he sware unto them.

³² For ask now of the days that are past, which were before thee, since the day that God created man upon the earth, and ask from the one side of heaven unto the other, whether there hath been any such thing as this great thing is, or hath been heard like it?

³³ Did ever people hear the voice of God speaking out of the midst of the fire, as thou hast heard, and live?

³⁴ Or hath God assayed to go and take him a nation from the midst of another nation, by temptations, by signs, and by wonders, and by war, and by a mighty hand, and by a stretched out arm, and by great terrors, according to all that the Lord your God did for you in Egypt before your eyes?

³⁵ Unto thee it was shewed, that thou mightest know that the Lord he is God; there is none else beside him.

³⁶ Out of heaven he made thee to hear his voice, that he might instruct thee: and upon earth he shewed thee his great fire; and thou heardest his words out of the midst of the fire.

³⁷ And because he loved thy fathers, therefore he chose their seed after them, and brought thee out in his sight with his mighty power out of Egypt;

³⁸ To drive out nations from before thee greater and mightier than thou art, to bring thee in, to give thee their land for an inheritance, as it is this day.

³⁹ Know therefore this day, and consider it in thine heart, that the LORD he is God in heaven above, and upon the earth beneath: there is none else.

⁴⁰ Thou shalt keep therefore his statutes, and his commandments, which I command thee this day, that it may go well with thee, and with thy children after thee, and that thou mayest prolong thy days upon the earth, which the LORD thy God giveth thee, for ever.

⁴¹ Then Moses severed three cities on this side Jordan toward the sunrising;

⁴² That the slayer might flee thither, which should kill his neighbour unawares, and hated him not in times past; and that fleeing unto one of these cities he might live:

⁴³ Namely, Bezer in the wilderness, in the plain country, of the Reubenites; and Ramoth in Gilead, of the Gadites; and Golan in Bashan, of the Manassites.

⁴⁴ And this is the law which Moses set before the children of Israel:

⁴⁵ These are the testimonies, and the statutes, and the judgments, which Moses spake unto the children of Israel, after they came forth out of Egypt.

WHAT DO WE OWE EACH OTHER?

"Love one another" ROMANS 13:8-14

Owe no man any thing, but to love one another: for he that loveth another ***hath fulfilled the law***. ⁹ For this, Thou shalt not commit adultery, Thou shalt not kill, Thou shalt not steal, Thou shalt not bear false witness, Thou shalt not covet; and if there be any other commandment, it is briefly comprehended in this saying, namely, Thou shalt love thy neighbour as thyself.

¹⁰ Love worketh no ill to his neighbour: therefore love is the fulfilling of the law.

¹¹ And that, knowing the time, that now it is high time to awake out of sleep: for now is our salvation nearer than when we believed.

¹² The night is far spent, the day is at hand: let us therefore cast off the works of darkness, and let us put on the armour of light.

¹³ Let us walk honestly, as in the day; not in rioting and drunkenness, not in chambering and wantonness, not in strife and envying.

¹⁴ But put ye on the Lord Jesus Christ, and make not provision for the flesh, to fulfil the lusts thereof.

What do we need to <u>do</u> to have eternal life?

Matthew 19, Mark 10 & Luke 10

What good thing shall I Do? How Did Yahushua response to his question?
Did he say Shalt or should NOT?
"Thou Shalt Not"

Matthew 19:17-21

And, behold, one came and said unto Him, **Good Master, what good thing shall I do**, that I may have eternal life? And He said unto him, Why callest thou Me good? there is none good but one, that is, **God: but if** thou **wilt <u>enter into life</u>, keep the commandments**. He saith unto Him, Which? Jesus said, *Thou shalt do no murder, Thou shalt not commit adultery, Thou shalt not steal, Thou shalt not bear false witness, Honour thy father and thy mother: and, Thou shalt love thy neighbour as thyself.* The young man saith unto Him, **All these things have I kept from my youth up**: what lack I yet? Jesus said unto him, **<u>If thou wilt be perfect</u>**, go and **sell that thou hast, and give to the poor**, and thou shalt have **treasure in heaven: and come and follow Me.**
"If he wanted to be perfect, more was required from him"

How Did Yahushua response to this question?
Did he say Shalt, should or Do NOT?
"Do not"

Mark 10:17-18

17 And when He was gone forth into the way, there came one running, and kneeled to Him, and asked Him, **Good Master, what shall I do that I may inherit eternal life?** 18 And Jesus said unto him, **Why callest thou me good? there is none good but one, that is, God.** 19 **Thou knowest the commandments, Do not commit** adultery, **Do** not kill, **Do** not steal, **Do** not bear false witness, **Defraud not, Honour** thy father and mother. 20 And he answered and said unto Him, **Master, all these have I observed from my youth.** 21 Then Jesus beholding him **loved Him**, and said unto him, **One thing thou lackest**: *go thy way, sell whatsoever thou hast, and give to the poor, and thou shalt have treasure in heaven: and come, take up the cross, and follow me.* 22 And **he was sad** at that saying, and **went away grieved:** for he had **great possessions**.

What Is The Love Of God?
{ Remember, For this is the love of God, that we keep His commandments: and His commandments are not grievous. 1 John 5:3 }

---

23 And Jesus looked round about, and saith unto **His disciples,** How hardly shall they that have riches enter into the kingdom of God! 24 **And the disciples were astonished at His words.** *But Jesus answereth again*, and saith unto them, **Children, how hard is it for them that trust in riches to enter into the kingdom of God!** 25 It is easier for a camel to go through the eye of a needle, than for **a rich man to enter into the kingdom of God.** 26 And they were **astonished out of measure, saying among themselves,**
Who then can be saved, with men it is impossible but not with God!

²⁷ And Jesus looking upon them saith, **With men it is impossible, but not with God**: for **with God all things are possible.**²⁸ Then Peter began to say unto Him, Lo, we have **left all**, and have **followed Thee**. ²⁹ And Jesus answered and said, Verily I say unto you, **There is no man** that hath left house, or <u>brethren,</u> or <u>sisters,</u> or **father, or mother, or wife, or children, or lands, for My sake, <u>and</u> the gospel's,**

³⁰ But he shall receive an hundredfold now in this time, houses, and brethren, and sisters, and mothers, and children, and lands, **with <u>persecutions;</u> and in the world to come eternal life**.

³¹ **B**ut many that **are first <u>shall be</u> last**; and *the last first.*

What will we receive in this life and how will we receive them?
Houses, and brethren, and sisters, and mothers, and children, and lands, with <u>persecutions;</u> and in the <u>world</u> to come eternal life

---

What did Yahushua say eternal Life was?
John 17:1-3
These words spake Jesus, and lifted up **His eyes to heaven, and said,** *Father, the hour is come;* **glorify Thy Son, that Thy Son also may glorify Thee:** ² As thou **hast given Him power over all flesh,** that He **should give <u>eternal life</u> to as many as <u>thou hast</u> given Him.** ³ **And this is life eternal**, that **they <u>might</u> know thee** *<u>The only True God</u>*, <u>and</u>
Jesus Christ, whom thou hast sent.

Who will go away into everlasting punishment?
Matthew chapter 25
&
Who will go away into life eternal?
Matthew chapter 25
And these shall go away into everlasting punishment: *but* **the righteous into life eternal. Matthew 25:46**

Master, what shall I do to inherit eternal life?
Paraphrasing and Summarizing
"Jesus appointed seventy other disciples"
Luke chapter 10

10:1 After these things The LORD appointed **other seventy also**, and **sent** them **two and two before His face into every city and place, whither he himself would come.** [2] **Therefore said He unto them, The harvest truly is great**, but the labourers are few: pray ye therefore The Lord of the harvest, that He would *send forth labourers into His harvest.*

[3] Go your ways: behold, I send you forth as lambs among wolves. [4] Carry neither purse, nor scrip, nor shoes: and salute no man by the way. [5] And into whatsoever house ye enter, first say, Peace be to this house. [6] And **if the son of peace be there**, your peace shall rest upon it: **if not**, it shall turn to you again. [7] And in the same house remain, eating and drinking such things as they give: *for the labourer is worthy of his hire.* **Go not from house to house.** [8] And into whatsoever city ye enter, and **they receive you**, *eat such things as are set before you:* [9] *And heal the sick that are therein*, and say unto them, **The kingdom of God is come nigh unto you**. [10] **But into whatsoever** *city ye enter, and they receive you not,* go your _ways_ out into the streets of *the same*, **and say,** [11] Even the very dust of your city, which cleaveth on us, we do wipe off against you: notwithstanding be ye sure of this, **that the kingdom of God is come nigh unto you**.

[12] But I say unto you, that **it shall be more tolerable in that day for Sodom, than for that city.**

[13] **Woe unto thee**, Chorazin! **woe** unto thee, Bethsaida! for **if the mighty works had been done in Tyre and Sidon, which have been done in you, they had a _great while ago repented_**, sitting in sackcloth and ashes. [14] But it shall be more **tolerable for Tyre and Sidon at the judgment, than for you.** [15] And thou, Capernaum, **which art exalted to heaven, shalt be thrust down to hell.** [16] **He that heareth you heareth Me; and** *he that despiseth you despiseth Me;* **and he that despiseth Me despiseth Him that sent me.**

In other words, if someone hates me because, I stand on the truth they are actually despising, abhorring and hating Yahushua the Messiah/Jesus Christ and if they despise Yahushua, they are really despising, abhorring and hating, Yahweh/God. Why because, the words we speak is **not ours** but **they came from Yahweh.**
Do scriptures support this statement absolutely?

John 12:48-50 *He that rejecteth Me, and receiveth not My words, hath one that judgeth him: the word that I have spoken, the same shall judge him in the last day. For I have not spoken of myself;* **but** *The Father which sent Me*, He gave Me a commandment, **what** *I should say*, **and what** *I should speak.* And I know that *His commandment is life everlasting:* whatsoever I speak therefore, **even as The Father said unto M, so I speak.**

Continuing in Luke chapter 10

[17] And **the seventy returned again with joy, saying, Lord, even** *the devils* **are subject unto us through**

Thy name. [18] And He said unto them, <u>**I beheld Satan as lightning fall from heaven**</u>.

[19] BEHOLD, I GIVE UNTO YOU POWER TO TREAD ON SERPENTS AND SCORPIONS, AND OVER ALL THE POWER OF THE ENEMY: AND NOTHING SHALL BY ANY MEANS HURT YOU.

[20] Notwithstanding in this rejoice not, that **the spirits are subject unto you;** <u>***but rather rejoice, because your names are*** **written in heaven.**</u> [21] In that **hour Jesus rejoiced in spirit, and said,** I thank thee, O Father, Lord of heaven and earth, <u>**that thou hast hid these things**</u> FROM THE *WISE AND PRUDENT*, AND **hast revealed them unto babes**: *EVEN SO*, **Father; for so it seemed good in Thy sight.**

It seemed good in His sight. Why

Because, It is the *glory of God* to conceal a thing: but the honour of kings is to **search out a matter.** Proverbs 25:2

Also, The secret things belong unto The LORD our God: **but** those things which are revealed belong unto us and to our children for ever, that we **may** <u>do</u> **all the** <u>words</u> **of this law.** Deuteronomy 29:29

Master, what shall I do to inherit eternal life?

Continuing in Luke chapter 10

[22] ***All things are delivered to Me of My Father***: and **no man knoweth who The Son is, but** The Father; <u>and</u> who **The Father is**, <u>but</u> THE SON, <u>AND</u> <u>**he**</u> to whom The Son will <u>reveal</u> Him. [23] **And He turned Him unto His disciples, and said privately,** BLESSED ARE THE EYES WHICH <u>SEE</u> THE *things* THAT YE SEE: [24] For I tell you, **that many prophets and kings have desired to see those things which ye see, and have not seen them;** and to hear those things which ye hear, and have not heard them.

[25] ***And, behold, a certain lawyer stood up, and tempted Him, saying, Master, what shall I do to inherit eternal life?***

[26] He said unto him, WHAT IS WRITTEN IN THE LAW? <u>HOW</u> READEST THOU?

[27] And he answering said, **Thou** *shalt* **love The Lord Thy God with** <u>***all thy heart,***</u> ***and with all thy soul, and with all thy strength, and with all thy mind; and thy neighbour as thyself.***

YAHUSHUA ASKED HIM WHAT IS WRITTEN IN THE LAW? *HOW READEST THOU*? **How did Yahushua respond to his REPLY?**

[28] **And he said unto him, Thou hast** <u>**answered right**</u>: **this do, and thou shalt live.** [29] **But he, willing to justify himself,** said unto Jesus, **And who is my neighbour?** [30] And Jesus answering said, A certain man went down from Jerusalem to Jericho, and fell among thieves, which stripped him of his raiment, and wounded him, and departed, leaving him half dead. **Please, continue to read this entire parable for a better understanding.**

My prayer and hope is that man will be enlighten, empowered and transformed.

THE REVELATOR AND TEACHING PRIEST, PROPHETESS AND PASTOR DR. MARY NEAL

Yahweh and Yahushua I thank and praise you for both The Holy Ghost and The completion of Quizzing. Praise Yah!

That all men **should** honour **The Son**, even as they **honour The Father.** He that **honoureth not** The **Son** honoureth **not** The Father which hath **sent** Him John 5:23

ABOUT THE AUTHOR

Prophetess and Pastor Dr. Mary Neal is the author of the book "A New revelation from God", A *CD "If You Want To Be Blessed"* A biblical game "Pick Up Your Cross Daily and Follow Me" She is also a songwriter and a writer of plays and poems.

She spent over eighteen years in ministry, ministering in churches, outreach ministries, ministering to the small as well as the great. Her passions are, searching the scriptures daily, teaching and preaching the Word of Yahweh/God, lending a helping hand as commanded in Isaiah 58 and Matthew 25. "Inasmuch as ye have done it unto one of the least of these my brethren, ye have done it unto Me" says, The Lord.

Number one goal, she says it is to make known the "Revelation of God's Son and the mysteries (hidden truths from the foundation of the world). To unify the body of The Messiah/The Christ that the church will be one body, mind, soul and Spirit as said in scriptures. John chapter 17 and Galatians teaches us that we are to be one as Yahweh/God and Yahushua/Jesus are "One" Meaning, having the same mind and Spirit.

She was born in Hayneville Alabama in 1947, the daughter of Ethel and Gilbert Wiley (both deceased).

Mary became a member of the church and was baptized; at the age of ten and she was refreshed (re-baptized) in the year of 1995. She relocated to Westbury New York in 1966 and Waco Texas 1992 where she currently resides.

She is a License and Ordained Prophetess and Pastor she also received her Doctorate degree in 2012.

She says that she has the Testimony of Jesus Christ, for this is the Spirit of prophecy as said in Revelation 19:10 and 13.

Founder and President of a non-profit organization, A Community volunteer, founder of "God's One People In Christ Ministries" "The House Of The Lord People Church" Gal. 3:28 and John 17 meaning, One in the Spirit but many members.

Founder of "One People Annual City-Wide Unity Day the last Saturday in May, 2013 will be our 12th Annual; we always receive an Annual Proclamation from the City.

Dr. Neal broadcasted six days a week for two years "This Is My Portion" KRMY "The Light" 1050 AM and www.krmyradio.com, broadcasting on BlogTalkRadio 24/24, she wrote articles for Black Christian News and two other local newspapers. She is The International Feed My Sheep Ambassador for the NPower International Ministry Network and she does live on-line International teaching weekly, Dr. Inetta J. Cooper, Founder/Visionary"

She pastor in two locations, preach and teach in three Nursing Homes, The County Jail, the Detention Center, youth ministry known as, TYC, feed the hungry both spiritual and physical every Saturdays and Sundays, provide clothing, shoes and household good when possible, she also send out and teach on-line Quizzing weekly for almost two years.

Preached on The Word Worldwide Network, she has interviewed and spoken out on local Radio and TV Stations many times and she supervised forty-four employees, is a high quality production lab.

Continuing 'Education

Fashion New York, HSM University Chicago IL, McLennan Community College Just-In Time Techniques, Career Track Self Discipline and Emotion Control, High-Impact communication Skills for Woman, Statistical Process Control for Leaders and Management Styles Austin Texas, Doctorate Degree NPower International Ministry. Nevertheless, best of all she said was studying and searching out "The Word of Yahweh/God" when she went to the best school "Holy Ghost School" from Gen.—Rev. from 1995 – present, for The Holy Ghost is the best Teacher says, The Word of Yahweh/God. When He Comes, He will teach you all things!

She does not believe in the separating of Yahweh's people. She said I am a Christ-ian meaning, a follower of Yahushua The Messiah/Jesus The Christ, one with The Father and His Son and His people.

She is the proud mother of one beautiful and successful daughter Sheila Neal Moore Regional manager for a large Company, Son-in-law Albert Moore who is also successful, Albert was on detail and assigned to three Presidents of The US. Mary has two beautiful grandchildren's who are twins' angels from Heaven she said, since they were two years old will tell anyone that ask them who Jesus is, they will tell you that He is The Son of God. In addition, they would say that they were going to be little preachers when they grow up but now they say, if it is The Lord's will, I can only say, Praise God!

Her own questions about the scriptures lead her to the searching and writing of the book. Armed with the Holy Spirit and the anointing, The Power of The Holy Ghost and a desire to learn the truth, she began this endeavor to search out the truth and help those that have questing and seek after answers. Her message to all is to pray, read the Holy Word daily and seek for wisdom and knowledge but above all get understanding. Walk in the Spirit and not in the flesh and "Let God be true and every man a liar".

OBJECTIVE:

To make a positive difference in the lives and future of the people around the World, to build a Godly family who lives by Godly principles. To tear down the walls of darkness that leads to discrimination and denominations between God's people who are to be "ONE"IN CHRIST JESUS. To build a people that will be blessed when they walk in The Spirit of God daily and take the power and the authority over evil as Yahweh and Yahushua has command us to do. Dr. Neal teaching that all in Christ Jesus should be one as said in the book of John 17:21-22, Galatians 3:28, and 1Corinthians12:12-20. Their Ministries reach out to the poor in spirit, the lost, homeless and the brokenhearted. For God has anointed me to preach the gospel to the poor: to heal the brokenhearted, to preach deliverance to the captives, and recovering of sight to the blind, to set at liberty them that are bruised, and to preach the acceptable year of the Lord as Jesus did in Luke 4:18-19 and Isaiah 61:1-3. Using The Name of Yahushua/ The Son of Yahweh to destroy every evil works of the devil as said in first John 3:8.

SALVATION & BAPTISM:

Baptized at the age of ten years old by man, adopted out of Egypt/The World and believed that Jesus was The Son of God at an early age. Around 20 years ago, I was refreshed and re-baptized a second time by man, most of all I have been born again and baptized by The Holy Ghost said Dr. Neal.

CREER HISTORY:

4/92-Present license Minster and Ordained Prophetess and pastor by Pastors and other Church leaders.
Ordained pastor and elder by, other elders, pastors, and the bishop of pastors, most of all, called and chosen of God and striving to be faithful to the calling, studying and searching the Scriptures Genesis through Revelation.
Preaching, teaching and fellowshipping with the body of Christ "Churches"
Writer for the Heavenly Messenger and Ankle News.

- Active member in jail ministries, nursing home ministries and outreach ministries
- Board member for Child Protective Services
- Mary Kay, Beauty Consultant.

Sales Associate:

- Provided customer with exceptional service, four years pacesetter, built a strong customer clientele, which resulted in a large customer return, markdowns inventory, transfers, stock keeping and trained other associates to perform the same task.
  1/80-4/92 Allergan Optical Inc., Waco, Texas Manufacturing Supervisor
- Supervised up to 44 employees in a high quality production environment, manufactured soft contact lenses in an ADA regulated operation, organized and directed work-flow to satisfy production demands, trained and evaluated department employees through safety training, counseling and motivating employees daily, developed a highly competent, cohesive, and flexible team to meet constantly changing requirements.
  Maintained employee discipline; by creating efficient work environment, which complies with GMP, SOP, and OSHA.
- Developed and initiated a procedure for cleaning assembly trays with recycling saline, which is now part of the company's procedure.
- Developed a procedure and cut cost 50% on HEMA solution and reduced daily paperwork.
- Developed, initiated, and achieved improvement to production saving the company $78K a year.

EDUCATION and EXPERIENCE:

Founded, coordinator and organizer of, "One People Annual City-Wide Unity Day"
Sunday school teach, vacation bible school and activities.
Pastor Assistant.

President and chair of the Board
C.E.I. Youth training teacher

Certificates of Achievement:

Certificate of Achievement Masterlife 1 October 1996
Certificate Mission 2 October 1993 and more.
HSM University, Chicago IL May 2000
McLennan Community College, Waco Texas Awarded Certificate of Achievement

- Just-In-Time Techniques April 1992
- Career Track "Self Discipline and Emotional Control" September 1992
- Statistical Process Control For Leaders January 1993

Allergan Quality Education System, Waco Texas January 1993 Management Styles, Austin Texas
February 1992